Family Values

Family Values

Subjects Between
Nature and Culture

Kelly Oliver

Routledge

New York and London

Published in 1997 by

Routledge
29 West 35th Street
New York, NY 10001

Published in Great Britain by

Routledge
11 New Fetter Lane
London EC4P 4EE

Library of Congress Cataloging-in-Publication Data is available from the Library
of Congress.

For Marion Ellen Long Aaberg

My Grandmother

(May 24, 1915–July 1, 1995)

contents

acknowledgments

Thanks to everyone whose questions, comments, or suggestions on earlier written or oral presentations of this work have challenged me to think through ideas and to be more precise, including: Natalie Alexander, Deborah Bergoffen, Teresa Brennan, Alison Brown, Charolette Burkowitz, Ed Casey, Harvey Cormier, Penelope Deutscher, Fred Evens, Tamsin Lorraine, Noëlle McAfee, Sharon Meagher, Mary Rawlinson, Marie-Jeanne Sanders, Jana Sawicki, Alan Schrift, Brian Schroeder, Benigno Trigo, Roberta Weston, Cynthia Willet, Iris Young, Ewa Ziarek, and the participants in my graduate seminar on Contemporary French Philosophy in the Spring of 1996.

Thanks to those whose continued professional support has been crucial in securing a position from which to teach and write, including: Robert Bernasconi, Teresa Brennan, Judith Butler, Nancy Fraser,

Elizabeth Grosz, Alice Jardine, Kathleen Higgins, Douglas Kellner, Alex Mourelatos, Henry Ruf, Robert Solomon, and Paul Woodruff.

Thanks to the American Council of Learned Societies for a summer grant to work on Part I of this book and thanks to the University of Texas at Austin for a summer grant to work on Part 2 of this book; this material support opened up the time and space in which to write.

Thanks again to Maureen MacGrogan, former senior editor at Routledge, for her patience and encouragement, and her dedication to feminist philosophy. Thanks also to David Auburn, production editor at Routledge, for his efficiency and good humor. Thanks to the *Journal of Medicine and Philosophy* for permission to reprint the first section of chapter one from an essay published there as "Which Came First? The Chicken of the Egg."

Finally, thanks to my friends and family, without whom I could not write and for whom I write. Special thanks to Beni Trigo, who has changed the entire landscape of my life and work; *tú eres mi cielo, tu sonrisa es mi estrella de norte.*

I wrote this book for my grandma Ellen. She was always there for me and I will always miss her.

family values

In *Family Values, Subjects Between Nature and Culture*, I examine the ways in which nature and culture have been defined in relation to sexual difference, articulated as the difference between mother and father. The opposition between nature and culture has been figured as a war between the sexes that plays itself out between mother and father. The rhetoric of the *war between the sexes* is making a strong comeback; and it is planting its roots in biology and psychology. For example, on February 1, 1995, ABC aired a special report on differences between the sexes called "Boys and Girls are Different: Men, Women, and the Sex Difference." Their advertising claimed that this broadcast would rekindle the war between the sexes. The program's host, John Stossel, belittled feminist analysis of sex differences, while deferring to the "facts" presented in biological research. In March, *Newsweek* ran a cover story entitled "The Science of the

Brain: Why Men and Women Think Differently" that discussed oppositions between men and women.[1]

The *New York Times* runs almost weekly articles on new studies in biology and psychology that reconfirm the battle between the sexes. For example, one article entitled "Fighting and Studying the Battle of the Sexes with Mice and Men" concludes that "even the genes of men and women may compete" and that "the desires of the mother and of the father may be at [biological] war with each other" in a "molecular arms race." Another article, "The Biggest Evolutionary Challenge May be the Other Half of the Species," describes mating in fruit flies and humans as a brutal war between the sexes.

At a time when women have proven that they can succeed in a man's world, that they are not just passive reproducers, either these studies implicity provide *scientific evidence* for women's passivity and natural inclinations toward reproduction and family life, or they figure women's activity as hostile and threatening to men. The stereotypes of women as passive virgins or aggressive bitches is not only still alive and well but is also becoming *scientific fact*. For example, recent discoveries that a woman's actions affect a fetus in her womb have been used by doctors, judges, and politicians to blame women for unhealthy or unhappy children; rather than acknowledge women's positive active role in reproduction, when women are seen as active agents, they are seen as dangerous or evil.

The rhetoric of *family values* is another example where women's active roles in family life and raising children are not praised or valued, but used to blame single mothers for urban crime, gangs, and drugs. There is an underlying prejudice that when women are in charge, of themselves or anyone else, that things will go wrong because women are either incompetent or malicious. Although women have been traditionally associated with the family, they are not seen as capable of providing the authority or regulation necessary to raise children; their place is in the home, but not as active agents even in the domestic sphere.

Most of us are familiar with the 1960s rallying cry of the contemporary women's movement in the United States: "The personal is political." This slogan provided a type of counterbalance to the old cliché "a woman's place is in the home." Implied in "a woman's place is in the home" is the belief that women belong in one certain place, and that this place—the home—is opposed to other places where men might belong. In the 1940s Simone de Beauvoir suggested both that the personal *is* political and that the personal *is not* political when she concluded that women should transcend traditional roles as mother and homemaker and engage in the properly political sphere, the public sphere, of men. In *The Second Sex* Beauvoir argues that as a result of patriarchal values girls are raised to concern themselves with their bodies rather than their minds; to this extent, the personal (domestic sphere) is the result of certain political values (Beauvoir 1989). She also maintains, however, that women need to overcome the values with which they were raised, concern themselves with their minds, and enter the social sphere, then occupied nearly exclusively by men; in this regard, Beauvoir, like many of her male predecessors, would agree that the personal or domestic sphere is opposed to the political or social sphere. When feminist activists say that the personal is political, they are insisting that the traditional roles of mother and homemaker operate within a properly political sphere. In fact, feminist theorists began to consider the relations within the domestic sphere, within the family, between husbands and wives, between parents and children, as political relations. As women began to see power relations in the family, women began to fight for civil rights as mothers and wives who would no longer be considered the private property of their husbands.

In her 1963 feminist classic, *The Feminine Mystique*, Betty Friedan, echoing Beauvoir, concludes that "we can no longer ignore that voice within women that says: 'I want something more than my husband and my children and my house.'" White middle-class women wanted something more than the domestic isolation of the suburbs; they wanted to enter the public sphere alongside men.[2] Even as feminists were arguing that the personal is political, women also wanted to make the public their own proper sphere. The family was not enough to make these women's lives meaningful. Today, after the women's movement has made considerable progress toward women's equal civil rights in both the public and the private spheres, again we hear the reactionary politics of "family values" and the implication that good women stay at home with their kids. At the same time that women are making career advances and leaving behind the patriarchal values that held them within the confines of the family and domestic sphere, politicians are running on platforms to reintroduce the "proper" moral values of the family into our "degenerate" society. The media is highlighting studies that once again "prove" that women are biologically destined to nurture children and care for men. Like the scientific theories of evolution and biological destiny in the nineteenth century that can be read as reactions to the early women's movement, natural and social sciences are "proving" once again that women's place is in the home.[3] In addition, career women are renegotiating the relationship between family and career; the last three decades have seen women's struggles to have both careers and families, to hold down jobs and raise kids.

The recent rhetoric of "family values" seems to be the antithesis of feminists' rallying cry "the personal is political." Throughout the 1960s and 70s many feminists insisted that the domestic sphere is political. They pointed to politics of domestic labor, sexual politics, and power relations between family members. Recently, once again, politicians and the media have made the domestic sphere a political issue. Unlike many feminists, however, who want to call attention to unfair practices and abuses of power *in* the domestic sphere, these politicians invoking family values are placing the responsibility for social injustice and abuse *on* the domestic sphere. The deterioration of family values is held responsible for crime, illegal drug use, domestic violence, and poverty. Within this rhetoric, the family is opposed to the state. The relationship between the family and the state runs only one way. The family is still expected to nurture the community; and it is blamed when the community breaks down. The correlation between the breakdown of the nuclear family and the breakdown of the community is read as a causal relationship in which the breakdown of the family causes a breakdown of the community.

The same conservative politicians who run for office on platforms of family values want to cut aid to dependent children, welfare services, government daycare services, education, summer work programs, and medical services. If the term "family values" does not mean supporting parents who are trying to raise children, providing health care, education, food, and training programs for those children, what does it mean? What does the term "family values" mean as it circulates in our media? When is the rhetoric of family values employed by politicians? What lies beneath the surface of this push for a morality based on family values?

The current rhetoric of family values is most directly employed when talking about abortion and inner-city violence. When the rhetoric of family values is employed in discussions about abortion rights, the rights of "unborn children," potential fathers, and potential families are pitted against a woman's right to make decisions about her body and her life. This use of the rhetoric of family values implies that "family values" has nothing to do with women's desires, women's rights, or women's health. Some politicians employing the rhetoric of family values want to deny abortion rights and medical aid for abortions, even in cases of rape and incest.

In the case of inner-city violence, the deterioration of family values is blamed for gang violence and drug-related violence. The suggestion is that if only these children had good nuclear families and fathers who kept them off the streets, then our streets would be safe again. At the same time that politicians employing the rhetoric of family values deny abortion rights and prohibit condoms or other contraceptives from being distributed in schools, they hold young women responsible for teenage pregnancy. While young women are held responsible for being *unwed mothers* and for the phenomenon of *teenage pregnancy*, we rarely hear of *unwed fathers* and there is no male analogue to *teenage pregnancy*.

Even while they cut welfare, food stamps, medical benefits, day-care facilities, and work programs, politicians employing the rhetoric of family values hold households headed by women, primarily women of color, responsible for crime and drugs. At the same time that politicians employing the rhetoric of family values maintain that good mothers should be home caring for their children and keeping them off the streets, they complain that poor mothers are taking advantage of welfare benefits to stay home. At the same time that politicians employing the rhetoric of family values discourage women from entering the work force by cutting work-training programs and promising to overturn affirmative action legislation, they argue that young single mothers should get jobs to support their families and get off public assistance.

The rhetoric of family values suggests that values would be safeguarded only when men are once again fully in power in both the public and domestic spheres. The rhetoric of family values does not, however, promote the rights of all men in public and domestic spheres. Implicit, sometimes explicit, in the rhetoric of family values is the association of homosexuality with a decline in moral values. Along with single mothers, people of color, feminists, and leftists, homosexuals are blamed for the deterioration of the moral fiber of the country. Like inner-city women of color—who are blamed for a degeneration of morals that leads to physical degeneration, drugs, and violent crime—homosexuals are not only blamed for spiritual or religious degeneration but also for disease. The family that is valued in this rhetoric is clearly a heterosexual family. Any alternative to the heterosexual nuclear family is seen as a threat to the family and, as a consequence, a threat to society.

Feminists and lesbians are also blamed for destroying family values and the moral fiber of the country. Women who choose not to have children are seen as incomplete and suspicious characters. Women who choose sexual relations with other women rather than men threaten the notion of community that demands that women provide emotional and domestic support for men; and without the domestic support from women, men's performance in the work force is threatened. Lesbians refuse to take up the role as domestic support for men. Within the rhetoric of family values, they, like single mothers and homosexuals in general, threaten a decline in morals.

In spite of the fact that women's domestic labor is what makes public labor possible, women are held responsible only for the threat that they pose to the community of men. Women's importance to the maintenance of both the domestic and public spheres is acknowledged only negatively by blaming women when something goes wrong, when fetuses are damaged, children injured, or morality weakened. The conservative deployment of the rhetoric of family values makes womankind the enemy of the community. The current conservative use of the rhetoric of family values assumes that families exist to support and nurture men and children. Women exist within this scenario only insofar as they perform their *natural* roles in the service of their men and children. Otherwise, they threaten the community. The rhetoric of family values is a reactionary stance against the gains that women have made in the last decade. Women's increased power in both the domestic and the public sphere is threatening; and conservative politicians are attempting to contain it.

In light of the frequent use of the cliché "family values," the real breakdown of the nuclear family in our society, and the renegotiation by women of career and family, it is time to re-examine the family and familial relations. For decades most feminists have avoided discussing the family and familial relations except to argue that the nuclear family and the institution of marriage exploit women; some feminists have maintained that both the family and marriage are patriarchal institutions that should be overthrown. Liberal feminists, radical feminists, Marxist and socialist feminists alike have argued against the nuclear family and its exploitation of women.[4] Yet, in spite of the realities of families headed by women, there is no denying that the fantasy of the nuclear family is still a centerpiece of our cultural imaginary. For this reason, we cannot merely dismiss the importance of the cultural ideal of the nuclear family. To diagnose the ways in which our notions of the family play into our conceptions of nature and culture, and our conceptions of the relationship between men and women, we need to reanalyze the place of the family and familial relations within the history and imaginary of our culture.

My methods of analyzing family relations in this book come from working within and against a contemporary discourse that has dual roots in phenomenology and psychoanalysis. This discourse, variously and unsatisfactorily referred to as *critical studies, post-structuralism*, or worse, *post-modernism*, is as influenced by Husserl as by Freud. Phenomenology and psychoanalysis, born in pre–World War II Germany, both make substantial studies of human subjectivity and consciousness in the name of objectivity and science, both engage in complex egology. From phenomenology, I inherit the concern to describe the essential structure of subjectivity. From psychoanalysis, I inherit the hypothesis that all of our relations, including our relation to ourselves, are modeled on our primary relations (at least as we imagine them). Yet, in their original formulations, both of these traditions have been seriously contested. Many of their theoretical descendants want to bury Husserl and Freud. In spite of the fact that ghosts of the dead always return to haunt their successors, there are important reasons to leave traditional phenomenology and psychoanalysis behind. The more interesting question might be, why keep them at all? Can we still use phenomenology and psychoanalysis to describe human relations? More specifically, can we use them to describe family relations?

If my own subjectivity is the foundation, and the transcendental ego the center-support, of traditional phenomenology, then contemporary developments have toppled phenomenology. So too, if the oedipal complex is the foundation of traditional psychoanalysis and penis envy its center support, then contemporary developments have toppled psychoanalysis. Can we give up the notions of a self-contained subjectivity, transcendental ego, oedipal complex, and penis envy and still have phenomenology and psychoanalysis? I believe that recent developments in this discourse at the intersection of phenomenology and psychoanalysis make it possible to give up some of their problematic notions and to formulate more promising ways to describe family relations and human relations in general.

The promise that I turn to is the promise of ethics, the promise of a more ethical way to describe human relations, the promise of a description of human relations that makes ethics possible. I use the language of the ethical to denote an obligation to engage in relationships without sacrifice, whether it is self-sacrifice or the sacrifice of another. Ethics, then, is the theory or study that frames the possibility of discussing and describing reciprocal and nonsacrificial relationships. In these terms, neither traditional phenomenology nor traditional psychoanalysis is ethical, nor can they set up the possibility of ethics.[5] Traditional theories of the subject, in both phenomenology and psychoanalysis, do not allow for the possibility of a reciprocal relationship between different people. In fact, in different ways, traditional theories of the subject describe a subject whose identity is dependent upon the hostile exclusion of any other person or particular groups of people. In turn, these identificatory or psychological exclusions have real effects on the exclusion and subordination of particular groups of people, and on the ways in which difference is inscribed in culture. In *Family Values*, I use unorthodox interventions into phenomenology and psychoanalytic theory in order to renegotiate familial relations and our notions of maternity and paternity towards values that are founded on reciprocity across differences.

the paradox of love

The popularity of self-help programs, various forms of therapy and counseling, anti-depressant drugs, and new-age religions suggests a widespread search for meaning, acceptance, self-esteem, and, ultimately, love.[6] Bookstores throughout the Western world have self-help sections filled with books discussing how to find love, how to maintain love, how to rekindle love, how to feel lovable, how to love yourself.[7] Why are we haunted with feelings that we are unloved or unlovable? Sidestepping issues of the prevalence of domestic violence, neglect, and children living in poverty, why are so many children who have so-called normal childhoods and normal relations with their parents growing up to suffer from depression, melancholy, or anxiety? If depression is becoming the norm, perhaps it is time to investigate our fantasies of normality.

While theories in psychology and psychoanalysis may actually perpetuate the fantasies that give rise to emotional suffering, they do not cause them. Still, examining psychoanalytic theories may help identify some of the problems. If we read psychoanalysis not as the study of the structure and dynamics of the *universal* human psyche, but as the study of the psychic manifestations of *particular aspects* of human cultures — which can be described according to structures, systems, and dynamics — then psychoanalysis might become a useful diagnostic indicator for various changes in symptomology across or within cultures. As an indicator of cultural symptoms, psychoanalysis is not limited to diagnosing individuals in relation to norms, but diagnosing those cultural norms themselves.

There are contradictions at the heart of psychoanalytic theory, contradictions that are telling for problems central to both philosophy and feminist theory, contradictions in our cultural stereotypes. Two contradictions fundamental to psychoanalytic theory and our cultural stereotypes are: 1. The belief that an infant's primary relationships become models for her subsequent social relationships and the belief that an infant's relationship with her mother is anti-social and must be broken off. 2. The belief that the father represents the authority of culture against nature and the belief that the father's authority comes from nature. Analysis of these contradictions will not only indicate some of the reasons why we do not feel loved, but also deconstruct the association between mother and nature and the association between father and culture.

Fundamental to psychoanalytic theory is the belief that our primary relationships become models for our subsequent relations. This is why in their sessions analysts return their clients to childhood relations in order to diagnose current relations; the idea is that by examining how early relationships developed, the analyst can diagnose problems in current relationships. Equally fundamental to psychoanalytic theory is the notion that in order to become social, children must separate from their mothers; they must be weaned from the antisocial dependence on their mothers' bodies. Psychoanalytic theory revolves around these issues of primary identification and separation.

These two issues come into conflict in such a way that the impossibility of maintaining both identification and separation sets up the impossibility of love. Our cultural norms for primary relationships, norms manifest in psychoanalytic theory, normalize the *impossibility* of love. In other words, our conceptions and images of our primary relationships exclude the possibility of being loved or lovable. Western images of conception, birth, and parental relationships leave us with a father who is not embodied, who cannot love but only legislates from some abstract position, and a mother who is nothing but body, who can fulfill animal needs but cannot love as a social human being.

Given the thesis that all of our relations are modeled on our primary relations, our relations should be modeled on our first relation, the relation to the maternal body. Yet, the way in which the maternal body is conceived within psychoanalytic theory, philosophy, and our culture in general prevents this relation from serving as a model for any subsequent social relation. The relation with the maternal body is imagined as antisocial, a nonrelation, which, if anything, threatens the social. If infants don't separate from their mothers' bodies, then there can be no society. The first relationship with the maternal body, then, is in the contradictory position of both providing the prototype for all subsequent relations and threatening the very possibility of any social relation.

The paradoxical position of the mother is the result of the imagined opposition between nature and culture. Western philosophy as we know it began with the birth of the soul. Plato proposed a dramatic and antagonistic relationship between body and soul. Aristotle followed by insisting that it is man's capacity for reason that separates him from the animals. Bodies and animals are governed by the laws of the natural world, but the mind and human beings are governed by the higher principles of reason. With its emphasis on reason against body, philosophy has insisted on a sharp distinction between nature and culture. Only human beings are properly social; only human beings have culture; only human beings love. The legacy of this mind/body dualism has been fraught with problems, not the least of which is the paradox of love.

When the bodily activities of procreation and sex are opposed to sociality, the infant is conceived in an antisocial space where love is reduced to biology and there is no love in nature; animals are incapable of love. Yet, only if our animality is *opposed* to our sociality are the bodily activities of sex and procreation relegated to an antisocial sphere. The reduction of procreation to nonsocial biology insures that the mother and child are trapped below the social until some cultural force ruptures that natural unity. If the mother–child relationship is natural and not social, then it is determined by animal instinct and not love.

The reduction of sex to nonsocial biology is another aspect of the opposition between body and culture. The identification of sex and nature leads to the philosophical notion of Eros as disembodied reason rather than embodied passion. Eros is opposed to sex just as mind is opposed to body. Recall Plato's gory description of the near death of bodily passion for true Eros in the *Phaedrus*. This abstract disembodied love is associated with the father as the representative of culture. But the infant, with its undeveloped reason, cannot *feel* this distant love. My contention is that our images of procreation and sex, and of maternal and paternal relations, leave us with an absent no-body father and an animal body mother, neither of which are capable of allowing the infant/child to feel loved.

If the mother's love is made paradoxical by the identification of mother and antisocial body, the father's love is made abstract or impossible by the identification of father and anti-body culture. Within Freud's account, the relationship between father and son is one of rivalry and guilt, while the relationship between father and daughter is one of envy and frustration; the father is the representative of threats and power. Within Lacan's account, the father is associated with the Name or No; that is to say, the father brings language and law to break up the primary dyad. The father's body doesn't matter: "For, if the symbolic context requires it, paternity will nonetheless be attributed to the fact that the woman met a spirit at some fountain or some rock in which he is supposed to live. . . . It is certainly this that demonstrates that the attribution of procreation to the father can only be the effect of a pure signifier" (Lacan 1979, 199). Why is the father's body irrelevant to procreation? How can paternity just as well be attributed to a spirit? What does this tell us about our cultural images of paternity in an age when so many fathers are absent from the lives of their children?

The absent father is fundamental to our image of fatherhood and paternity. In important ways the necessity of the father's absence is imbedded in recent rhetoric of family values and manly responsibility. The association between the father and the law, name, or authority makes the father an abstract disembodied principle. Patriarchy is founded on the father's authority. Paternal authority is associated with culture against maternal nature. But, in both philosophy and psychoanalytic theory, it turns out that the paternal authority that legitimates culture and breaks with antisocial nature is founded on the father's *natural* authority because of his *natural* strength or aggressive impulses. The paternal authority of culture is founded on the father's *naturally* stronger body: might makes right. After grounding the father's authority in nature, our philosophers and psychoanalytic theorists have disassociated the father from nature by disembodying him. The father is physically absent from the family scene because he is part of culture.

Even when he is present in the lives of his children, the father is present as an abstraction; his body is merely the representative of abstract authority or law. The association between father and culture, and the opposition between nature and culture or body and mind, disembodies the father. His body must be evacuated to maintain images of his association with culture against nature; his body threatens a fall back into nature. From Plato to Arnold Schwarzenegger, paternal Eros has been figured as virility. With Plato, bodily virility is replaced with intellectual virility; the body is dismissed from love, which becomes abstract contemplation. With Arnold Schwarzenegger and the cult of body building, the body becomes a thing, a possession, muscles worn like the latest fashion or a shield. The virile subject circumvents any real relationship by defining the other or beloved in terms of his own power, potency, or property. As mere property or product of a virile subject a child cannot feel loved. Just as our stereotype of the mother–infant relationship as an antisocial natural relationship does not permit love because love is social, our stereotype of the disembodied abstract father who represents the authority of culture cannot provide love because love is concrete and embodied.

In the first part of *Family Values, Subjects Between Nature and Culture* I discuss the ways in which the body, especially the maternal body, has been associated with nature and opposed to culture. Analyzing texts from biology, medicine, philosophy, and psychoanalysis, I exploit inconsistencies in the ways that these discourses have constructed the natural body and I argue that the body is social and that the infant's relation with the maternal body sets up the possibility of subsequent social relations. In the first chapter, "Animal Body Mother," I present a genealogy of biological and medical discourses on the maternal body and its relation to the fetus in order to demonstrate the ways in which the maternal body has been constructed as passive and threatening. From the beginnings of Western medicine the father has been figured as the active agent and guardian of culture and the mother has been figured as a passive container that threatens culture from the side of nature. Philosophy and psychoanalysis also disseminate images of the mother, the feminine, and woman locked into a crypt of nature and the father, the masculine, and men liberating their sons from the crypt of nature by sacrificing women so that men can escape. Biology, philosophy, and psychoanalysis present a war between the sexes that is fought within the family where culture itself is at stake.

In the second chapter, "Maternal Law," I read texts by Jacques Derrida and Sarah Kofman that stretch the connection between mother and nature and begin to suggest a connection between mother and law. The descriptions and images of mothers in these texts suggest that the mother is not antisocial but rather associated with language and law. Moving beyond what I see as the limitations of these texts, I present a notion of identity that is not postulated as the exclusion or annihilation of difference or the other. I analyze the relationship between desire and identification in order to provide an alternative to theories of identity based on the abjection of what is other. In the last section, "Body Language," I make the case that the body, especially the maternal body, is social and that language and law are operating on a bodily level.

In the second part of *Family Values, Subjects Between Nature and Culture* I discuss the ways in which the body, especially the paternal body, is absent from culture. Analyzing texts from philosophy, psychoanalysis, and law, I diagnose some contradictions inherent in the association between the father and culture, an association that is based on the exclusion of the paternal body. In chapter three, "No Body Father," I begin by developing a notion of virile subjectivity and demonstrating that the history of philosophy is built on subjectivity as virile. The virile subject is the subject who relates to the world and others as objects of his knowledge and control. By tracing the notion of ownness in phenomenology, I suggest that the traditional phenomenological subject is a virile subject. I show how the authority and power of the virile subject have been based in notions of paternal authority grounded in a fundamental contradiction over the father's relation to nature. Looking at eighteenth- and nineteenth-century political theory, I show how the association between father or man and culture is based in an argument from nature. In addition, I develop a notion of an *abject father* to explain why the paternal body has been evacuated from culture. Finally, I give examples of how the father's body is turned into an abstract idea in legal discourses and some of the rhetoric of the men's movement and the rhetoric of responsibility among African American men.

In chapter four, "Paternal Eros," using texts by Levinas, Ricoeur, Derrida, and Kristeva, I explore alternatives to traditional discourses that associate the father with law, culture, and responsibility. These texts suggest that the father is also associated with promise and love. Still, these promising alternatives to stereotypes of paternity continue to disregard or deny the paternal body. And, many of them continue to privilege the father—son relationship as the promise of paternal authority. Throughout the second part of the book I argue that culture, language, and law are embodied and their authority is grounded in the body. In the end, I suggest that we need to bring the paternal body back into our discourses and images of fatherhood. I conclude the book with some speculations on the ways in which my analysis of the social body and embodied culture could impact ethics. Finally, I suggest new ways to think of the relationship between family and values.

part one

social body

animal body mother

It is in maternity that woman fulfills her physiological destiny; it is her natural "calling,"
since her whole organic structure is adapted for
the perpetuation of the species. But we have
seen already that human society is never aban-
doned wholly to nature.

(Simone de Beauvoir, *The Second Sex*)

Biological Imaging [8]

Although Foucault's remarks on the maternal body itself are
extremely limited, his analysis of biology, medicine, and techniques
employed in various institutions in order to discipline the body and
make it docile can be useful in analyzing the history of biological
and medical theories of the maternal body. [9] Analyzing the diseased
body in *The Birth of the Clinic*, Foucault describes the processes through
which the medical gaze constitutes an individual, specifically the sick
individual. There he maintains that "the gaze is no longer reductive,
it is, rather, that which establishes the individual in his irreducible
quality" (Foucault 1975, xiv). I will indicate how the medical gaze
has established the fetus as *the individual* and the placenta as the key to
the irreducible quality of individuality itself, while the maternal
body fades into the background.

In *The Birth of the Clinic*, Foucault traces some of the complex lines between the visible and the invisible. In contemporary medicine and biology it seems that scientists can inspect an organism and simply "see" what it is and what it does. Seeing is knowing. Yet, as Foucault points out, even with the advance of medical technologies that enable scientists and doctors to "see" parts of the human body never seen before, their seeing involves an interpretation of that which they "see." What becomes visible through technological advances does not eliminate the invisible, rather it merely rearranges the visible and invisible. As Foucault says:

> What was fundamentally invisible is suddenly offered to the bright-ness of the gaze, in a movement of appearance so simple, so immedi-ate that it seems to be the natural consequence of a more highly developed experience. It is as if for the first time for thousands of years, doctors, freed at last of theories and chimeras, agreed to approach the object of their experience with the purity of an unprej-udiced gaze. But the analysis must be turned around: it is the forms of invisibility that have changed. (1975, 195)

In the Preface to *The Birth of the Clinic*, Foucault begins his discussion by comparing Pomme's mid-eighteenth-century account of his bath cure for a hysteric to Bayle's mid-nineteenth-century account of brain lesions. Foucault points out:

> Between Pomme, who carried the old myths of nervous pathology to their ultimate form, and Bayle, who described the encephalic lesions of general paralysis for an era from which I have not yet emerged, the difference is both tiny and total. For us, it is total because each of Bayle's words, with their qualitative precision, direct our gaze into a world of constant visibility, while Pomme, lacking any perceptual base, speaks to us in the language of fantasy. But by what fundamen-tal experience can I establish such an obvious difference below the level of our certainties, in that region from which they emerge? . . . From what moment, from what semantic or syntactical change, can one recognize that language has turned into rational discourse? What sharp line divides a description that depicts membranes as being like "damp parchment" [Pomme] from that other equally qualitative, equally metaphorical description of them laid out over the tunic of the brain, like a film of egg whites [Bayle]? (1975, x–xi)

As the practice of autopsy and examination of human cadavers became common in the nineteenth century, scientists no longer had to fantasize about the internal organs of the human body. Artists were no longer required to create visual representations of those organs from their imaginations. Rather, the scientists could draw, even photograph, what they saw. Medicine had moved from fantasy to truth. The invention of the microscope revealed previously hidden worlds to the scientific gaze. Even more recently, the invention of ultrasound imaging, magnetic resonance scanning devices, and various invasive scopes have made the internal workings of the living animated body available for inspection. The scientists' metaphors, as strange as they may be, take on a truth that they could not previously have had because these technicians can "see" the object itself. As long as they are looking at it, the human body can no longer withhold its mysteries.

In the case of the maternal body, as the gaze of the physician or biologist moves from the body of the mother to images of the fetus, that fetus becomes the individual constituted through the medical gaze. As the fetus becomes more visible, the maternal body becomes more invisible. Although technology has changed over the last 2000 years, and our views on reproduction have changed dramatically, the role attributed to the maternal body in reproduction has changed very little. In fact, technological advances—and the changing focus of the gaze—have turned the mother into a subject only insofar as she has a responsibility for her child, both before and after its birth. The history of medical and biological accounts of conception and gestation construct the maternal body as a passive container that exists for the sake of the "unborn child." And, as new technologies make it possible to view the fetus *in utero*, it becomes an individual, the active subject of its own gestation and birth.

Jana Sawicki, Gena Corea, and others have argued that new reproductive technology makes women subjects of their own reproductive choices as they never have been before, while at the same time subjecting them to disciplinary techniques employed through the institutions in which these technologies are developed and deployed (Sawicki 1991). And, although she does not explicitly employ a Foucaultian framework, Nancy Tuana has done excellent work to describe a history of theories of reproduction that have been used to support arguments for women's biological inferiority to men

13

(Tuana 1993). Drawing on some of this research, I would like to take a different path. I am interested in how theories of reproduction, particularly the relationship between the maternal body and the fetus, both construct and manifest the changing discourse of the individual or person.

In the first chapter of the 1989 text book *Biology of the Uterus*, Elizabeth Ramsey attributes the errors in ancient representations of the uterus to the fact that no one had "set eyes on one" (in Wynn and Jollie 1989, 1). She explains:

> Since the human uterus, at least in its gross anatomy, is not a particularly complicated organ, one may wonder why anyone who had once held a uterus in his hand and perhaps made a simple sagittal section through it would have failed to grasp its pattern. That of course is the crux of the matter. The early physicians did not hold the uterus in their hands; many never even set eyes on one. Religion and law forbade dissection of human bodies until surprisingly recent times, and all concepts of reproductive tract anatomy were based on findings in animals. Since most of the animals observed had duplex or bicornuate uteri, extrapolation to the human produced many erroneous and bizarre theories. (1)

Theories of the bicornuate, or two-chambered, uterus were held through the sixteenth century. From Hippocrates in the fourth century BC through the sixteenth century, "the uterus was believed to consist of a number of cavities exhibiting angulations and horns, and its lining studded with 'tentacles' or suckers'" (Wynn and Jollie 1989, 1). Elizabeth Ramsey identifies the illustration in figure 1 as the earliest known representation of the uterus from the ninth century. This representation shows a circular uterus with earlike chambers at the top (fig. 1). An illustration from Mondino dei Luzzi, who, according to Ramsey, performed the first authorized public dissection of a human body for scientific purposes in 1315, still represents a compartmentalized uterus even after supposedly "setting eyes on one" (fig. 2).

Ramsey does not explain how the setting on of eyes fails to yield the pattern of this "simple organ." Perhaps, seeing is not believing. What the scientist "sees" is affected by what he expects to see. Yet, Ramsey's attitude towards the developments in biology—that seeing is knowing—seem representative of not only ancient presumptions

fig 1.

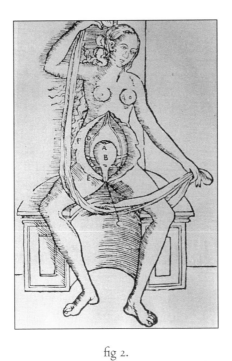

fig 2.

about medicine, but also contemporary presumptions. Luzzi held a human uterus in his hand and still saw compartments there.

Without the benefit of holding a human uterus in his hands, based on his study of animals, like Hippocrates, Aristotle believed that the human uterus had compartments. In addition, Aristotle provides one of the first known theories of the epigenesis of the embryo. He maintained that the embryo developed gradually as a result of the combination of male and female principles: "What the male contributes to generation is the form and efficient cause, while the female contributes the material" (Aristotle 1984, 729.a.10). The male principle contributes the soul while the female principle contributes the less perfect body (738.b.25). The male element creates the individual or person within the maternal body. On this account, the maternal body provides merely the fertile soil within which the male seed implants itself and grows. The female principle is passive while the male principle is active.

In the first and second centuries AD, Rome produced several important physicians who contributed to the theories of reproduction. Rufus and Soranus (both of Ephesus, eventually practicing in Rome) continued the tradition of the bicornuate uterus, while Galen improved Aristotle's explanation of the inferiority of the female contribution in conception (see Wynn and Jollie 1989, 2–3). Like Aristotle, Galen held that both males and females have semen, but the female semen is not as "hot" as the male semen, both in its temperature and its perfection. Galen explains that "the female must have smaller, less perfect testes, and the semen generated in them must be scantier, colder, and wetter (for these things too follow of necessity from the deficient heat)" (Galen 1968, 14.II.301). Females are the result of the coldest and most impure combination of male and female elements. According to Galen, "the left testis in the male and the left uterus in the female receive blood still uncleansed, full of residues, watery and serous, and so it happens that the temperatures of the instruments themselves that receive [the blood] become different" (14.II.306). And when a seed from the left testis in the male combines with the left uterus in the female, then a female child is the impure result. Nancy Tuana notes:

> Galen's anatomical error provides the explanation, missing from the
> Aristotelian account, of why woman is deficient in heat. Although

Aristotle based all of woman's imperfections on this defect, he failed to provide any account of the mechanism that causes it. Galen's creative anatomy provides this mechanism: the impurity of the blood out of which female seed is generated accounts for woman's inferior heat. Since woman is conceived out of impure blood, she is colder than man. Due to this defect in heat, her organs of generation are not fully formed, and the seed produced by them is imperfect. (1993, 134)

As Tuana points out, Galen's account of conception justified women's biological inferiority. Galen's theories held with only slight modifications through the twelfth century. Sometime during the twelfth or thirteenth century physicians at the school at Salerno in Sicily developed the notion of a seven-chambered uterus (shown here in a text from the sixteenth century) (fig. 3). Expanding on Galen's theories, they held that male embryos develop in the three right chambers, female embryos in the three left chambers, and hermaphrodite embryos in the middle chamber (see Wynn and Jollie 1989, 5).

In the seventeenth century, however, the Aristotelian doctrine of epigenesis—the doctrine that the embryo develops—was called into question. In its place, scientists began to propose theories of

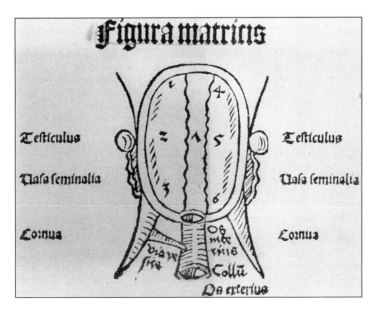

fig 3.

preformation: that the human animal is preformed in miniature and merely grows rather than develops gradually. The notion of preformation was developed in accordance with the theory that there is no generation in nature, only the growth of what is already there (see Tuana 1993, 148). Using microscopes, scientists confirmed the preformation theory. With primary access to chicken eggs, anatomists "saw" tiny organs already present in chicken embryos. They hypothesized that these organs merely grow during gestation.

Once Louis Dominicus Hamm observed human sperm under a microscope and "saw" "spermatic animalcules," and a new version of preformation took hold. Several other scientists claimed to confirm the findings of Hamm. In 1699 Plantade "saw" the preformed human animal in sperm under his microscope: "For while I was examining them all with care one appeared which was larger than the others, and sloughed off the skin in which it had been enclosed, and clearly revealed, free from covering, both its shins, its legs, its breast, and two arms, whilst the cast skin, when pulled further up enveloped the head after the manner of a cowl" (cited in Cole 1930, 69). In 1694 Nichlaus Hartsoeker illustrated a spermatic animalcule (fig. 4). With the theory of preformation of the "spermatic animalcule," the male element provides *both* the form and the material of the child in miniature and the tiny person merely grows in the maternal

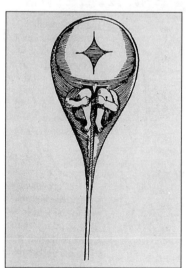

fig 4.

womb as the seed grows in the soil. The microscope had provided proof that the male principle is superior and that all individuals exist preformed in the male element. The trouble with this theory was explaining why so many preformed individuals had to perish so that one might implant itself in the womb.

In spite of the seemingly regressive theory of preformation of the seventeenth century, the sixteenth century brought some changes in anatomical theory. Vesalius, Colombo de Cremona, and Fallopis da Modena, all eventually working in Italy, gave greater detail to theories of the uterus. Vesalius first used the terms "uterus" and "pelvis," Colombo named the "labia," "vagina," and "placenta" (Colombo called the after-birth "placenta" to describe its cakelike appearance in 1559, although the word did not acquire its present meaning until the latter half of the seventeenth century) (Steven 1975, 12) and Fallopio named the Fallopian tubes (Wynn and Jollie 1989, 8–9). By this time dissection and autopsy of human cadavers was more commonly practiced. Still, the study and dissection of the pregnant maternal body was limited. Cadavers were obtained by gravediggers and from the poor who did not benefit from burial and funeral rituals. Prior to the eighteenth century, most of the theories of the operations of the uterus and placenta during pregnancy were still based on dissection of pregnant animals.

In the second century, for example, Galen had described the exposure of a living goat fetus *in utero* in *On Anatomical Procedures* (see Steven 1975, 1). He had identified four stages of embryonic development: 1. coagulum of male semen and female semen (menstrual blood); 2. Formation of the heart, liver, and brain; 3. rudimentary formation of all body parts; 4. embryo fully formed. Over 1000 years later, in 1554, Jacob Rueff illustrated Galen's theory in his *De Conceptu et Generatione Hominis* (fig. 5). Rueff also illustrated the attachment of the fetus to the placenta and its attachment to the uterus. This illustration was derived from Vesalius's earlier illustrations in *De Humani Corporis Fabrica* (1543). This drawing shows a human fetus attached to a zonary placenta which, as twentieth-century biologists have shown, is not the shape of a human placenta but rather an animal such as a dog.[10] Vesalius's early illustrations and Rueff's copies appear to be based on observation of chicken eggs, the egglike shape, and animals with zonary placenta, the ribbon around the womb (fig.

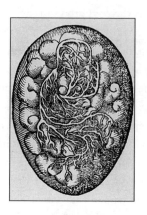

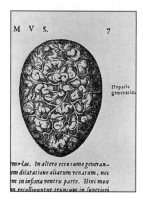

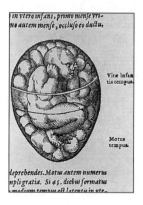

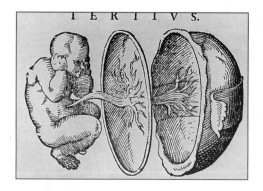

fig 5.

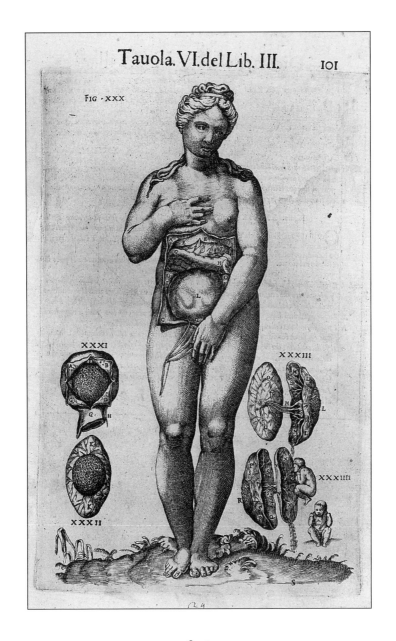

fig 6.

5). Twelve years later, Vesalius corrected his drawings to indicate the discoid placenta of the human as distinct from the zonary placenta of the dog and the multiplex placenta of the buffalo.

In the sixteenth century the debates over the nature and function of the placenta began. Until the end of the eighteenth century it was widely held that the maternal and fetal vessels were anastomosed end to end in the placenta and that the two bloodstreams were continuous (Wynn and Jollie 1989, 9). In 1587, Arantius published *De Humano Foetu* in which he compared the operation of the placenta to the function of the liver. He is unclear about the relation between the fetus, placenta, and maternal body. His contemporary Hieronymous Fabricius of Aquapendente published *De Formato Foetu* seventeen years later in which he refutes any suggestion by Arantius that the fetal and maternal blood vessels are not continuous. Following the long accepted theories of Aristotle and Galen, he maintains that the placenta acts as a kind of sealant to insure that the maternal and fetal blood vessels do not separate under the weight of the fetus; the placenta is a type of glue (Steven 1975, 7).

In 1626, Adrianus Spigelius published his *De Formato Foetu* in which he too confirms the thesis that "the umbilical vessels are roots which carry nutriment from the uterus to the foetus, and that foetal and maternal vessels are united within the substance of the placenta" (Steven 1975, 13). Spigelius' treatise remained popular due to its elaborate illustrations prepared by the artist Julius Casserius (fig. 6). But, as human dissection became more typical in the eighteenth century, and the compound microscope had been perfected, scientists no longer needed to employ the creative imagination of the artist in order to describe and illustrate what the eye could see. Now, printed anatomies were drawn at the scene of the dissections of pregnant women (see Adams 1994, 128). Fantasy was becoming "reality."

William Hunter's *Anatomy of the Human Gravid Uterus*, published in 1772, was extremely popular due to its graphic illustrations and his claims to have revealed "the object as it was actually seen" rather than as "a figure of fancy" or as it is "conceived in the imagination." (Adams 1994, 129). He claims that his images are superior to those of his predecessors because each image "carries the mark of truth, and becomes almost as infallible as the object itself" (Hunter 1772, ii) (fig. 7). He insists that "every part is represented just as it was found;

TAB. XXVII. *Undecimum Cadaver, mense quinto ineunte.* Fig. I. *Uterus cum appendicibus. foetus apparet.* Fig. II. *Utero omnino aperto, membrana Decidua Reflexa, Chorion involv.*

fig 7.

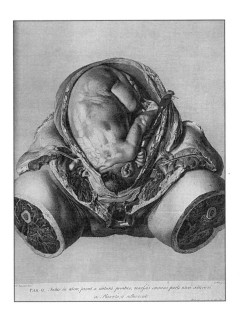

TAB. G. *foetus in utero, prout a natura proditus, resectis omnino parte uteri anteriori a. Placenta a. adhaerente.*

fig 8.

not so much as one joint of a finger having been moved to shew any part more distinctly, or give a more picturesque effect" (Adams 1994, 132). In addition, Hunter claims that his representations are more accurate because they are based on his vast access to pregnant cadavers: "opportunities of dissecting the human pregnant uterus at leisure very rarely occur. Indeed, to most anatomists, if they happened at all, it has been but once or twice in their whole lives." But Hunter claims that he has had "numerous opportunities," so many that he could not include all of the drawing in his masterpiece (130). [11]

In Hunter's drawings the fetus is always shown intact while the maternal body is always shown dissected. The maternal body is cut up so that it can be ordered and analyzed while the fetus remains an untouchable unit. Hunter maintains that the fetus is "the individual in his most complete opacity" (Adams, 132). The maternal body appears as merely the house of this individual. Using more persuasive evidence based on "seeing" the human fetus *in utero*, Hunter continues to justify the passivity of the maternal body. In fact, his representations present even more vivid images of the maternal body as merely a container for the fetus. While the fetus always maintains its integrity as an individual in Hunter's images, the maternal body is cut up and truncated (fig. 8). [12]

By the end of the nineteenth century, the human placenta, which contemporary biologists refer to as the "placenta of man," was studied in its own right . Scientists began to classify various types of placenta and study their functions. The old theories of the continuity of fetal and maternal bloodstreams gave way to more complicated accounts of the function of the placenta and the relation between fetus and maternal body. As scientists began to view the placenta as a type of barrier between fetus and maternal body, instead of the glue that held them together, the relation between the fetus and maternal body became one of opposition. In his 1876 "Lectures on the Comparative Anatomy of the Placenta," William Turner describes the placenta as a barrier that presents a "mechanical obstruction" to theories that propose that the fetus gets oxygen and nourishment through the placenta (Steven 1975, 21). He describes two placentas which appear to operate together in an uneasy opposition: "The foetal placenta possesses an absorbing surface: the maternal placenta a secreting surface. The foetus is a *parasite* which is nourished by the juices of the mother" (Steven, 21, my emphasis).

Many contemporary accounts of the relation between the fetus and the maternal body continue this language of opposition. For example, in her 1975 textbook *The Placenta of Laboratory Animals and Man*, Elizabeth Ramsey attributes the formation of the placenta to the invasion of the fetal conqueror with its army of wandering giant cells:

> Both cytotrophoblast and syncytiotrophoblast participate in the formation of a basal trophoblastic shell which constitutes the junction between the maternal and fetal tissues. By virtue of the cytolytic activity by which the trophoblast *destroys* the endometrium as it invades it, a wide and irregular band, the junctional zone, is created just outside the shell in which *degenerated and degenerating* maternal cells are mixed with extravasated blood and strands of fibrinoid. . . . Further *penetration* of the endometrial stroma is achieved by individual *wandering trophoblastic giant cells.* . . . *Penetration* into the lumina of the ueteroplacental arteries by trophoblast occurs in early implantation stages. A little later the intraluminal cells *invade* the arterial wall and replace its normal fabric. Similar *invasion* occurs also from without by *wandering giant cells.* Appreciable *weakening* of the wall results, occasioning dilation of the channel. (Ramsey 1975, 84, my emphasis)

The fetus has gone from parasite to conquerer, still at war with the maternal body. In the twentieth century this battle between the fetus and the maternal body has become not just a fight over nourishment, but also a battle over rights and the ownership of the placenta itself: whose right to life or happiness takes priority? who controls the placenta? the fetus or the maternal body?

Grosser's influential classification of placenta in 1909 attributed all placental functions in the human placenta to the fetus. He classified types of placenta according to layers; he divided the layers into fetal and maternal layers. And in human placenta he identified three fetal layers and *no* maternal layers. The placenta was essentially an extension of the fetal circulatory system. Grosser proposed that the mere number of layers present in the placenta determined the permeability and the free exchange from fetal to maternal circulation. With three layers, as compared with six layers in the horse, for example, the exchange between fetus and maternal circulation in the human animal is relatively unobstructed (Steven 1975, 34–35). Grosser's classifications were confirmed as late as 1942 by Flexner and Gellhorn (22).

The fetus, once only imagined floating innocently in the mother's womb like a cherub in the clouds (remember Jacob Reuff's 1554 drawing [fig. 5]), has become an autonomous individual controlling its own development and birth within the hostile maternal environment. Although many biologists now believe that chemical changes in the placenta trigger labor, Johnson and Paine's entry in the on-line encyclopedia maintains that labor is induced by the release of a hormone from the "baby's" pituitary gland. The fetus is already a "baby" who controls his own birth.

Most contemporary theories postulate a complex placental circulatory system which acts as an exchange between the maternal body and the fetus. Yet, many biologists continue to describe the placenta as an extension of the fetal cirulatory system and figure the relationship between the maternal body and the fetus as a hostile relation. As the fetus becomes seen as an individual at odds with the maternal body, it must be protected by external controls placed on the maternal body. The maternal body must be monitored not only to protect the pregnant woman but also to protect the unborn individual. Women have a new responsibility to restrain their desires, appetites, and cravings for the sake of this unborn individual. While she is an active agent insofar as she is held responsible for any harm to the fetus, the mother is still merely the passive container for fetal development.

With the development of ultrasound techniques, fetal imaging, and fetoscopic cameras, the fetus can be seen living within the womb. We no longer have to rely on the graphic images of Hunter's dead fetuses cut from their unfortunate mothers' dissected bodies; we have Lennart Nilsson's photographs of fetuses going about their business in the "maternal environment," which have become so familiar to us on Right to Life posters. [13] Nilsson's *A Child is Born* is a very carefully edited selection of photographs that often show a picture of a fetus with an inset picture of a baby on the same page. Yet, when asked by David Van Biema of *Life* magazine when life begins, Nilsson responds, "Look at the pictures. I am not the man who shall decide when human life started. I am a reporter, I am a photographer" (quoted in Adams 1994, 142). Pictures do not lie. Once again, seeing is knowing. For most of the people who use Nilsson's work, these photographs prove that the fetus is an individual, an unborn child who needs to be protected from the whims and vices of his mother.

As Alice Adams points out, the womb has become the mere backdrop of these representations of the fetus as unborn individual, an individual at odds with his environment:

> Some physicians describe the fetus as a parasite who takes over the mother's body; others describe it as a prisoner of the mother's psychological and physical pathology. Prisoner, parasite, philosopher, astronaut, hermit, patient—all the identities ascribed to the silent fetus have this in common: they are based not on a model of cooperation or union between mother and fetus but on a model of maternal–fetal opposition. They all ascribe to the fetus a degree of intention, a modicum of mature consciousness, and awareness of self and other. Whether subordinate or superior, invader or captive, the fetus is always alienated from its immediate (maternal) environment. (Adams 1994, 143–144; see also 137, 156–7)

The fetus has become the superior individual in the relationship between the maternal body and the fetus. Judges force women to have cesarean sections for the sake of the unborn child. Judges and legislators regulate abortions for the sake of the unborn child. Pregnant women have become subjects only insofar as they are responsible for providing the proper prenatal care for their unborn child. Their behavior is monitored in order to protect this unborn patient. Not only is the fetus an individual, a patient requiring prenatal care, an unborn child with rights to life and *quality* of life, the fetus takes priority over the mother. Before the fetus and maternal body were represented as opposed to one another, the concern was for the health of the mother. If mother and fetus were one, then to take of the mother is also to care for the fetus. But, if the mother and fetus are at odds, then the health of the fetus begins to take priority over the health of the mother. In fact, the mother becomes suspect and responsible for any defects, both physical and psychological, in the child.[14]

New technology and medical advances make it possible for doctors to perform fetal surgery. As doctors focus on the fetus, we lose sight of the mother and the maternal body. Some illustrations in articles in the *New York Times* on fetal surgery are revealing (fig. 9). The mother's body is not present in the illustration, or the article, and the surgeon is shown holding the fetus's hand. Ann Kaplan points out the fetus is represented as a baby with developed facial expressions (Kaplan 1992, 206). She also discusses some of the popular representations of the fetus that give priority to the fetus over the mother. In Amy Heckerling's film "Look Whose Talking," for example, the fetus is shown talking while in the womb. The fetus is made into a fully developed person. These representations help support arguments about a fetus's individual rights.

As the electromicroscopic gaze has turned to the placenta itself, it has become the key to the individual's individuality. In 1978 biologist George Birdwood presented the following concluding remarks to a conference on Placenta—The Largest Human Biopsy:

> As some of the studies reported here have shown, the human placenta is not simply human in the sense that it represents the average cross-section, much less the lowest common denominator, it is *highly individual*—in its norms, and no doubt in its responses. That individuality is not, of course, wholly genetic in origin; it also reflects the interaction between the unique genetic heritage of the *fetoplacental unit and the maternal environment* throughout the whole duration of pregnancy. . . . Assuming that the individuality of the placenta corresponds, at least in certain respects, with the individuality of the newborn baby it has fostered *in utero*, placental studies could provide a precise means of investigating individual susceptibility. In time, this information could contribute to a "congenital profile," characterizing each individual, as a basis for personalized prescribing and health counseling. (Beaconsfield and Birdwood 1982, 151–2; italic is my emphasis)

Note that in Birdwood's description the fetus and placenta work together as a unit within the "maternal environment" and that the placenta fosters the newborn baby. The placental–fetal unit is the active agent in gestation and birth, while the maternal body is the passive environment. Although the conception of the fetal–placental–maternal relation is more complex than the early theories of Aristotle, Galen, and Hamm, the maternal body is still represented as the passive element in this relation.

The placenta is "highly individual," not because it is one, or corresponds to one human being, but because it holds the key to the human being's uniqueness; it is his individuality itself. Now the individual exists as a code in the genetic material; from the moment of conception the individual's life is biologically determined. To crack that genetic code is to uncover the individual in his individuality; it is to look into an individual at what makes him unique. Indeed, as Birdwood suggests, the placenta could serve the newborn baby by providing him with a genetic profile that would indicate whether he would get lung cancer if he smoked a pack of cigarettes a day for 30 years, which could be very handy information (see Beaconsfield and Birdwood 1982, 152).

While Birdwood suggests that the placenta operates along with the fetus, some biologists maintain that the placenta is autonomous. For example, biologist Olga Genbacev talks about the autonomous and "self-regulating nature" of the placental organ (11). Rebecca Beaconsfield refers to the placenta as an "experimental animal," divorced from either the mother or the fetus; she calls it the "largest human biopsy" (Beaconsfield and Birdwood 1982, 1). Dorothy Villee says that the placenta is an organism separate from the fetus and the mother, "a world unto itself" (Beaconsfield and Birdwood 1982, 149). Peter Beaconsfield and Claude Villee have edited a book entitled *Placenta—A Neglected Experimental Animal*. The placenta no longer exists just for the sake of the fetus; it has become "an experimental animal," "the largest human biopsy," an autonomous and self-regulating organism whose secrets, like those of other animals and organisms, will reveal themselves under the dissecting electromicroscopic gaze of the scientist. [15]

These theories of the autonomous placenta suggest that there is no immediate relationship between the fetus and the maternal body. The relationship is arbitrated by this third party, the placenta. This model is replicated in the courts and hospitals, where third parties—judges, doctors, and husbands—often decide whose rights or concerns will take priority, the pregnant woman's or the fetus's. In most of these cases, those third parties are men who decide the fate of women by appealing to science and medicine, which have for centuries perpetuated representations of the maternal body that already render the pregnant mother passive. The descriptions given by many contemporary biologists (including Birdwood, the Beaconsfields, the Villees, Genbacev, Ramsey) suggest that either the fetus is in control of gestation and birth, or the placenta as autonomous agent is in control. The maternal body has been stripped of any possible agency. In addition, the relation between the fetus and the maternal body is figured as a hostile relation which requires an outside arbitrator to protect the fetus *against* the maternal body.

There are some biologists, however, who see the placenta as a medium of exchange, even communication, between the fetus and the maternal body. Biologist Hélène Rouch, for example, describes the placenta as the medium through which the maternal body and fetus have a relationship. It regulates the maternal metabolism, "transforming, storing, and redistributing maternal substances for both her own and the fetus' benefit" (Rouch 1993, 39). Exchange between fetus and maternal body takes place through the placenta. She describes the relationship as one of exchange and mutual cooperation rather than a hostile takeover by an alien parasite.

One implication of my analysis of the different metaphors used to describe the maternal body, placenta, and fetus is that the role of vision in medical research and biology needs to be questioned. Physicians and biologists, even with the most advanced technology, can see many different things. What they see is constructed through their gaze as much as it appears to them. As some things become visible through this gaze, others become invisible. Often tied to traditions, scientists see what they expect to find. Biologist Laurence Longo calls on his fellow scientists to "avoid the easy phenomenological approach. Too often, we scientists fall into the easy approach of doing the experiment we know how to do. We look where the light already is, so to speak, instead of where the truth lies" (Beaconsfield and Birdwood 1982, 158). Even while challenging his colleagues to break away from traditional experiments, Longo believes that the truth always lies hidden in the darkness waiting for the scientist's illuminating gaze. But as the light shifts, so does the darkness: what was foreground becomes background, and something gets cut off.

This genealogy of the biology of the placenta shows how the maternal body is represented as a passive receptor and container for the man's issue and the fetus. Ancient conceptions of conception represented the womb as the fertile ground in which the male planted his seed, the form of the potential person. As advances in biology proved that female and male elements both contribute to the development of the potential person, the womb became represented as the house of the fetus. And, insofar as the maternal body may be figured as active, it is figured as hostile. Recent studies use metaphors of war and battles to describe conception and fetal development. Not only is the fetus at war with the maternal body, but also the male's contribution is at war with the female's. Biologists talk about the genetic development of the fetus as a war between the sexes.

The *New York Times* reports that "even on a genetic level the desires of the mother and of the father may be at war with each other. By Dr. [David] Haig's theoretical framework, a mammalian father has one aspiration—that his offspring grow as big and strong as possible in the womb, to give them a headstart in life. The mother, it so happens, has a slightly different plan. She wants healthy offspring as well, but she also wants to preserve her future fecundity, which means that any one embryo must not be permitted to grow so cumbersome that it weakens and depletes her." [16] Instead of figuring this interaction between male and female genes as a negotiation or compromise, it is figured as a "war," an "innate conflict of interest," and "the molecular arms race."

Another recent article describes an evolutionary battle of the sexes in which males and females are at war over who will dominate. The reporter tells us that

> a new study indicates that it is during the actual act of mating that males and females are having what appears to be their most *vicious, knock-down drag-out fight* of all, an *evolutionary struggle* cloaked in the deceptively cooperative act of consummation. One scientist [William Rice] has managed to uncover the *power of this battle* in an ingenious study of fruit flies. . . . He did it by preventing females from evolving, effectively tying their hands in the evolutionary struggle. With male fruit flies unleashed to do their best, or worst, they quickly evolved a number of *nasty tricks*, including a seminal fluid so potent that is was not only much more effective at preventing females from producing offspring with any other males but it actually shortened the females' lives. The new work is the latest and most striking of a growing number of studies on *the power of the conflict between males and females* of various species during mating. Some of the most interesting and controversial studies are revealing aspects of *human mating battles*.[17] (my emphasis)

Rice describes the adaptation between males and females through the evolution of mating as physiological attack and defense strategies similar to adaptations by predator and prey. (Of course, the female fruit flies are the prey.) The article goes on to talk about the "daughters," "sons," and "mothers" of fruit flies, "face-offs" between the sexes, naïve fruit flies, chemical warfare, sperm as weapon, kamikaze sperm, and rape, divorce, and prostitution among ducks. The use of these kind of metaphors to describe behaviors that could be described using many other metaphors and models perpetuates particular world views while discounting others.

Scientific representations (and their public dissemination) are both the products and are in the service of various political forces and power relations. Just as a doctor's beliefs influence what he sees, what he sees influences public opinions and conceptions. Medical knowledge and truth are produced through an emphasis on vision that isolates, and erases the context of, the gaze by presuming that seeing is neutral and independent of political forces and power relations. As the technology for looking into the previously hidden interior of the human body advanced, so did the truth. Scientists' descriptions of what they see are more true now that they have high tech imaging devices than they were when they had only primitive microscopes.

But is the notion that a "congenital profile" could be read off of the genetic material in the placenta any less fantastic than the preformation theory that the individual exists in full form in the sperm? Are the notions of wandering giant cells and weakening walls any more scientific than notions of colder and warmer semen? Whereas eighteenth- and nineteenth-century scientists opened dead bodies in order to discover the secrets of life, contemporary scientists gaze at living bodies in order to discover the secrets of death who will die of lung cancer if they smoke, who will die of sclerosis of the liver if they drink.

In the case of the maternal body, as the fetus *in utero* becomes more visible, the maternal body becomes more invisible. As the fetus or fetal-placental unit is constructed through the medical gaze as an active individual, the maternal body is constructed as a passive container or environment. As the fetus gains rights, the mother loses rights. The fetus and maternal body are opposed to one another and the mother becomes a (suspect) subject only insofar as she is responsible for her child.

Foucault points out in *The History of Sexuality* that "the hysterization of women, which involved a thorough medicalization of their bodies and their sex, was carried out in the name of the responsibility they owed to the health of their children, the solidity of the family institution, and the safeguarding of society" (Foucault 1980, 146–147). The same could be said of the medicalization of reproduction and birth; the institutions of medicine and biology have constructed the pregnant woman as a passive, docile body in order to discipline this body in the name of woman's responsibility to "the health of their children, the solidity of the family institution, and the safeguarding of society."

Early medicine justified women's inferiority, which in turn justified her lack of citizenship and rights. The superiority of the male element in procreation justified paternity rights, which enabled men to control and possess children as resources on their farms and in their shops. Today, as raising children has become expensive and disruptive to careers, mothers are granted custody of children so that men are free from that responsibility. Still, as women fight for equal rights, their rights are undercut by their responsibility to reproduce and care for children. Women's reproductive rights and freedom are still pitted against the rights of men and fetuses. So, called Right to Life organizations continue to use medical and biological justifications to attempt to deny women the right to reproductive freedom. Representations of pregnant women as passive environments for the developing individual are used to discipline pregnant women and monitor and control their behavior.[18]

These few examples indicate the politics of representation involved in the medical gaze. What is at stake is not only the regulation of our behavior and the legislation of our bodies but also our very conceptions of bodies and of ourselves as individuals. If our first relation with a woman's body is figured as a relation with a passive container that exists for our own sake, then what does this imply for our subsequent relations with women and women's bodies? If the first human relation is figured as a hostile relation between two autonomous subjects fighting over nutrition and civil rights, then what does this imply for subsequent relations between people? If, on the other hand, the relation between maternal body and fetus is figured as a cooperative exchange, not between two autonomous subjects, or one identical subject, or one subject who takes priority over the other, but between what Kristeva calls "subjects-in-process" who are constituted through their relationships, then the woman is constituted as pregnant and gestating through her relation to the fetus, while the fetus is constituted as a viable individual through its relationship to the maternal body. Through their shared experience of birth, the woman becomes a mother and the fetus becomes an infant. Perhaps our conceptions of ourselves and our subsequent relationship to each other would change. At this point, we can only imagine how changes in medical and biological representations of the relationships between fetus and maternal body might affect reproductive technologies, laws governing reproduction, and the mores of motherhood; or how new technology, new laws, and new mores might effect medical and scientific representations. Our very conceptions of ourselves and our relationships with others hangs in the balance.

Crypt of Nature

Hegel's Antigone [19]

In the previous section, I analyzed some of the ways in which medical discourse has rendered the maternal body and mothers passive and invisible. My analysis suggests that as the medical gaze becomes fixed on the individual subject with agency, or citizen with rights, the maternal body fades into the background. In this section, I will analyze some of the ways in which philosophical and psychoanalytic discourses have rendered the maternal, feminine, and women as passive and invisible. Taking Hegel as an example, I will diagnose the way in which woman fades as culture emerges within philosophical discourse. At the end of this chapter, I will engage psychoanalytic discourse in order to challenge associations between the maternal or woman and passive, antisocial, nature.

Making the transition from individual consciousness to the community, in the *Phenomenology of Spirit*, Hegel says that the family is "a *natural* ethical community," which is opposed to the properly cultural ethical community, the Nation (Hegel 1977, 268, § 450). The first and immediate duties of ethics unconsciously bind family members to each other. Yet, these duties are properly ethical only insofar as they are not merely natural and unconscious, but rather willed and conscious (270, § 452). Rational moral judgment arises out of ethical duties that are given in natural relations that do not have their justification in Reason. The family, then, is in the paradoxical position of both challenging rational moral judgment and giving birth to rational moral judgment, challenging the nation and giving birth to the nation. It is through the family, and for the sake of the family, that individuals move outside of the family to do business; individuals work outside the home, and enter the larger community, to support the family. But, if the individual is concerned solely with the family, then he does not care about the nation; his interests are opposed to the nation except insofar as he sees his family as part of the larger community. In fact, Hegel maintains that it is sometimes necessary for the nation to go to war to unite families in a common goal outside of the family itself (272, § 455). For Hegel, the family serves the function of providing a transition from an unconscious immediate ethical order to a conscious ethical order mediated by reason.

The project of the entire *Phenomenology* is to conceptualize consciousness. Hegel maintains that philosophy is the conceptualization of consciousness. In his preface he makes fun of Descartes' light of nature or philosophy according to intuition (Hegel 1977, 42, § 68). Also, he derides philosophy as common sense, philosophy as categorizing or pigeon-holing, and philosophy as formalism (42, § 68; 32, § 53; 9, § 16). For Hegel, philosophy is the activity of articulating the concept of consciousness, or articulating what we mean by consciousness. To put it simply, the goal of philosophy is to articulate fully the meaning of consciousness such that there is no difference between that meaning and its articulation. If this goal is reached, nothing remains unconscious or unspoken. To say that the rational is the real and that the real is the rational is to say that only what can be conceptualized is real and that everything real can be conceptualized.

In order for Hegel to reach his goal in *Phenomenology*, the ethical order of the family must be superseded and yet brought to consciousness through articulation and conceptualization at a later stage in the dialectic. Otherwise, there is some aspect of the real that is not, or cannot be, conceptualized. I argue that woman gets left behind as the unconscious of the family upon which all subsequent dialectical movements of the conceptualization of Spirit rest; she is never resuscitated or preserved in the later stages of the dialectical movement of consciousness. She is the spirit behind the Spirit, the ghost that haunts Hegel's *Phenomenology*.[20]

Hegel's insistence that even the ethical actions of family members towards each other are ethical only insofar as they are not natural is in keeping with his emphasis on conceptualization. The natural, unconscious, and inner is opposed to the cultural, conscious, and outer (Hegel 1977, 268, § 450). So, they are not natural feelings of love that ethically bind family members to each other (269, § 451). In fact, in Hegel's analysis it turns out that not all familial relations are capable of properly willed ethical duties; not all family relations are ethical relations. Relations between husbands and wives or between parents and children are not ethical because they are always infused with emotions and natural feelings (see Hegel 1977, 273, § 456).

Ethical relations are relations that take the individual beyond nature and move him into culture. The family is responsible for this transition between nature and culture in two distinct ways. First, paradoxically, the natural blood relations of the family produce ethical duties between some family members, duties that these family members recognize as duties to the family. Second, the family has the responsibility of rescuing the individual from nature through the rituals of burial. By engaging in burial rituals, family members symbolically stave off the forces of nature and reinsert the individual into culture; the dead individual's bond to the community is reasserted through burial rites.

If we look closer at Hegel's text, it becomes apparent that the individual who moves into culture through this double operation of the family is always and only the male; and, the family members who do the necessary work in order for this movement to take place are always and only female. First, with regard to burial rites, the individual loses his particularity (his body), and at death burial rites guard against the consumption of the body by nature by reclaiming the individual as a cultural particular. Through the burial ritual the family protects the corpse from "unconscious appetites": "The Family keeps away from the dead this dishonoring of him by unconscious appetites and abstract entities, and puts its own action in their place, and weds the blood-relation to the bosom of the earth, to the elemental imperishable individuality. The Family thereby makes him a member of a community which prevails over and holds under control the forces of particular material elements and the lower forms of life, which sought to unloose themselves against him and to destroy him" (Hegel 1977, 271, § 452). What are these unconscious appetites and lower forms of life which try to destroy man? Obviously, the lower life forms to which Hegel explicitly refers are parasites that destroy the corpse. But what are the unconscious appetites and abstract entities to which he refers?

In the paragraphs preceding this passage, Hegel describes the necessity of action for moving the dead man from irrational nature with its abstract processes of death to consciousness and the particularity bestowed on man through this action which installs man into the community.[21] Through the actions of his family on the unconscious and abstract processes of nature, man is transformed through the mixture of his universality and the individuality of the action taken into a particular individual. At death, the man is freed from his individual reality, his sensuous body, and becomes a universal (Hegel 1977, 270, § 451). It is only after the action of his family, ultimately the action of women, installs man back into civil society that man becomes a particular individual. "But because it is only as a citizen that he is actual and substantial, the individual, so far as he is not a citizen but belongs to the Family, is only an unreal impotent shadow" (270, § 451).

Nature is associated with unconscious, abstract elements that manifest themselves as unconscious ethical relations in the family. The family is associated with this unconscious, abstract, sensuous nature. The family is associated with the body. But, as it turns out, it is primarily woman, as wife, mother, and sister, who is identified with these unconscious and irrational aspects of the family. She is associated with the body and its needs; she fulfills man's sexual needs, nourishes him, and protects his body after death through burial. Yet, the threat from which she protects man turns out to be the threat of nature and all of its associations, which she embodies within the family. In this sense, the threat against which woman protects man is the threat of the feminine. She protects his virility, his potency, by remaining in the shadows.

It could be argued that although the *figure* of woman and the feminine get left behind in Hegel's dialectic, the *principle* of the feminine, individuality, is sublated in man's move through that principle into the community as a particular individual. In other words, the feminine or woman can be negated so that her principle, individuality, is preserved in man. Although I accept that this is how Hegel describes the dialectical movement of the conceptualization of consciousness such that all unconscious or unarticulated elements of consciousness come to consciousness and become articulated, I maintain that Hegel's feminine is *in its principle* unconscious and inarticulate; the way in which the feminine embodies individuality is dependent on its identification with the unconscious, and it is in principle inarticulate. It seems that the feminine is not unique in this regard within Hegel's *Phenomenology* and that this fact might provide evidence that the negation of the feminine does not, any more than any other negation, undermine Hegel's project. But, although every stage of Hegel's *Phenomenology of Spirit* involves the coming to consciousness of unconscious elements or the articulation of that which had not yet been articulated, implied in each of these stages—and all of *Phenomenology* for that matter—is the notion that the unarticulated unconscious elements of consciousness can in principle be brought to consciousness; the feminine is one element that cannot in principle be brought to consciousness.

Unlike the master or slave, the feminine or woman does not contain the dormant seed of its opposite. Rather, the masculine or man comes to conscious articulation against the feminine, which he necessarily leaves behind. Whereas the slave triumphs through his work and preserves the mastery of the master, woman's work leaves her nowhere. If, at the earlier level of self-consciousness, the master had triumphed through the slave's work, then the dialectical movement from universal through individual to particular would have been short-circuited; the first negation of the universal by the individual would not take place, and so the subsequent negation of the negation which yields the preservation of the principle of mastery in the individual work of the slave would also not take place. Yet, at the level of the ethical order, man triumphs through woman's work. How is it that she who works is left behind?

Just as woman is in the paradoxical position of protecting man against the threat that she presents, the ghost of woman both protects and threatens Hegel's project in the *Phenomenology*. For Hegel, in spite of the fact that the rest of the dialectical progression of Spirit is built on her unconscious and inarticulate impulses, she must be left behind precisely because she is in principle unconscious and inarticulate. In "The Ethical Order" the unconscious is associated with the feminine. Even the sister, who is the most promising woman in the family, is not conscious of her ethical duties: "The feminine, in the form of the sister, has the highest *intuitive* awareness of what is ethical. She does not attain to consciousness of it, or to the objective existence of it, because the law of the Family is an implicit, inner essence which is not exposed to the daylight of consciousness, but remains an inner feeling and the divine element that is exempt from an existence in the real world" (Hegel 1977, 274, § 457).

It is the feminine unconscious that threatens to destroy man and the community. For Hegel, Antigone's challenge to Creon and civil society exemplifies woman's threat. Hegel makes woman's threat explicit when he identifies the government with "the manhood of the community" and woman as "the everlasting irony [in the life] of the community." Throughout the section on the ethical order, the family threatens the community with its bodily impulses (Hegel 1977, 287, 288, § 475). Woman's threat to the community is implicit in her association with nature, inarticulate inner feelings, the unconscious, and the body. Yet, these associations give her the power to nurture the community. Woman's role in the burial ritual is an example of her paradoxical relation to man. Through nature, woman protects man from nature. She protects his body against the impulses of the body. Mother earth, the womb of being, threatens to consume the corpse of man and reclaim him for nature. Mother nature both gives birth to man and threatens to consume him. The burial rites performed by women guard against that threat. As Derrida points out in his engagement with Hegel in *Glas*, "when a man *binds himself* to a woman . . . it is a matter of entrusting her with his death" (Derrida 1986, 143). The family bond that gives rise to the ethical bond is a pact with a dead man.

In considering various familial relations that might move the individual from the natural into the cultural, Hegel considers three types: relations between husbands and wives, relations between parents and children, and relations between brothers and sisters. I will consider each relation in turn. Relations between husbands and wives are ruled out because although there is self-recognition in this relationship, it is natural and not ethical. The relationship is based on love and not law, which prevents the relationship from ever becoming fully conscious and thus ethical. As mother and wife, the woman finds her vocation and her pleasure as an individual in her universal duties to her husband and children (Hegel 1977, 275, § 457). These duties are natural and universal duties that are never particularized for the woman: "It is not a question of this particular husband, this particular child, but simply of husband and children generally" (274 § 457).[22] Women, it seems, love only the role of mother and wife, for their duty does not emanate from the love for a particular individual. In the husband, however, the universal and particular are separate. As a citizen (already promoted to the level of culture through the devotion of his wife), he possesses the self-conscious power of the universal; thereby he acquires the right of desire and a guarantee of freedom with regard to it (275, § 457). In other words, because he is a citizen, he has a right to satisfy his desires whenever he wants. The particular individual who is his wife is a matter of indifference to him; when he has desires, he simply wants them satisfied. His wife becomes merely the vehicle through which he satisfies his desires so that he can continue his properly ethical duties as a citizen without distraction. This relationship is not a relation of self-recognition and not a properly ethical relation, because it is a relation between a woman's natural desire to nurture and a man's natural desire for sex, or what Hegel calls "love."

Hegel maintains that the self-recognition in the husband–wife relationship is merely a representation or image of true self-recognition. Earlier in the section on Reason, Hegel makes a distinction between picture or image thinking and conceptual thinking. The relation of sexual desire between husband and wife is not conceptual but merely natural and therefore picture thinking; the sexual relation between husband and wife is a mere image of the properly ethical relation. Yet, Hegel's metaphors betray him when in the section on Reason he has already figured conceptual thinking as like the fulfillment of sexual desire:

> The *depth* which Spirit brings forth from within—but only as far as
> its picture-thinking consciousness where it lets it remain—and the

ignorance of this consciousness about what it is really saying are the same conjunction of the high and low which, in the living being, Nature naïvely expresses when it combines the organ of its highest fulfillment, the organ of generation, with the organ of urination. The infinite judgment, *qua* infinite, would be the fulfillment of life that comprehends itself; the consciousness of the infinite judgment that remains at the level of picture-thinking behaves as urination. (Hegel 1977, 210, § 346)[23]

In the husband–wife relationship, there is no consciousness of the ethical relationship but only a mere shadow or image of that relationship, and therefore at this level consciousness "behaves as urination." To continue to extend Hegel's metaphor, ironically, it is in the desireless relationship between brother and sister that the ethical relationship becomes conscious of itself and attains the level of its highest fulfillment and behaves like a (male) sex organ. Not only is the organ of generation the highest fulfillment of nature, but also the reproduction of the nation (through the birth of children) is the "actual existence" and *raison d'être* of the husband–wife relation (Hegel 1977, 273, § 456).

The relations between parents and children are not properly ethical because they too are mixed with emotion. The parents begin to feel alienated from their children as they see them grow up and become independent, while the children feel dependent on their parents from whom they have derived their existence. The relation between parents and children is not a relation of mutual recognition because it is asymmetrical and too emotional; the duties between parents and children are still too natural to be properly ethical.

For Hegel, the relationship that brings the possibility of mutual recognition, and the move to the properly ethical, is the brother–sister relation. Unlike parents and children, brothers and sisters are not dependent on one another. Moreover, unlike the husband–wife relation, the brother–sister relation is not tainted by sexual desire: "They do not desire one another" (*Sie begehren daher einen der nicht*); their relationship is "unmixed with any natural desire" (*unvermischt mit natürlicher Beziehung*) (Hegel 1977, 274, § 457; 1970, 336; 1977, 275, § 457; 1970, 337). In the brother and sister the same blood has "reached a state of rest and equilibrium" (1977, 274, § 457). It is the lack of natural (sexual) desire that makes the settling of blood possible. Without the interference of desire, the brother–sister relation-ship provides the possibility of mutual self-recognition: "In this relationship, therefore, the indifference of the particularity, and the ethical contingency of the latter, are not present; but the moment of the individual self, recognizing and being recognized, can here assert its right, because it is linked to the equilibrium of the blood and is a relation devoid of desire" (*begierdeloser Beziehung verknüpft ist*) (1977, 275, § 457). Yet, earlier in the *Phenomenology*, at the level of self-conscious-ness, desire (*begierde*) makes mutual recognition possible. Hegel says that "self-consciousness is Desire" (*es [Selbstbewußstein] ist* Begierde) (1977, 109, § 174; 1970, 143). In the brother–sister relation, however, mutual self-recognition is possible precisely due to the lack of desire.

Much of Hegel's analysis makes little sense without one footnote to Sophocles' *Antigone* in "The Ethical Order" of *Phenomenology*.[24] The example of Antigone makes sense of the double operation with which the family moves the individual into the properly social and ethical realm. Antigone is bound by an implicit ethical duty to her brother to give him a proper burial.[25] In the character of Antigone we have both an example of the function of an ethical duty to blood-relations and the institution of the burial rites. By symboli-cally burying her brother, Antigone saves his body from the uncon-scious elements. And her act out of duty guarantees that he is recognized as social and ethical. Antigone also provides an example of the unconscious inner feelings that threaten the community and man, especially the manliness of man.

Once again, Hegel's metaphors and examples betray his project when he chooses the relationship between Antigone and Polynices to figure the desireless brother–sister relationship in which the blood has reached an equilibrium. The brother–sister relationship can be ethical because it cannot be incestuous; and yet Antigone and Polynices are born out of the incestuous union of Oedipus and Jocasta. In fact, Antigone has three brothers, Polynices, Eteocles, and Oedipus; the last is both her father and her half-brother. What of Antigone's relationship to her father/brother Oedipus? What can we say of the balance of blood in this relationship? In fact, as Tina Chanter points out, the sacrifice that Antigone faces is in part due to her bad blood (Chanter 1994, 106–107). Antigone and Polynices pay with their lives for their bad blood.

For Hegel, the potential ethical relationship cannot take place between two brothers or between two sisters. The relationship between brothers is a competition, a fight to the death (Hegel 1977, 286, § 473). After all, Polynices and Eteocles kill each other in battle over the throne of Thebes. Hegel suggests that brothers are always in conflict and that this conflict is the downfall of both. If brotherhood is impossible and leads to death, sisterhood is nonexistent. Hegel never mentions Antigone's sister Ismene. What of Antigone's duty to her?[26] What of Antigone's duty to her other brothers? In Hegel's scenario, the fledgling ethical relationship must be a relationship between brother and sister in which there is only one brother. The primary ethical relation necessitates sexual difference without sexual desire. It must be a relation between two different sexes who serve two different functions in the ethical order.

Hegel maintains that "the loss of the brother is therefore irreparable to the sister and her duty toward him is the highest" (Hegel 1977, 275, § 457).[27] The relation is not, however, reversible. Given Hegel's analysis, there is no reason to believe that the loss of the sister is irreparable to the brother and that he also has a duty to her; even if he has a duty toward her, it is her duty toward him that is "the highest." Like most of Hegel's "arguments" in this section, the claim that the brother is irreplaceable is based on Sophocles' *Antigone*, where Antigone says:

> If I had been the mother of children
> or if my husband died, exposed and rotting—
> I'd never have taken this ordeal upon myself,
> never defied our people's will. What law,
> you ask, do I satisfy with what I say?
> A husband dead, there might have been another.
> A child by another too, if I had lost the first.
> But mother and father both lost in the halls of Death,
> no brother could ever spring to light again.
>
> (Sophocles 1982, 105)

Although for Hegel the family represents divine law and divine duty, only the duty of sister to brother can challenge the civil law. The divine law avenges Antigone when King Creon's son Haemon,

Antigone's fiancée, kills himself upon seeing Antigone dead and Creon's wife, Eurydice, kills herself upon hearing of her son's death. Still, Antigone loses her life in her struggle with the civil law.

The tension between the divine law and the civil law is figured by Hegel, following Sophocles, as a tension between feminine and masculine. For Hegel, woman is the keeper of the family and the divine law, while man is the citizen of the community subject to, and maker of, the civil law. Antigone acts on the divine law that commands her to bury her brother, while Creon as king embodies the civil law. In Sophocles' *Antigone*, however, Creon is as much threatened by Antigone's womanhood as he is by her defiance of the civil law. Not only the civil law but also Creon's manliness are at stake. The struggle between the family and the community turns out to be the battle of the sexes. As Creon says:

> We must defend the men who live by law,
> never let some woman triumph over us.
> Better to fall from power, if fall we must,
> at the hands of a man—never be rated
> inferior to a woman, never.
>
> (Sophocles 1982, 94)

Hegel follows Sophocles in identifying the divine law with the inner feelings of the individual (*Moralität*) and its conflicting principle, the civil law, with the outer behavior of citizens of a community (*Sittlichkeit*). Woman embodies the divine individual law, and man (through woman's work) embodies the civil law of the community. Even for Hegel, the government of that community is a manifestation of manliness (Hegel 1977, 287, § 475).

In Hegel's analysis, the domestic is the antithesis of the political, and the dialectical tension between them gives rise to their synthesis, the modern nation. The family—that is, woman—while necessary to nurture the political, is a threat to it. Analyzing why Antigone feels bound to her treasonous brother (Polynices) to the same, perhaps greater, extent than to her loyal brother (Eteocles), Tina Chanter concludes that "the political significance of the deeds enacted by her brothers is not at stake for her. Politics is not her province; the family is" (Chanter 1994, 98–99). Chanter points out that while Antigone's loyalties to a traitor have bothered other commentators, Hegel is content that Antigone's duties have nothing to do with politics.

With the loss of Polynices, Antigone can fulfill her divine ethical duty to her brother and the family by performing the burial rites through which she reclaims his body from the devouring elements of mother nature and through which she reclaims his manliness from her uncle Creon. Antigone performs the highest duty because she realizes her duty to the family through the special blood relation to her brother and she performs the burial ritual at the same time. Through this double operation, she moves her brother from the family into the community, from the divine law into the civil law. She defies the civil law in order to bind him to it. Hegel maintains that "the brother is the member of the Family in whom its Spirit becomes an individuality which turns toward another sphere, and passes over into the consciousness of universality." "He passes from divine law, within whose sphere he lived, over to human law" (Hegel 1977, 275, § 458, 459).

The brother is able to pass over to the human, masculine, or civil law from the natural, feminine, or divine law through the ethical agency of his sister. Recall the passage where Hegel claims that "the feminine, in the form of the sister, has the highest *intuitive* awareness of what is ethical. She does not attain to *consciousness* of it, or to the objective existence of it, because the law of the Family is an implicit, inner essence which is not exposed to the daylight of consciousness, but remains an inner feeling and the divine element that is exempt from an existence in the real world" (Hegel 1977, 274, § 457). Antigone's ethical act of burying her brother reclaims him for the properly ethical world of the community, yet she is not conscious of the ethical imperative upon which she acts. She acts out of intuition and feelings. At the same time, Hegel maintains that Antigone suffers because she necessarily acknowledges the civil law and her guilt before it (Hegel 1977, 284, § 470–471). She recognizes the community's consciousness of her ethical duty to the family, but she herself is not conscious of her duty as ethical.

As Luce Irigaray points out, Antigone is in the paradoxical situation of both knowing her crime, committing it intentionally, and remaining ignorant and unconscious of the law: "*What an amazing vicious circle in a single syllogistic system.* Whereby the unconscious, while

remaining unconscious, is yet supposed to know the laws of a consciousness—which is permitted to remain ignorant of it—and will
become even more repressed as a result of failing to respect those
laws" (Irigaray 1985, 223). Recall that for Hegel the feminine is
unconscious of ethical laws; she "knows" her duty intuitively. For
Hegel, intuition is inferior to the ability to conceptualize ethical
duty. Woman cannot reach this higher level of conceptualization
because of her nature. Paradoxically, it is because she is bound by
her nature that man can escape nature and enter culture.

How is it that, even while she is guiltier because she knows her
crime, she remains unconscious of the law or her duty? Hegel maintains that "the ethical consciousness is more complete, its guilt more
inexcusable, if it knows *beforehand* the law and the power which it
opposes, if it takes them to be violence and wrong, to be ethical
merely by accident, and like Antigone, knowingly commits the
crime" (Hegel 1977, 284, § 470). How is she both guilty by virtue of
her intent to commit a crime and ignorant by virtue of her unconsciousness of the law? We might speculate that this is a stage at
which woman becomes conscious within the Hegelian dialectic. Yet,
within the Hegelian scenario this is impossible because woman,
unlike man, cannot escape (her) nature.

It becomes clear in "The Ethical Order" that the unconscious
desires that must be suppressed for the sake of the community are
women's desires, especially women's sexual desires, which cannot
exist if the community is to survive. The only woman in whom a
man can recognize himself and thereby leave the family to enter the
social is the sister. This sister necessarily has no sexual desire. And,
in fact, Antigone never can because she sacrifices her life for her
brother before she can wed or have a family of her own. The relation
of mutual recognition between brother and sister turns out to be a
morbid recognition of the dead brother by the sister for the social.
But who recognizes her after her death? Who buries her? Ultimately,
in spite of Hegel's claims, there is no mutual recognition in this
sacrificial relationship.

Unlike the master–slave relationship of the earlier section on
self-consciousness, the ethical order requires death. Like the master–slave relation, however, the feminine fulfills the function of the
body and keeper of the body (like the slave), while the masculine

fulfills the function of the mind or spirit (like the master). Yet, the brother–sister relation is not a relation between master and slave because it is not the potential fight to the death. The sacrifice made by the sister is not the slave's submission necessary to the onset of self-consciousness. The battle between mutually recognizing self-consciousnesses that ends in the master–slave relation can be fought only between men. In Hegel's *Phenomenology of Spirit*, only men fight; women do not fight. More than this, at the stage of the ethical order, only men are self-conscious; women are not.

Luce Irigaray suggests that it is precisely because Antigone does not participate in the master–slave dialectic that she is a threat to the community and to the dialectic itself; she threatens from outside. "Antigone is silenced in her action. Locked up—paralyzed, on the edge of the city. Because she is neither master nor slave. And this upsets the order of the dialectic" (Irigaray 1993a, 119). The master–slave dialectic provides the mutual recognition of manliness, a willingness to fight to the death. Antigone does not fight; she willingly faces the consequences of her illegal action. Yet, she poses a greater threat to the city than an invasion by the enemy. Her threat to Creon is even greater than Polynices' attempt to take over the city and the throne by force. The force of Antigone's threat is that she is a woman. Creon proclaims "I am not the man, now: she is the man if this victory goes to her and she goes free" (Sophocles 1982, 83). Later, Creon explains that "she destroys cities, rips up houses, breaks the ranks of spearmen into headlong rout. But the ones who last it out, the great mass of them owe their lives to discipline. Therefore we must defend the men who live by law, never let some woman triumph over us. Better to fall from power, if fall we must, at the hands of a man—never be rated inferior to a woman, never" (94). It is not so much the fact that Antigone breaks the law that threatens anarchy; rather it is her femininity that threatens the patriarchy. Her femininity and feminine sexuality must be suppressed if men are to maintain the community and civil society, and if civil society is to maintain its manliness. Woman's place is outside of the community, outside of the dialectic. Woman's place is in the home. It is her nature.

"Nature, not the accident of circumstances or choice, assigns one sex to one law, the other to the other law; or conversely, the two ethical powers [divine and civil] themselves give themselves an individual existence and actualize themselves in the two sexes" (Hegel 1977, 280, § 465). Nature assigns the divine law to the feminine and the civil law to the masculine. It is this elemental connection that makes Antigone's threat to the civil law so powerful. The civil masculine law exists, and maintains itself, by consuming the feminine divine law:

> Human law in its universal existence is the community, in its activity in general is the manhood of the community, in its real and effective activity is the government. It *is, moves,* and *maintains* itself by consuming and absorbing into itself the separation of the Penates, or the separation into independent families presided over by womankind, and by keeping them dissolved in the fluid continuity of its own nature. . . . Since the community only gets an existence through its interference with the happiness of the Family, and by dissolving self-consciousness into the universal, it creates for itself in what it suppresses and what is at the same time essential to it an internal enemy—womankind in general. (288, § 475)

Culture and community are maintained by making an enemy of womankind. Feminine desire must be suppressed to the point of vilifying it.

Hegel calls womankind the everlasting irony of the community because the feminine threat is necessary to sustain the community. The community becomes a community by warding off the threat of the feminine—which gives priority to an individual family over the community—by unifying all families into one community through war (Hegel 1977, 288, § 475). "The community, however, can only maintain itself by suppressing this [feminine] spirit of individualism, and because it is an essential moment, all the same creates it and, moreover, creates it by its repressive attitude towards it as a hostile principle" (288, § 475). Within Hegel's scenario, the community is possible only by virtue of the sacrifice and repression of the feminine.

Womankind and her divine law of the family are consumed by mankind and his civil law of the State in order to protect man from being consumed by nature. Man consumes woman so that he won't be consumed by mother nature. The woman, especially the mother, threatens to suck him back into nature, both in the natural unity of the family and the natural soil of the earth. Recall that woman performs the burial ritual to protect man's corpse from being consumed by mother earth and various unconscious desires. Those unconscious desires turn out to be woman's desires, especially her sexual desires. As Hegel describes it, women have an ironic relationship to the community; they laugh at the government's attempts to replace divine, or natural, law with civil law. Moreover, these women find their pleasure in virile young men and not the old men ruling the state. The ironic consequence is that the old impotent rulers send the virile young men off to battle as revenge against their women and thereby prove the importance of the virile young men to the protection of the state (Hegel 1977, 289, § 275).

Implicit in Hegel's analysis is the assumption that women's sexual desires for virile young men threaten the state and lead to war. Certainly, within *Phenomenology of Spirit*, women's sexual desires are threatening: the sister's sexual desires are denied; the wife's sexual desires are denied. Yet, women cannot be properly ethical or social because they cannot overcome their natural desires. The natural desires of women lead to anarchy or war. For Hegel, when they lead to war, there is hope of restoring the community against woman's spirit of individualism. Implicit in his analysis is an association of this spirit of individualism and woman's sexual desires: she wants to keep her brave young men for her own pleasure. But, if we look at history we see that in cultures that send their brave young men to battle, it is during times of war that women can gain some independence. For example, in the United States during World War II women took over many of the jobs previously reserved for men only. An irony that Hegel overlooks is that sending the young male workers off to war makes the community dependent on women to work outside the home. If we extend Hegel's analysis, the result is that the community makes war in order to protect itself from women's desires (to consume women's desires) and in the process assimilates women into the community as properly ethical and social workers.

Hegel's dialectic denies the possibility of woman entering the community as properly ethical and social. He denies her this possibility because of her sex. Yet, as Irigaray argues, even while Hegel bases his theory of the ethical order on sexual difference, he denies sexual specificity:

> The practice of that law, which Antigone was the last to perform, already bears the stamp of the male universe. . . . Already Antigone is working in the service of the god of men and of their *pathos*. She tries to make up for their crime, to brush error aside so as to appease the gods of the dead and leave the living with no trace of crime. It is no longer a case of her fulfilling her role as a member of the *female gender*. Antigone already serves the state in that she tries to wipe away the blood shed by the state in its bid for power and human right through *sacrifice*. Thus the female has already ceased to serve her own gender, her dialectic. . . . Antigone is already the desexualized representative of *the other of the same*. (Irigaray 1993b, 110-111)

Irigaray suggests that Antigone is not serving the "natural female" role assigned to her by Hegel when she buries her brother: she is stepping out of her duty to the family by serving the dead for the sake of the community. For Hegel, woman's only function with regard to the dead is to protect him from nature and preserve him for culture. If, however, her ethical duty is the intuitive duty to the family and not to the community, then why would she serve the dead at all? The community gains from the burial rituals; the individual gains his social status. But what does the family gain? Irigaray points out that Antigone is already serving the state by trying to right their wrongs. Her challenge to the state is the challenge created by the state and vice versa, as Hegel maintains. Antigone is the feminine against which the masculine can define itself; but, as Irigaray argues, that feminine is always only the other of the same. This is to say that the feminine against which man defines himself is his own creation; it is everything with which he doesn't want to identify. And by exiling or repressing that with which he won't identify, and calling it feminine, he protects his masculinity. As Irigaray claims throughout her writings, there is only one sex in patriarchal cultures, and it is the masculine.

If man assimilates or consumes woman in order to protect himself, then there is no feminine sex apart from the one that man prepares for himself. If she is consumed, then there is no sexual difference and no sexual dialectic (see Irigaray 1985). Go back to my earlier example of women entering the work force during World War II. Once the men returned from the war, many women were forced back out of the work force. While the men were away, the women did not need to be "feminine." But once the men returned, the women needed to be "feminine" once again so that the men could be masculine. American culture still has a difficult time negotiating femininity, motherhood, and women's skills in the work force. If a woman is successful at work, she is seen as just one of the boys or as a threatening prima donna; on the other hand, if a woman is seen as feminine at work, her career can suffer. The difficulty negotiating between femininity and the public sphere is a result of the split between nature and culture, perpetuated in Hegel's *Phenomenology*, in which the feminine is associated with nature and the masculine is associated with culture. If femininity is associated with nature, then it threatens culture. If masculinity is associated with culture, then women in the work force must be masculine.

Hegel's dialectic between the sexes is necessarily fixed in favor of the masculine. The relationship between the sexes cannot be a dialectical relation without reducing one sex to the other and figuring the relation between the sexes as an opposition. As Irigaray says in *Sexes and Genealogies*: "Hegel's method is based on contradiction, on contradictory propositions. Yet sex does not obey the logic of contradiction" (Irigaray 1993b, 139). Dialectical logic always pits two terms against each other, and the conflict is resolved by negating one term and then negating that negation so that the synthesis can take place. The affirmation of one term is possible only through the negation of the other. In the case of the dialectic between sexes, the masculine affirms itself by negating the feminine.

Hegel describes this war between the sexes when he traces the brother's trajectory into the community. For Hegel, at first, the brother–sister relationship is without desire, and therefore in it the relation between the sexes reaches an equilibrium. This equilibrium, as I have discussed above, already favors the masculine. After the brother leaves the family behind to enter the public sphere, he leaves his sister behind. He denies his relation to the family for the sake of his community. From the vantage point of the community, womankind becomes hostile and threatening. The once stable relation between the sexes becomes a hostile opposition, which, according to Hegel, is only temporarily resolved through copulation (Hegel 1977, 278-280, §§ 463-67).

While the brother remains within the divine law of the family, the relationship between the brother and his sister, between masculine and feminine, is merely a natural sexual difference. The irony is that this sexual difference has the potential to move beyond nature because it is exempt from sexual desire. Once the brother moves into the community, however, this innocent sexual difference becomes the war between the sexes. Sexual difference becomes opposition. Once the community becomes conscious of the ethical, thanks to the unconscious ethical acts of women, then the community also becomes conscious of the threat women pose to the properly ethical. The Hegelian dialectic shows no gratitude for the domestic labor performed by women in the service of the public sphere; rather, woman is left behind.

Hegel's project in the *Phenomenology of Spirit* requires a reconciliation of masculine and feminine; without such reconciliation, some part of the phenomenology of consciousness would not be preserved as we move to the higher levels of description. As I indicated earlier, Hegel's project in the *Phenomenology* is to conceptualize all of conscious experience. In the section "The Ethical Order," he describes how consciousness moves from individual self-consciousness to social consciousness. If there is some part of the experience of consciousness that cannot be conceptualized, then Hegel's project is called into question. Then, the real is not rational. If the feminine is not conceptualized and brought into the level of the social and all subsequent levels of the dialectical progression of consciousness, then there is an element that is left behind by the *Phenomenology*. Hegel's analysis of the feminine in "The Ethical Order" undermines the entire project of the *Phenomenology of Spirit*.

In the *Phenomenology*, women are unconscious and limited by their natural roles as wives, mothers, and sisters. Yet, the ability of men to become conscious of themselves and their relation to their community is dependent on women's work. As it turns out, then, the conceptualization of consciousness seems to be dependent on the unconceptualizable, unconscious, feminine law. Consciousness is dependent on unconsciousness. Moreover, this unconscious and unconceptualized feminine law never becomes conscious or conceptualized. Only in the masculine does silent, unconceptualized nature wait to be transformed into rational, conceptualized culture through the work of the feminine, which in principle cannot be conceptualized. Hegel's *Phenomenology* is a phenomenology of masculine consciousness that is possible only by setting up feminine "consciousness" as the negation of masculine consciousness and then suppressing the feminine.

As Irigaray points out, Hegel's feminine is nothing other than the negation of the masculine, and as such it must be excluded from the story of masculine consciousness. On Hegel's account, "neither of the two [sexes] is by itself absolutely valid," and yet, as we have seen, the feminine is sacrificed for the masculine. There is no real exchange or mutual recognition or mutual interdependence within the dialectical movement of the "Ethical Order." Hegel's insistence that "these two *universal* beings of the ethical world have, therefore, their *specific* individuality in *naturally* distinct self-consciousnesses" leads me to suspect that if there are two naturally distinct self-consciousnesses, then only one of them is described in *Phenomenology of Spirit* (Hegel 1977, 275, § 459). Hegel's is a phenomenology of masculine consciousness; woman remains unconscious in his account. Unburied by her brother, she is the ghost who haunts the *Phenomenology*.

Psychoanalysis's Natural Childbirth

Not only in philosophy—which traditionally has claimed to be immune to sexual difference in the quest for universal knowledge—but also in various other disciplines, including psychoanalysis—which begins by recognizing sexual difference—woman, feminine, and maternal have been associated with nature and opposed to culture. Women have been reduced to their reproductive function, which is seen as a natural function, and thereby confined to a natural role. Men, on the other hand, can escape or sublimate their nature in order to perform higher functions. Freud defines civilization as the sublimation or repression of drives that women, because of their anatomy, cannot fully experience and therefore cannot sublimate. In addition, he argues that civilization is the result of the repression or sublimation of aggressive drives, drives which are primarily related to the infant's relationship with the maternal body.

For Freud, the infant can leave its dyadic dependence on the maternal body only through the agency of the father. The father threatens the child with castration if it does not leave its mother. The male child takes these threats seriously and sublimates his desires for his mother. But he must also give up his identification with his mother; it is this identification that threatens his ability to become social. He is coaxed into identifying with his father with the promise of a future satisfaction of his incestuous desire for his mother with a mother substitute. The male child identifies with his father's virility and with his father's ability to satisfy himself and the child's mother. The male child must give up his primary identification with his mother because she is stuck in nature and he will be too if he doesn't leave her. More than this, she is feminine and he cannot be masculine unless he gives up his identification with her. Freud ties himself into knots trying to explain the relationship between femininity and masculinity and transitions from one to the other with his bisexuality thesis. In *Womanizing Nietzsche: Philosophy's Relation to the "Feminine,"* I argued that Freud's bisexuality thesis and his theories of feminine sexuality manifest a fear of the femininity in men and ultimately a fear of birth, the fear that men where once part of a female body.[28]

For Freud, the female child must separate from her mother to become autonomous and social, and yet to become feminine she must continue her identification with her mother. Because she continues her identification with her mother, and because she cannot completely fear the threat of castration from the father since she is already castrated, the female child does not become fully social. She has an inferior sense of justice since she doesn't have a fully developed superego, which is the result of her inability to fear castration. She gains what autonomy she has by resenting her mother for not having a penis and envying her father for having one. The female child, along with the mother, is stuck in nature because her anatomy prevents her from feeling the father's threats.

The move from nature to culture is a move from the mother to the father. It is motivated by the father's threats, which are effective only if one has a penis. Culture, then, on Freud's account, is necessarily and by nature patriarchal. Yet, it is nature that culture leaves behind. Because she is associated with nature, the mother must be left behind, killed off, in order for the child to become social. The mother is so unimportant to culture and the development of the psyche that Freud hardly mentions her. In his theory, she, too, is left behind. By now, Freud's theory of the Oedipus complex is a familiar story; it is a story of active men fighting over passive women. Like Hegel, Freud locks women into the crypt of nature.

In the twentieth century, Jacques Lacan and his followers have continued to promote theories that associate the mother with nature and the father with culture, theories that demand that proper development includes leaving the mother behind. For Lacan, the mother is associated with a realm of need and nature that is left behind as soon as the paternal agent intervenes and introduces the infant to language. For the infant, the mother is initially the satisfaction of its needs. She is not an object or a person for the infant; yet she provides more than the satisfaction of *natural* needs like food. But when the infant begins to experience a lack of satisfaction, when its needs are not met automatically, then it begins to sense that its mother is distinct. Under threats of castration, translated by Lacan into threats of the lack of satisfaction, the infant substitutes demands, or words, for its natural longings or needs. But there is always a gap between the need and the demand that expressed that need. Ultimately, what the infant *needs* is to have its needs met automatically without having to ask; it *needs* to feel at one with the satisfaction of its needs; it *needs* to be one with its mother, its satisfaction. So, with the onset of language and culture, the infant can no longer get what its needs. Lacan calls this gap between need and demand desire. Desire is unfulfillable. The infant is forced into a painful world of unfulfillable desires through threats and prohibitions instituted by the father.

In both Freud and Lacan's theories the separation between nature and culture is ultimately unbridgeable.[29] The maternal body falls on one side of the abyss and the father and his law and language falls on the other. For Lacan, desire is the result of this gap. Language is always at odds with the maternal body; it is always nothing more than a frustrated attempt to articulate need, an impossible demand for love.

But, what if we need to commune with other people? What if we need to be social? Then, perhaps, language does more than fail to articulate bodily drives or needs. Even assuming that it fails to communicate needs, perhaps language succeeds in forming communion between bodies. Language brings us together because it is an activity that we engage in with each other and not because it does or does not succeed in capturing or communicating something in particular. We keep talking not just because we can never say what we are trying to say—that is, what we need—but also because we need to be together through words. For Lacan, demands are always demands for love; and as demands, they can never succeed in getting us what we want. This view of the relationship between love and demand seems to presuppose that language is merely a feeble container for something else. Yet, words are not just symbols that contain various conscious and unconscious significations; they are also part of a process of communicating, in the sense of communing, with each other. Language is not just something we use or something that uses us; rather, it is something we do, something that we do together.

Many of Freud's successors have challenged his Oedipal story with its silent mother and threatening father. Psychoanalysts and psychologists have been concerned with psychic dynamics that develop before the onset of language and the resolution of Freud's Oedipal complex or the onset of Lacan's mirror stage. Melanie Klein offered the first significant alternative to Freud's account of the infant's development. She focused on the pre-Oedipal stage of development in order to describe the ways in which the mother–child relationship was formative to the infant's development. Turning the focus from father to mother, Klein proposes that the infant's ego is developing almost from birth through its relationship with its mother's body, especially her breast (Klein 1986, 179). Nursing becomes crucial in explaining the infant's psychic development.

Klein describes the infant as occupying a paranoid–schizoid position in relation the maternal body. In this position, the infant wants "to possess himself of the contents of the mother's body and to destroy her by means of every weapon which sadism can command" (Klein 1975a, 219). This position is described as schizoid because the infant experiences the maternal body as part objects. It is paranoid because the infant assumes that some of these part objects have the same sadistic motivations that it has towards them. In this way, the infant splits the maternal body into good and bad parts. The fundamental split occurs between the good and bad breast. The good breast is the one that is freely given and satisfies hunger, the bad breast is the one withheld that leads to frustration. The impulses to incorporate the good parts and destroy the bad parts are outgrowths of Freud's notion of Eros and Thanatos, or the life drive and the death drive.

On Klein's account, the infant moves into another position in relation to the maternal body when it realizes that its mother is whole and not a series of part objects. Klein calls this position the depressive position because, once the infant realizes that its mother is whole and that both the good and bad are parts of one and the same mother, he feels guilty about wanting to destroy part of his mother. In this position, even though the infant has a sense of a whole object instead of part objects, it doesn't have an image of its mother as separate from its father. Its identification of a whole is an identification of a combined mother–father, what Kristeva will call the imaginary father identified with Freud's father of individual prehistory. Klein, unlike Freud before her or Kristeva after her, associates the infant's recognition of wholeness with the mother and not the father.

Once the infant experiences the guilt associated with its fantasies of destroying the bad parts of the maternal body, it tries to make amends and engages in what Klein calls *reparation*, through which it adopts a less sadistic and more loving relation to its mother. For Klein, contra Freud, the mother and the infant's fantasies about the mother play a fundamental role in psychic development. For Klein, even the superego, the mark of civilization, is developed through an incorporation of both mother and father: "The imagos of his mother's breast and his father's penis are established within his ego and from the nucleus of his super-ego. To the introjection of the good and bad breast and mother corresponds the introjection of the good and bad penis and the father. They become the first representatives on the one hand of protective and helpful internal figures, on the other hand of retaliating and persecuting internal figures, and are the first identifications which the ego develops" (Klein 1975b, 409). For Klein, culture and language are not instituted through the father's castration threats, the importance of which are significantly diminished in her work, but through the introjection of the good and bad mother and father. The mother is not associated with anti-social nature; rather, the mother–infant relationship is the prototypical social relationship.

In opposition to Freud's theory of penis envy in girls, Klein proposes a kind of womb envy in boys. She argues that infants of both sexes are primarily feminine insofar as they are identified with the maternal body. The male's identification with the feminine leads to a femininity complex in the male because he lacks the powers of birth. He resents this lack and blames it on his mother, which gives rise to envy and hostility towards femininity. For Klein, it is the mother's and not the father's body that is associated with power and privilege.

Following Klein, D.W. Winnicott further emphasizes the mother-infant relationship, almost to the exclusion of all others. In his essay "The Mirror-role of Mother and Family in Child Development," he maintains that the infant's subjectivity is formed in the mother–infant dyad, in which the infant experiences his mother as an extension of himself. The mother is a kind of mirror for the infant that allows him to organize his perceptions. In his essay "The Theory of the Parent–Infant Relationship," he develops a notion of the "good enough mother" who is responsible for the infant's ego development. The good enough mother is one who is neither absent nor too invasive; she is the median between the extremes that will lead to problems in the infant's development.

Unlike Klein, who discusses the child's unconscious fantasies and images of its mother, Winnicott discusses the maternal environment and maternal responsibility. He moves from an analysis of physic development centered in the infant to one centered in the mother. Finally, the mother is an active agent in mothering. Yet Winnicott's identification of maternal responsibility became the grounds for regulating the maternal environment. If mothers did indeed have as much control over the development of children as Winnicott proposed, then mother's must be watched, instructed, and chastised. Doane and Hodges argue in *From Klein to Kristeva* that "at first it might seem that distinguishing the 'object mother' from the 'environment mother' empowers the mother by acknowledging her subjectivity and her work as nurturer. Yet, while creating mothers as agents, Winnicott simultaneously creates them as objects for the regulatory discourse of experts" (Doane and Hodges 1992, 21). Winnicott's theories gave rise to a whole genre of "how to" manuals for mothers. And while mothers are rarely praised for producing healthy happy offspring, they are blamed for producing unhealthy or unhappy offspring.

Like Klein and Winnicott before him, John Bowlby also criticized Freud's theory that the mother–infant relationship is not social and must be interrupted by the social force of the paternal agent. By studying the effects on its psychological development of various amounts of attention that an infant receives, Bowlby concludes that social interaction is crucial to development.[30] The development of infants who were separated from adult caretakers and did not receive affection was hindered, while the development of infants who received social stimuli was enhanced. Daniel Stern confirms Bowlby's findings when his studies demonstrate the importance of touch and social contact for infant development. Stern maintains that the mother–infant relationship is social from its beginnings; that the infant is never one with its mother. And that the interaction between mother and infant is a complex social relationship that includes communication and preverbal exchanges of smiles, looks, sounds, and movements.[31]

Jessica Benjamin has continued to work to demonstrate that the primary relationship between mother and infant is already a social relationship. Following attachment theorists (e.g., Bowlby) and object relations theorists (Klein, Winnicott), Benjamin maintains that from the beginning infants are interested in the world and are not part of an antisocial mother–infant dyad. Infants naturally want independence and take pleasure in developing autonomy. They do not have to be pulled away from their mothers by paternal threats. Benjamin concludes that if "we believe that infants take pleasure in interpersonal connection and are motivated by curiosity and respon-siveness to the outside world, we need not agree to the idea that human beings must be pulled by their fathers away from maternal bliss into a reality they resent" (Benjamin 1988, 174). Benjamin also points out that real mothers work to help their children gain their independence rather than threaten the possibility of autonomy. In addition, it is usually the mother who sets limits for the child and inculcates "the social and moral values that make up the content of the young child's superego" (152).

Rather than identify the superego solely with the father, Benjamin also identifies it with the mother. Usually, the child's sense of limits comes from its interactions with its mother because mothers are still primary caregivers in our culture. Contrary to the theories of Freud and Lacan, Benjamin maintains that law and regulation, the markers of civilization, come from the child's interactions with its mother.[32]

While Benjamin calls this primary relationship between mother and infant an *intersubjective* relationship, in *Maternal Ethics and Other Slave Moralities* Cynthia Willett describes it as a type of subjectless sociality.[33] She argues that sociality can occur before the infant is a subject and thus before the onset of intersubjectivity (Willett 1995, 18), and that this sociality is not linguistic but instead should be understood as more akin to music and dance (40, 47). Beginning in this social song and dance, the infant's self-recognition, or the separation of child from mother, is not egoistic but intersubjective. Willett says that an awareness of the face is fundamental to intersubjectivity and that infants respond to their caretakers' facial expressions with smiles at about two months of age (27). Self-recognition is derived from this face-to-face play with parents.

Willett reinterprets Lacan's mirror stage as a derivation of earlier face-to-face play in which the infant encounters his own image and responds jubilantly recalling the face-to-face play with his parents. While Lacan associates the mirror stage with the infant's frustration at the discrepancy of seeing itself whole in the mirror and yet experiencing itself as fragmented, Willett emphasizes the infant's pleasure, which is not the result of a static image of wholeness but the result of the recognition of the animation of interactive intersubjectivity. The infant recognizes agency and movement in the mirror image of his body rather than Lacan's static image of wholeness. This stage is still nondiscursive and, following psychologist Daniel Stern, Willett describes the interaction between infant and parent that *sets up* intersubjective interaction as "nondiscursive affect attunement" (Willett 1995, 89). She suggests that the development of language and language skills grows out of this affect attunement that originally expresses itself in primordial forms of music and dance.

If sociality is possible before the acquisition of language and if a sense of subjectivity and agency comes through touch and bodily interaction, then we must rethink the relationship between the body and language, between nature and culture. Language becomes possible only because of bodily drives which become speech, drives which move between bodies in an affective attunement that is the basis for sociality, language, and culture. The first bodily relationship between mother and infant sets up rather than threatens the social.

maternal law

> We need to discover a language that is not a
> substitute for the experience of corp-à-corp
> as the paternal language seeks to be, but
> which accompanies that bodily experience,
> clothing it in words that do not erase the
> body but speak the body.
>
> (Luce Irigaray, *Sexes and Genealogies*)

In this chapter I will critically analyze texts from Derrida, Kofman, Irigaray, and Kristeva that present alternatives to traditional associations between mother and nature. I begin with two texts by Derrida, *Of Grammatology* and "Circumfessions," in which he challenges the association between mother and nature and (against Lacan) reassociates the mother with the name and the law. Next, I turn to Kofman's *Rue Ordener, Rue Labat* to analyze another figure of maternal authority or law that replaces paternal authority. In the section "Identification, Desire, and Abjection" I formulate a notion of self-identity that is neither opposed to desire nor built on the abjection or the exclusion of the Mother or any other. Finally, in the last section of this chapter, I use works by Irigaray, Kristeva, Brennan, and Willett to begin to articulate a notion of maternity as social and to begin to renegotiate the relation between bodies and language such that bodies, maternal bodies in particular, are not necessarily sacrificed to culture.

The First Lady Of Grammatology

> But the distance of the commentary is not neutral. What he comments upon is consonant with a whole network of affirmations which are his, or those of him, "he." Furthermore, the position of commentator corresponds to a choice to at least accompany and not displace, transform, or even reverse what is written in the text that is commented upon. (Derrida 1991, 42)

In the second part of *Of Grammatology*, Derrida attempts to reverse Rousseau's privileging of speech over writing and thereby challenge the whole history of philosophy as the history of a metaphysics of presence. He does so by deconstructing Rousseau's notions of an original and a supplementary mother, what we could call a natural mother and a cultural mother. He claims to expose a blind spot in Rousseau's text by making visible the movement of the supplement which is invisible to Rousseau's text, but without ever leaving that text. And, by so doing, he exposes the logic of supplementarity that motivates and undoes the metaphysics of presence. He exposes the operations of an other within the text which goes some distance to explain the tension in Rousseau's writings between what he declares and what he describes. Yet, while he does more than merely comment upon those writings, while he works from within the texts to reverse them, transform them, designate their impossibilities, and thereby escape metaphysics by a "hairsbreadth," his remarks are "consonant with whole network of affirmations which are his" (see Derrida 1976, 314; and 1991, 42). Where does Derrida choose his alliance with Rousseau? Which Rousseau? Might his own maternal blind spot be located there?

Through Rousseau, Derrida reads the substitution for the mother as the original supplement upon which all culture is founded: "The displacing of the relationship with the mother, with nature, with being as the fundamental signified, such indeed is the origin of society and languages" (1976, 266). Derrida suggests that for Rousseau, the mother stands at the beginning of a chain of substitutions, the first of which is Rousseau's imaginary mother, the one whom he can control in his passionate fantasies. On Derrida's analysis, the supplement (substitution or addition) of this fantasy mother does not replace an absent mother but creates the absent mother. The desire to possess an original mother is produced through the operation of imaginary supplementarity. The fantasy mother produces the myth of the original. "The absolute present, Nature, that which words like 'real mother' name, have always already escaped, have never existed" (159). The mother, the "true-mother," herself turns out to be a supplement produced by a chain of supplementary meditations which "produce the sense of the very thing they defer" (157).

Yet, is it the relationship with the mother, or the mother in herself, which is the original supplement? And isn't it only from the child's perspective that these can amount to the same thing? Furthermore, who is the child in Derrida's text, Derrida or Rousseau? The chain of substitutions that begins with the passionate fantasy of the mother and motivates both writing and taking lovers assumes that substitutions take place between signifiers, including *mother, lover, sister, wife*, within the play of signification as it captures the child, who for his part remains the active agent manipulating his imaginary substitutions for his own enjoyment. He is the omnipotent child whose mother is nothing other than his fantasy of her; she is always already *his* fantasy. From Rousseau's text to Derrida's, neither the child's subject position nor his sexual identity is displaced, transformed, or reversed: the child is still presumed to be the active male child in relation to the passive maternal body.

Although Derrida remarks on Rousseau's passionate feelings for his mother, a passion as strong as the passion of lovers, and thereby reinscribes a trace of sexual difference, at the same time he affirms Rousseau's effacement of sexual difference in his discussion of the child. The child is both sexed and prior to sex. Analyzing Rousseau, Derrida says that the "great substitution" is the "child's becoming-man" and the "mother's becoming-woman" (1976, 175). Is "child," then, another word for "son"? Taking up Derrida's question to Levinas in another context, I ask, "If so, whence comes that equivalence, and what does it mean? And why couldn't the 'daughter' play an analogous role?" (Derrida 1991, 39–40). Sexual difference is a chain of signifiers all re-marked feminine from mother to sister. This chain begins for the child who is always already marked as masculine; it is his masculinity, his virility, that insures the inaugural substitution.

In a later text, Derrida himself asks, "How can one mark as masculine the very thing said to be anterior, or even foreign, to sexual difference?" (Derrida 1991, 40). In other words, doesn't the substitution or chain of substitutions that makes the child a man and the mother a woman already suppose masculine virility? Is masculine virility also a supplement in this text, or is it the true original? Isn't it the case that *she* is always already a representation because *he* is presumed to be more than a representation, because *he* is a representor? And if *he* is a subject who can never fully return to himself, can never become present to himself, isn't it because of *her*? And yet *she* turns out to be only a figment of *his* imagination. In the end, does his encounter with the other, who both returns him to himself and prevents the possibility of any such return, turn out to be an encounter with only himself? Isn't he just masturbating, after all? (Recall that in *Of Grammatology* Derrida identifies the logic of supplementarity with masturbation.)

Doesn't the economy of the supplement ally itself with the economy of the proper when its fundamental metaphor is one of the substitution of women? The circulation of signs within society and from one culture to another is like the circulation of money; and the economy of arbitrary signs and abstract circulation begins with the exchange of the abstract mother, the fantasy mother, for the "real mother." The mother can belong to a system of supplementary exchanges only if she is abstract, imagined, possessed by him. Like signs and money, she becomes his property. Like signs and money, she has value only while in circulation. Rousseau worried that substituting his fantasy mother for his real mother, supplementing auto-eroticism for his passion for her (or one of her substitutes Thérèse) was evil or diseased; on Derrida's analysis this evil is the same danger that Rousseau associates with substituting writing for speech. It could be said that Rousseau seems to fear that (even as it protects him from suffering her violence) the logic of the supplement does violence to the other and that this violence is evil or diseased. Yet Derrida reassures us that the violence of supplementarity is beyond good and evil, and that "one can no longer see disease in substitution when one sees that the substitute is substituted for a substitute" (1976, 314). So, one need no longer fear that substitution does violence to the original, to the other, once we have done away with her altogether.

The feminine other, the other of sexual difference (who within Derrida's *Of Grammatology* is always feminine), does not exist. She is already a representation—even Rousseau knew that: "The natural woman (nature, mother, or if one wishes, sister), is a represented or a signified replaced and supplanted, in desire, that is to say in social passion, need. She is in fact the only represented, the only signified whose replacement by its signifier Rousseau prescribes thus exalting the sanctity of the interdict [against incest]" (1976, 266). The prohibition against incest commands substitution—the wife must be substituted for the mother. As Derrida points out, there is no incest. Before the prohibition, it does not exist because it is not recognized as prohibited. And after the prohibition, it is prohibited and does not exist. He is interested in how Rousseau describes the transition from preprohibition to prohibition, from presocial to social. Insofar as any analysis of the origin of the social already presupposes the conditions for the social and therefore presupposes the social, we cannot identify the origin. The origin is a myth, the prohibition creates incest, the present determines the past. The only explanation is that the onset of the social is an accident, an antinatural accident of nature, like the wet dream that introduces the possibility of masturbation.

Even as he sheds light on Rousseau's confusion, the blind spot around the origin does not disappear from Derrida's text. It is not completely clear in *Of Grammatology* whether the absence of the mother necessitates the substitute or whether the substitute appears by accident and produces the effects of both absence and presence. He says, "It is at the moment when the mother disappears that substitution becomes possible and necessary. The play of maternal presence or absence, this alteration between perception and imagination must correspond to an organization of space" (1976, 153). The space of this play is organized according to the logic of the supplement which seems to undermine any distinction between perception and imagination. Who is the mother of perception once the imaginary mother takes her place? How can the mother disappear before the appearance of her substitute if the appearance of the substitute produces the effect of her presence? How can her displacement produce society if she is produced through the operation of displacement (cf. 1976, 266)? Is this Derrida's point? The operation of displacement, or the logic of the supplement, is primary; which is to say, the logic of the secondary is primary.

If the secondary is primary, then there isn't any original second. Writing, masturbation, metaphor, taking a lover, all amount to the same operation, an operation of substitution and addition, a supplementary operation. Yet, in Derrida's text, the mother is maintained as the first second. In spite of Rousseau's description of the incest taboo as a prohibition against sexual relations between brothers and sisters, Derrida insists that the incest interdict prohibits relations between children (sons) and their mothers. Derrida refuses the sister and substitutes the mother. Rousseau describes the propagation of primitive humans through unions between brothers and sisters: "they became husband and wife without ceasing to be brother and sister" (Rousseau 1966, 45). Derrida notes that Rousseau "does not mention the mother at all, only the sister" (Derrida 1976, 263). And in a note called forth by the word "sister," Derrida explains that, for Rousseau, before the incest taboo there is need but no passion. For Rousseau, passion and love are possible only after the incest taboo. In this note, Derrida quotes a passage from Rousseau that suggests that the "child" has no passion for his sister; his relation to her is like his relation to a watch or a dog. Derrida asks if Rousseau would say the same thing about the child's relationship to the mother. Although Derrida does not say as much, perhaps his question is motivated by the passage he quotes earlier from Rousseau's *Confessions*, in which Rousseau describes his feelings towards his mother as those of the most passionate lover, inconceivable and unintelligible, it seems, because of the incest taboo.

On the basis of nothing more than his suggestive question in this footnote, Derrida substitutes the mother for the sister, "the natural woman (nature, mother, or if one wishes, sister)" (Derrida 1976, 266). If someone else wishes, he may choose the sister, but Derrida prefers the mother. And in the next paragraph the sister disappears, as it is the relationship with the mother that must be displaced at the origin of society. The incest interdict as the beginning of culture becomes the command to substitute for the mother. Although

Rousseau does not mention the mother in connection to incest, Derrida claims to show her place in Rousseau's text: "Society, language, history, articulation, in a word supplementarity, are born at the same time as the prohibition of incest. That last is the hinge between nature and culture. This statement does not name the mother in Rousseau's text. But it shows her place all the better" (1976, 265). Derrida must replace the sister with the mother—maintaining that the sister was always already the mother's replacement all along—in order to make his argument about the impossibility of identifying an origin of language in Rousseau's texts.

The prohibition must be a prohibition against the relation with the mother because of the passion in this relation. Derrida shows that in Rousseau's text the social already infects the presocial by pointing to a passion before the origin of passion, a passion that confuses the morrow and eve of the origin of culture. This passion is the passion for the mother which is dangerous and must be replaced. So dangerous is this passion that the substitution itself must be hidden and shown only indirectly (Derrida 1976, 266). Even the substitution commanded by the incest prohibition is guilty because it conjures the forbidden "original" passion for the mother. Derrida's substitution of mother for sister in his reading of Rousseau, however, suggests a blind spot between Derrida's *declarations* of his own displacement, transformation, or reversal of an identification of the origin of culture or an original supplement and his *description* of the operations of the logic of supplementarity. Derrida declares that the logic of supplementarity designates the impossibility of locating an origin, yet in his description of the operations of the logic of supplementarity Derrida continually returns to the mother. Even when Rousseau's text refuses to identify the mother as the origin of the incest prohibition, Derrida returns her to the place of the original. Even as he declares the notion of an original supplement or primary second an impossibility, he continually replaces the mother in this impossible position.

Derrida's Maternal Operation [34]

Perhaps Derrida's most complicated and compelling text on the mother is "Circumfession," written to his own mother. Derrida's autobiographical essay "Circumfession" is written in response to a request from Geoffrey Bennington, author of the accompanying exposition on Derrida's corpus, to disrupt or surprise Bennington's neatly packaged outline of Derrida's work, in his book entitled *Jacques Derrida*. "Circumfession" runs along the bottom margin of Bennington's text, all the while looking (up) to say something unrecognizable in the terms of that text. Like Saint Augustine, who turns his eyes upward to God to confess his life after the death of his mother, Derrida confesses his life to God, to Geoffrey, and to Georgette (his mother) as she lies dying. "Circumfession" is presented as the (anti-) code, logic, or grammar that defies the logic or grammar of Derrida's corpus as set out by Bennington. Even with its symbols, "G" (God, Geoffrey, Georgette . . .), "SA" (Saint Augustine, *Savoir Absolute* . . .), "FP" (facial paralysis . . .), "Circumfession" confesses something in excess of any symbolic system, any language; it confesses what cannot be confessed and as such it fails. It fails to confess the blood of the living body, the living maternal body.

Just as Bennington sets out Derrida's corpus as a dead corpse, without even a quotation from one of his texts, Derrida can at best present dead bits of himself in his writing, like so many bits of skin ritually removed from his body. Just as Saint Augustine asks how he can confess anything to an omniscient God, Derrida asks how he can confess to "G" who knows everything there is to know about his texts and has, after all, catalogued them nicely and identified their underlying logics and grammars. Bennington's text circumscribes Derrida's corpus and makes it a proper body of work. Derrida compares this ritual of circumscription to the ritual of circumcision which marks the male child's proper entrance into the Judaic culture and reaffirms the community's alliance with God. What remains after the event of circumcision is the mark on the body, the mark of the proper; but what cannot be recuperated through the mark or scar is the blood shed at the time of the ritual. What is always in excess of any text, any symbolic ritualized mark, any culture or language, is warm blood.

Derrida's challenge, then, is to return to the text that which cannot be returned, the blood from the living body as it performs the ritual of writing; he tries to recall the blood that is shed at the circumcision. His autobiography is the attempt to graft warm blood to words on a page that are the left-over dead skin from the ritual of circumfession. His challenge is to present an uncircumcised text, "a supposedly idiomatic, unbroachable, unreadable, uncircumcised piece of writing" (Derrida 1993, 194). *Circumcision* means to cut short, cut round, limit, cut off, circumscribe; *circumscribe* means to draw a line around, encircle, mark off borders, limits, restrictions.[35] Does Derrida try to write an unlimited text, a text without borders? A text without borders is an unreadable text. Insofar as circumcision marks the community's recognition of its proper member, Derrida tries to write an unrecognizable text. Insofar as the ceremony surrounding the circumcision is also the Hebrew naming ceremony and the circumcision marks the proper Hebrew name, he tries to write an unnamed text.

The name is what is at stake in "Circumfession": "In a story of blood, at the point where I am finally this cauterized name, the ultimate, the unique, right up against what, from an improbable circumcision, I have lost by gaining, and when I say that I want to gain my name against G., that does not mean the opposite of losing" (Derrida 1993, 43–44). Derrida is trying to regain his name against "G" (Geoffrey) and for "G" (Georgette). Geoffrey offers up a total recognition of the proper name "Derrida" and in so doing does not recognize his friend Jacques; Georgette, Derrida's mother, no longer recognizes him or remembers his name.

In "Circumfession" both the name and the circumcision, recognition and blood, come back to the mother: "The role of the mother in circumcision for if she who desires, sometimes commits circumcision with the inhibited desire for child-murder, she is indeed in the position of obsequence (*Glas*, with its circumcisions, guillotines, incisions, still illegible tattoos), figure without figure, armed extra who is no longer present among us at the operation she now delegates after having previously performed it herself" (Derrida 1993, 188–190). By and for the mother, circumcision is the ritual renewing the alliance with God and is traditionally a prerequisite for the marriage alliance. In his writing, Derrida performs a ritual circumcision by and for his mother, trying to preserve the blood shed from the body:

> Sucking up the blood through a lightweight cloth, the tight filter of a white dressing around the penis, on the seventh day, when they would put on orange-flower water in Algeria, with the theory, among so many others, that by mingling with the blood right on that wound

that I have never seen, seen with my own eyes, this perfumed water attenuates that pain which I suppose to be nil and infinite, and I can still feel it, the phantom Burning, in my belly, irradiating a diffuse zone around the sex, a threat which returns every time the other is in pain, if I identify with him, with her even, with my mother especially, and when they claimed that orange-flower water has an anesthetic virtue, they were believed, anesthetic they said for the wounded baby, of course, not for the mother kept at bay, sometimes in tears, so that she could not see, in the next room, and I spread out here this white cloth all bloodied in consoling a mother in order to console myself without forgetting all the theories according to which circumcision, another word for peritomy, that cutting of the surround, is instituted by the mother, for her, the cruelty basically being hers. (66–68)

The relation of the mother to the name and the circumcision is all the more dramatic in Derrida's case, where his name is lost to his mother who no longer recognizes him. He writes "Circumfession" to his mother; he wants to reclaim his name against Geoffrey in order to give it back to his mother. Insofar as he is unrecognizable to his mother, in order to write a text unrecognizable to Geoffrey, Derrida attempts to confess his mother and his own lost name, his Hebrew name, Elijah. Elijah is the prophet who condemned the Israelites for breaking their alliance with God (see Derrida 1993, 81). As the angel of the covenant, Elijah supposedly attends the circumcision to oversee the renewal of the alliance. He is also one of the only prophets who did not die; he was translated to Heaven in a chariot of fire. And he will return as a forerunner of the messiah.

While Elijah is the heavenly guardian of the alliance between God and Israel, the wife and mother is the earthly guardian of the alliance. The renewal of the alliance is foreshadowed in Exodus 5:24–26 when Zipporah circumcises her own son in order to save Moses from God's wrath. Zipporah's role in Exodus is not only to renew the alliance of the convenant, but also to renew the marriage alliance, which was also an alliance between the Levites and the Midianites. Zipporah's father Reuel or Jethro was the priest of Midian (Exodus 2:18, 3:1). Moses had been raised as an Egyptian after the Pharaoh's daughter had rescued him from the water and from the order that her father had issued which commanded the death of all male children born of the Israelites. Once Moses saw the suffering of his people, he left Egypt and went to Midian. There Reuel gave him his daughter Zipporah after Moses protected Reuel's sheep from some hostile shepherds. Until Exodus 4:25–6 there is no mention of Moses' circumcision (he was raised as an Egyptian), which would symbolize his proper entrance into the people of Israel and renew their alliance with God; nor is there mention of Moses' marriage, which would symbolize his alliance with Zipporah and the alliance between the Levites and the Midianites. In Exodus 4:25–6 the alliance between man and woman, between one tribe and another, and between man and God is reaffirmed through Zipporah's circumcision of her son and her symbolic circumcision of Moses: "Then Zipporah took a flint, and cut off the foreskin of her son, and cast it at his feet; and she said: 'Surely a bridegroom of blood art thou to me.' So he let him alone. Then she said: 'A bridegroom of blood in regard of the circumcision.' "[36] David Rosenberg translates the passage: "On the way, at a night lodging, Yahweh met him—and was ready to kill him. Zipporah took a flinty stone, cutting her son's foreskin; touched it between Moses' legs: 'Because you are my blood bridegroom', she said, 'marked by this circumcision.' "[37]

Zipporah not only circumcises her son but also symbolically circumcises Moses by touching the blood to his legs and proclaiming him a blood bridegroom. Some commentators maintain that Zipporah refers to her son when she says "bridegroom of blood." Bridegroom was a title that women used to refer to their newly circumcised sons, following the earlier tradition of circumcision just prior to marriage.[38] In her study of Moses, Dorothy Zeligs points out that when in Exodus Zipporah says a blood bridegroom by virtue of circumcision, that circumcision is plural in the Hebrew.[39] If the Hebrew word for circumcision is plural, then this provides more reason for interpreting Zipporah's circumcision as a dual circumcision of her son and Moses. In addition, as Charlotte Berkowitz points out, the Hebrew Bible displaces the genitals to the thighs and feet.[40] This is yet another reason for interpreting Zipporah's touching Moses's thighs with the bloody foreskin as a symbolic circumcision of Moses himself. With this ritual Zipporah circumscribes her union with Moses and his union with God and the Israelites. By so doing, she saves Moses' life.

There have been various speculations on why God suddenly threatened Moses' life. When God calls upon Moses, he protests that he is not the candidate to speak on behalf of the Israelites because he is slow or heavy of speech and tongue (Exodus 4:10). Could it be that God means to punish Moses for his hesitance to serve Him? Berkowitz argues that Moses' protest that he has a heavy tongue "affiliates his words with the 'mother tongue'" since the Hebrew word for heavy is the same as the word for glory, and Moses' Hebrew mother's name was Yokheved, glory of God (Berkowitz 1995, 50). This reference to his mother reminds us that Moses had two mothers, his birth mother, Yokheved, and the Pharaoh's daughter.[41] He also had two mother tongues. His heavy tongue is Hebrew.

After God threatens Moses' life, he protests again that the Pharaoh won't listen to him because even the people of Israel refuse to listen to him: "Behold, the children of Israel have not hearkened unto me; how then shall Pharaoh hear me, who *am* of uncircumcised lips?" (Exodus 6:11 King James). Why would Pharaoh listen to him as a representative of Israel when he was not even recognized by the Israelites? Perhaps Zipporah's ritual circumcision of Moses is also meant to address his "uncircumcised lips." The circumcision marks him as a child of Israel, Israel who was identified in Exodus 4:22 as the son of God. Earlier, after his first protest, God reassures him by telling him that Aaron "shall be to thee instead of a mouth, and thou shall be to him instead of God" (Exodus 4:16). In Moses' next conversation with God, God tells him to tell Pharaoh that Israel is His son, even his first born, and if Pharaoh doesn't free His son, then He will slay Pharaoh's son, even his first born.

The strange scene of the circumcision at Exodus 4:25 prefigures the last plague set upon Egypt when God makes good on his promise to slay the first-born sons of Egypt. The Israelites mark their doors with blood so that the angel of death will pass over their houses and spare their sons. Immediately after God announced to Moses that he will kill Egypt's first born, He sought to kill Moses and then Zipporah circumcised her son and symbolically circumcised Moses. She marked Moses with blood, the blood of Israel, so that he would be spared. She proclaims Moses a bridegroom of blood recalling the covenant between God and Moses based on Moses's blood and the blood of his fathers. Israel is the son of God by blood. And the patrilineage is ritually marked by the circumcision which circumscribes the male organ of generation as within the boundaries of, and for the sake of, Israel.

In a sense, Zipporah's son is named after Moses; his name is Gershom as a sign that Moses has been "a stranger in a strange land" (Exodus 4:22; see also Exodus 18:3). With the circumcision, Zipporah circumscribes Moses, and their son, into the community of Israel. Moses, a Hebrew raised as an Egyptian, is a stranger in both communities. With the circumcision, Zipporah proclaims Moses a bridegroom of blood or a husband of blood to indicate that they are blood relatives. They are by blood Israelites. This bond of blood is stronger than all others. It is frequently invoked to symbolize the strength of the covenant and eventually to symbolize the binding strength of God's law on Israel. After Moses receives the ten commandments and subsequent laws, he kills an oxen and sprinkles the people of Israel with its blood to remind them that they are bound to God and His laws by blood. Israel is the son of God. The ritual circumcision, insisted upon in preparation for the night of Passover at Exodus 12:44-48, binds the sons of Israel to God through blood that signs a pact of regeneration.

Images of Zipporah appear in Derrida's "Circumfession": the mother with the foreskin of her son in her teeth (Derrida 1993, 97), the loved woman circumcising the son in an act of fellatio (218). In Derrida's images in "Circumfession," Zipporah circumcises her son with her teeth by biting off the foreskin: "Zipporah, the one who repaired the failing of Moses incapable of circumcising his own son, before telling him, 'You are a husband of blood to me,' she had to eat the still bloody foreskin, I imagine first by sucking it, my first beloved cannibal, initiator at the sublime gate of fellatio" (68–90). In the simulated castration of circumcision the mother wounds her baby to inscribe his name—the name that connects him to his community—on his body, on his sex (see 66, 72, 153). She is responsible for this ritual which inscribes the proper name on the body and insures its proper entrance into the social contract. Derrida points out that when spoken the Hebrew *milah* means both word and circumcision (89). So, Zipporah's symbolic circumcision of Moses redresses his protests of speaking with a heavy (mother-) tongue and addresses his uncircumcised, wordless, lips.[42] The circumcision gives him words, *milah* gives him *milah*. In "Circumfession," the mother's tongue is the guarantor of the mother tongue; the mother's tongue marks the male body, makes it proper, so that the alliance, the social contract, can be renewed.

In his "Circumfession," Derrida mentions the notebook for a book on circumcision, "The Book of Elijah," that he had planned to write in 1976. On the cover of this notebook Derrida writes the Hebrew *milah* (Derrida 1993, 89). Possibly it makes no difference that he has not written "The Book of Elijah" since, as he says, circumcision is "all I've ever talked about" (70). Derrida describes writing as a ritual of circumcision. He says that the desire for literature is circumcision (78). He calls the attic where he stores all of his writing "the sublime" that contains all of the "skizzies" of his circumcision (134). The text is the mark of circumcision, the skin cut from the body, from the sex—the skin without blood. Derrida dreams of a pen that could write the living body in warm red blood. He confesses that he has always dreamed "of a pen that would be a syringe" so that he could write himself into a sentence and find himself there (10). But this is something that neither he nor Geoffrey can do. *He* is not the proper name that signs the text, the name that is circumscribed by the circumcision. What is lost in this symbolic ritual is the blood; the blood is shed:

> I have been seeking myself in a sentence, yes, I, and since a circumbygone period at the end of which I would say I and which would, finally, have the form, my language, another. . . . I call it circumcision, see the blood but also what comes, cauterization, coagulation or not, strictly contain the outpouring of circumcision, one circumcision, mine, the only one, rather than circumnavigation or circumference, although the unforgettable circumcision has carried me to the place I had to go to, and circumfession if I want to say and do something of an avowal without truth turning around itself . . . the pulsion of the paragraph which never circumpletes itself, as long as the blood, what I call thus and thus call, continues its venue in its vein. (14–15)

How can Derrida write this blood, the blood shed in the ritual circumcision? Especially given the mother's role in, and relation to, circumcision? The blood shed in circumcision is both started and stopped by her (tongue). The mother's tongue is what makes his language possible. He has come to language because she properly marked him for the social. She sacrifices him to the social, which can know nothing of her pain. It is her sacrifice. It is her pain. What mixes prayer and tears with blood is what Derrida must write, but cannot (Derrida 1993, 20). Blood exceeds any writing. Moreover, in "Circumfession" blood, tears, and prayers are always of the mother, for her child. She weeps for her child and his pain. It is what mixes *her* blood with prayers and tears that he must confess but cannot.

Now, Derrida laments that his mother can no longer weep for him. She does not recognize him and therefore she cannot weep for him. He no longer exists for her. Yet, what is most troubling for him is that if he died before her, she could not mourn his death. Forgetting his immortal namesake, Elijah, Derrida is obsessed with his own death. For his mother, he is already dead. He is already absent to her and even his absence is not present. How can he confess this absence that is not even present as an absence? This confession, the confession of his absence to his mother, is the uncircumcised text. He has no name for her. His name has slipped her mind. It is this slipping away of the name for the mother that shakes Derrida. It is the double sense of the slipping of the name *for* the mother that rocks him: her name like the name of god is unpronounceable (Derrida 1993, 58, 264), and his name no longer exists for her—for the rest of her life he has no name (22). At least in the circumcision there is a mark, a trace, of the blood shed from the body. But where is the mark, the trace, of Derrida on the body of his mother? Does her body exist only for the sake of her son? She provides the name and marks the body for it. But where is her body, the maternal body, in his "Circumfession"?

Except in the photographs where his mother's body is young and beautiful, when it makes an appearance in the text of "Circumfession," his mother's body appears as scarred, immodest, already dead (Derrida 1993, 24, 25, 82, 101, 108). In this text, her body is slipping away, already gone: "Now she is becoming—I'm with her this 18th of June—what she always was, the impassability of a time out of time, an immortal mortal, too human inhuman, the dumb god the beast, a sleeping water in the henceforth appeased depth of the abyss, this volcano I tell myself I'm well out of . . ." (80). As his mother, "G" is not embodied; she is outside of time," a god," "a beast," "a volcano," "a sleeping water." She is outside of culture, outside of the realm of the name, the guarantor, but not the beneficiary, of both.

Derrida writes: "I began with this fear, with being scared of her bad blood, with not wanting it, whence the infinite separation, the initial and instantaneously repeated i.e. indefinitely postponed divorce from [d'avec] the closest cruelty which was not that of my mother but the distance she enjoined on me from [d'avec] my own skin thus torn off, in the very place, along the crural artery where my books find their inspiration, they are written first in skin." (1993, 227–28). But this skin cannot contain the blood of a living body, especially the maternal body, particularly the mother's "bad blood." The blood-mark of the broken hymen is also a reminder of the menstrual blood and the blood of childbirth.

Derrida says that "for 59 years I have not known who is weeping my mother or me—i.e. you" (1993, 263). He writes the circumfession "for the death agony of my mother, not readable by her but the first event to write itself right on my body . . ." (120). The pain of "Circumfession" is the pain that Derrida cannot feel, the pain of his mother, that is written on his body, on his sex. The guilt that he confesses is the guilt of his murderous mother who wounds her own son in the ritual of circumcision. The pain of his mother's guilt serves as a salve for his own guilt, the guilt of killing her in writing her before she has died: "from what wound is it waiting for me, me who, among other remorse with respect to my mother, feel guilty for publishing her end, in exhibiting her last breaths . . ." (36). Yet, he has to write his mother because he would be guiltier if he did not (37). Writing both kills her as the warm-blooded woman whom he called "maman," and saves her from herself, from loss of memory, from association with nature, from devouring mother-earth.

Confessing his mother's guilt is a type of revenge against the murderous ritual of circumcision, the ritual that marks the male infant's entrance into the social and simulates the threat that makes him leave his mother behind. He murders her in writing not only because he writes her death before it has happened, but also because through his writing he can only "de-skin" himself; he cannot remember his mother and her warm blood. He can only confess that he is haunted by the image of embalming his mother alive (1993, 260). The only mother that he can confess is a bloodless mother who is already dead. Still, only through his murderous confession ritual can he try to acknowledge, remember, or recognize she whose blood gave him life.

The blood in excess of Derrida's confession is maternal blood. The lost memory of the blood shed at his own circumcision is a lost memory of the blood of his birth, his mother's blood. His pain for his mother is his impossible memory of the pain of childbirth. "Circumfession" is the confession of a phantom pain in his sex that is associated with the forgotten pain (a phantom memory) of his own circumcision, a pain that he attributes to his mother. Yet, is this phantom pain in his sex the phantom memory of the pain in his mother's sex? Perhaps even the pain of his birth? With Derrida, we can "follow the traces of blood" in "Circumfession" back to the mother:

> the first I remember having seen with my own eyes, outside, since I was and remain blind to that of my seventh or eighth day, which happens to be the day of my mother's birth, July 23, that first blood that came to me from the sex of a cousin, Simone 7 or 8 years old, the day when the pedal of a toy scooter penetrated her by accident, *Verfall*, with the first phantom sensation, that algic sympathy around my sex which leads me to the towels my mother left lying around, "marked" from red to brown, in the bidet, when as I understood so late, she was having her own "period". (1993, 108)

Here the traces of blood lead Derrida back to the blood of his own circumcision—to which he is blind—which happens to be on the day of his mother's birth (her birthday or perhaps also the day she gives birth). He traces his first blood to the sex of his cousin accidentally penetrated and this trace leads to his mother's menstrual blood. All of these traces bring with them the (sympathetic) phantom memory in his sex of his own circumcision and his mother's blood. He is blind to the blood of his circumcision, but he sees the marks of his mother's blood. But what ritual shed this blood whose trace remains in the mark? How can Derrida trace this maternal blood? He remembers seeing the marks of his mother's blood on towels; he sees her blood coagulated in bedsores on her heels, hips, and sacrum, blood that is not properly contained by skin (1993, 82). But can he see the warm blood of the maternal body? Even if he can sense it and imagine it, he cannot write it.

His autobiography is only a trace of his life and of she who gave him life; like the marks on a towel or discarded skin, the words on the page are leftovers from the life of the body. While telling the story of a life, an autobiography speaks only death; its violence is murderous. Even in the attempt to tell the story of dying—the only story left to tell, it seems—the autobiography automatically graphs the other of life to its trace. By grafting lifeless traces of the life and death of the body into its other, the mother tongue immortalizes man's life. The mother tongue both protects and threatens the social and the divine alliance. It is her tongue that reaffirms her son's alliance with God, with culture, and with woman. He enters the alliance because he has the mother tongue with which to speak.

Following some of this other texts, Derrida figures this alliance with images of the hymen.[43] The hymen occupies a precarious place in Derrida's corpus; it operates both as the sign of the alliance or marriage and the sign of the impossibility of the alliance. Within the economy of Derrida's corpus the hymen is a marriage and an undecidable "concept" that calls any alliance into question. Even while traditionally the circumscription of the hymen in marriage rituals marks the proper entrance of the woman into the marriage alliance and transfers her as unspoiled property from her father to her husband, within Derrida's corpus "hymen" becomes associated with an economy that operates outside of the economy of the proper.

Circumcision, as simulated castration, marks the economy of the proper, property. The mark or scar of circumcision is a reminder of the threat of castration that, within Freudian psychoanalytic theory, forces the male child to enter language and culture. Circumcision circumscribes the castration threat and writes the paternal prohibitions that secure the social onto the body. In Derrida's description of the ritual of circumcision the taboo that raises the threat of castration, incest, is also present; the mother simulates the paternal threat of castration in an act of fellatio. The ritual of circumcision simulates both the prohibited act and the punishment for that act. The ritual of circumcision circumscribes both the social alliance and the threat to that alliance. And both its security and its threat come from the mother. She necessarily stands outside the alliance as it guarantor and its impossibility.

Woman occupies a similar position in the burial ritual. In his analysis of Hegel in *Glas*, Derrida diagnoses "the feminine operation of burial" within which the man entrusts his death to the woman and the woman is responsible for his corpse. For Hegel this is an appropriate task for the woman who is accustomed to the night and the subterranean world of the earth. In addition she is a guardian within the family of an ethics of the singular. Through the burial rituals she protects the singular body of man, his proper individuality, from being eaten by the earth. Paradoxically, the burial ritual, as a symbolic system, separates man from the animals and thereby guarantees that even though his body dies, his spirit does not and he is thus protected from the cannibalism of the earth; his singularity will not be eaten by worms. On Derrida's analysis, however, the feminine operation of burial "does not oppose itself to the exteriority of a nonconscious matter; it suppresses an unconscious desire. The family wants to prevent the dead one from being 'destroyed' and the burial place violated *by this desire*" (Derrida 1986, 144). And although Hegel does not indicate which unconscious desires are to be guarded against, Derrida does. The dead man is not only subject to the threat of material cannibalism but also imaginary cannibalism: "The two functions of (the) burial (place) relieve the dead man of his death, spare him from being destroyed—eaten—by matter, nature, the spirit's being-outside-self, but also by the probably cannibal violence of the survivor's unconscious desires. That is, essentially, the women's, since they, as guardians of (the) burial (place) and the family, are always in a situation of survival" (146). So at the same time that woman desires to incorporate the dead husband into her memory or into herself, she protects him against her own violent cannibalistic (not to mention necrophiliac) desires. She prevents herself from ingesting, incorporating, his pure singularity which has already become universal spirit. She prevents him from returning to nature by remaining within nature and tending to his needs from the outside. She is responsible for the details of maintaining the symbolic rituals which maintain the symbolic system, but only so long as (and in order that) she remain outside of that system guaranteeing its survival. When she threatens to move inside, the system seems to collapse and death destroys both the man and his system. Woman, then, provides both the threat and the security against the threat.

Like the hymen, the woman/mother circumscribes the alliance by breaking it. The hymen, intact, is a sign that the woman is a virgin and can properly (in the sense of *propre*, clean and proper) become the property of another man. Traditionally the marriage ritual involved breaking the hymen to seal the alliance and displaying the resulting blood as proof of the consummation. This blood-mark on a sheet, like the circumcised foreskin, can only serve as a reminder of the blood shed during the ritual, a reminder of the living body that is *not* property. The broken hymen, a membrane skin, with its bloodstained sheet, like the circumcised foreskin with its bloodstained cloth, is a dead skin, a dry parchment, upon which the social ritual is written. These rituals that make the body *propre* leave only traces of life.

If the maternal body is a blind spot in Derrida's texts, it is not only because the life of the body cannot be written, but also because he associates the maternal body with nature or God. The maternal body becomes the speechless mother tongue and the nameless mother's name, the faceless figure of a figurant: "No woman or trace of woman, if I have read correctly—save the mother, that's understood. But this is part of the system. The mother is the faceless figure of a *figurant*, an extra. She gives rise to all the figures by losing herself in the background of the scene like an anonymous persona. Everything comes back to her, beginning with life; everything addresses and destines itself to her. She survives on the condition of remaining at bottom" (Derrida 1985, 38).

The association of the mother with nature, God, or origin is what distinguishes remembrance of the mother from nostalgia for the mother. Nostalgia is always for something that is forever lost because it was never present. Nostalgia for the mother is a longing for an impossible return to the peace of the maternal womb, the silence of a tongue that does not speak, a return to mother earth associated with the death drive (cf. Derrida 1993, 150). Derrida diagnoses such nostalgia in his analysis of Rousseau in *Of Grammatology*. Remembering the mother, on the other hand, is recalling her as a desiring, speaking subject, to whom we are indebted for life. Autobiography attempts to remember, to give birth to life's story, to give words to a silent tongue, to rescue the body from death. Autobiography attempts the impossible. Perhaps, like G. in Derrida's "Circumfession," autobiography only acknowledges without remembering or recognizing.

Derrida's autobiography is the attempt to write an unrecognizable text, a text that is not a remembering because it is not linear like
Bennington's text that sits on top of it. His autobiography is the
attempt to write the impossibility of writing autobiography by
acknowledging that his life is unrecognizable to her who gave him
life, his mother, G. Yet, doesn't the acknowledgment of the debt of
life always bring with it the danger of making the mother into a
god? Of draining her blood and embalming her alive?

Paternal Mother

The Enigma of Sarah Kofman

Implicit in Sarah Kofman's *The Enigma of Woman: Woman in Freud's
Writing* is a diagnosis of the restrictive phallic economy within which
Freud describes feminine sexuality and the mother. One of the central theses of this work is that penis-envy is a screen solution that
serves to cover up man's incestuous and matricidal desires. It is only
with the theory of penis-envy that Freud can explain how men come
to desire women. In fact, Kofman maintains that without the theory
of penis-envy, heterosexuality in men is necessarily pathological,
while fetishism and homosexuality are normal consequences of the
horror that the boy experiences at the sight of his mother's genitals.

Freud asserts that boys feel horror at the sight of female genitals
because of castration anxiety. In his essay "The Uncanny" he also
indicates that "neurotic men declare that they feel there is something uncanny about the female genital organs" (Kofman 1985, 82).
Departing from Kofman's analysis, in *Womanizing Nietzsche* I have
identified the *heimlich* and yet *unheimlich* experience described by Freud
as Freud's fear of birth, his fear that because they were once part of
their mothers' bodies, men may be feminine. The mother's genitals
are uncanny, both *heimlich* and *unheimlich*, because they recall the boy's
original home in his mother's womb. The womb is the origin of his
life, but an identification with the maternal body threatens castration and ultimately death. The physical identification with the
maternal womb threatens to take away that which makes him
different from the mother. The image of a return to the womb also
threatens death insofar as for Freud death is figured as a type of

return to the womb of nature. For the boy, the mother's womb promises both life and death.

Kofman takes up the connection between the mother and death. She suggests that Freud attempts to sublimate death by sublimating the mother. She begins by analyzing Freud's dream of the "Three Fates" in which, after going to bed tired and hungry, Freud dreams of three women in a kitchen, and one of them is making dumplings and tells him that he will have to wait; he is impatient and tries to put on his overcoat to leave, but the coat is too long, its fur trim and embroidery suspicious, and seems to belong to another man. In his analysis of the dream, Freud identifies the woman making dumplings with his mother. His dream appears to him as the wish fulfillment of the basic need for food and love, which he claims come together in the mother's breast. In his analysis, however, no sooner is the maternal figure in his dream associated with love and nourishment than she becomes a messenger of death. Freud associates the dumpling-making hand motion with an experience from his child-hood, when his mother convinced him that everyone dies and returns to the earth by rubbing her hands together as if making dumplings to show him the "blackish scales of *epidermis* produced by the friction as a proof that we are made of earth" (Freud 1967, 238).

In Kofman's analysis Freud's dream becomes representative of maternal pedagogy whose primary lessons are death and deferral. Since the mother is associated with nature and therefore silent, the maternal pedagogy is always only a visual pedagogy later made scientific through male articulation (Kofman 1985, 76). Science, including psychoanalysis, has its origin in this maternal pedagogy. In Freud's dream, the mother tells him that he will have to wait, thus teaching him the lesson of deferred gratification.[44] He will have to wait for a mother substitute in order to fulfill his wish for the life-giving maternal breast that brings together love and nourishment. Next, the mother shows him that the gift of life has to be paid for with death, death in the hands of his mother.

Kofman identifies Freud's interpretation of his dream of the Three Fates as his attempt to master the mother and thereby master death. By translating or sublimating the mother/death into his scientific discourse, Freud tries to claim as his own the lessons learned from his maternal pedagogy and thereby assume the position of master. The mother remains a silent image associated with natural bodily needs, which are later sublated through the intervention of paternal agency into socially acceptable forms of communication and love. The relation with the maternal body is forbidden and dangerous. It is associated with a return to nature that threatens murder and death. To deny the maternal pedagogy, however, is to try to insist that one is born without a mother; it is to try to insist that one gives birth to oneself. To deny that the mother knows or teaches the lessons of science is to commit matricide. But, as Kofman asks, is the mother/ death sublatable? Can science re-present either the mother or death, either the experience of birth or the experience of death?

The sight of the mother's genitals awakens the fear of experiences over which the boy is not the master, the experiences of birth and death, and ultimately incestuous desires. Freud compares the mother's sex to Medusa's head. Men cannot bear the sight of Medusa's head; it turns them to stone. It scares them stiff. Freud claims that the fear is the result of castration anxiety. The boy sees that his mother has been castrated and he fears that he will suffer the same fate; the sight of his mother's sex also awakens sexual desires that reassure him that he has not been castrated. Like Medusa's head, the sight of the mother's sex causes the boy's own sex to turn to stone, which reassures him that he is not castrated like her.

Kofman argues that penis-envy is what completes masculine sexuality. Only penis-envy can guarantee that the boy has not suffered castration. If women, including the mother, envy his penis, that proves both that they don't have one and that he does. It proves that women are castrated and men aren't. The sight of women's "castrated" genitals actually proves that man is not castrated. Kofman once again invokes Medusa: "Penis envy, one might say, plays the same role as the hair on Medusa's head, so often represented by serpents substituted for the penis, the absence of which is the essential cause of horror. Penis envy is seen as equivalent in a way to the symbolic multiplication of man's penis. And if horror in the face of woman's genital organs always has as its *apotropaic* (displacing or turning away) counterpart the erection of the male organ . . . we can then understand how what was *supposed* to draw man away from woman is always at the same time what brings him closer to her" (Kofman 1985, 85; first italics is my emphasis).

Yet, penis envy is merely a screen solution to Freud's more fundamental problem, incestuous desires for the mother and resulting matricide. Kofman suggests that the enigma of woman leads Freud back to the mother, but he stops short of uncovering the mother when he maintains that female sexuality is the bedrock and limit of psychoanalysis (Kofman 1985, 94). Kofman claims that "to respond 'truly' to the riddle of female sexuality would have been in one way or another to dis-cover the Mother, to commit incest" (94). Freud avoids revealing the mother by setting up screens to cover her nakedness, to cover her sex, not because of castration anxiety but because of incestuous and matricidal anxieties. Kofman suggests that unlike Oedipus, who uncovers his mother's sex and satisfies his incestuous desires (which lead to Jocasta's suicide), Freud cannot face the maternal sex because of his incestuous desires and his fear of *her* death (94–95). So, he tries to sublate his incestuous desire into a desire for scientific research on sexuality, which leaves the fundamental riddle of feminine sexuality unanswered. The enigma of Freud's work is the way in which he devises complicated theories with which to *protect* his mother from death by castrating and killing her.

Taking Kofman's analysis one more turn, we can say that Freud learns too well the maternal lesson that the gift of life must be repaid with death. For, he repays his mother's gift of life with death; he sacrifices her out of gratitude. He kills her so that she won't die. In a sense, by defining her in terms of a masculine phallic economy, the economy of the son, he tries to kill her off before he is born so that he won't have to love her and leave her, so she won't leave him. He gives birth to himself out of the phallic economy that motivates the Oedipal drama and his Family Romance. Implicit in Kofman's criticism is the belief that Freud might have found a better way to repay his mother for the gift of life—and to protect her from his own incestuous desires—than castrating her and killing her.

Within the phallic economy, castration, fetishism, or matricide are the only alternatives. Either the boy admits the mother's castration and suffers castration himself by continuing to identify with her; or he denies that she is castrated and puts fetishes, penis substitutes, in the place of her missing organ, which allows him to identify with a phallic mother. Or, he denies any identification with the mother and commits matricide. Kofman suggests that insofar as the mother is defined within a phallic economy, matricide is unavoidable. In some of her early work on Nietzsche, Kofman presents an alternative to the castration, fetishism, or matricide entailed by Freud's phallic economy.

In *Nietzsche and the Philosophic Scene* (*Nietzsche et la scéne philosophique*), Kofman reads Nietzsche's Dionysus as an undecidable figure who "crosses himself out (*se rature*) of the distinction between the veiled and unveiled, masculine and feminine, fetishism and castration" (Kofman 1988, 198). Kofman relies on a passage from *The Gay Science* in which Nietzsche says: "Perhaps truth is a woman who has reasons for not letting us see her reasons? Perhaps her name is—to speak Greek—Baubô?" (Nietzsche 1974, Preface §4, 38). Baubô makes Demeter, the goddess of fertility, laugh by pulling up her skirts and showing her a drawing of Dionysus on her belly. Kofman says that "whenever a woman lifts her skirts, she provokes laughter and flight, such that this gesture can be used as an *apotropaic* means. The belly of the woman plays the role of the head of Medusa. By lifting her skirts, was not Baubô suggesting that she go and frighten Hades, or that which comes to the same, recall fecundity to herself? By displaying the figure of Dionysus on her belly, she recalls the eternal return of life" (Kofman 1988, 196—197, my emphasis). Baubô represents fecundity and the eternal return of life. She is the female double of Dionysus (197).

Dionysus is both male and female, but cannot be reduced to either one or the other. He is beyond this metaphysical distinction (Kofman 1988, 197). He skirts both castration and fetishism by refusing to commit to the phallic economy of truth where it is either there or it isn't. He prefers masks and does not pretend to uncover or cover the secrets of nature/woman. Kofman identifies Nietzsche with Dionysus when she maintains that Nietzsche's reversal of the Platonic notions of unchanging and changing is not only a reversal but also a challenge to this oppositional way of thinking (187). Nietzsche calls into question dogmatism and asserts perspectivism, which, according to Kofman, he can do only because he sees from a dual perspective, "having inherited from his father and his mother opposing evaluations" (187). Like Dionysus, "he is always his own double" (187).

Kofman suggests that by having it both ways, Nietzsche/ Dionysus can give birth to himself without killing off the mother; rather he gives birth to himself through his identification with her fertility. By having it both ways, he does not have to suffer castration nor set up fetishes as penis substitutes in order to identify with his mother.[45] He is his mother and his father. As Nietzsche says in *Ecce Homo*, "The good fortune of my existence, its uniqueness perhaps, lies in its fatality: I am, to express it in the form of a riddle, already dead as my father, while as my mother I am still living and becoming old. This dual descent as it were, both form the highest and the lowest rung on the ladder of life . . . I know both, I am both" (Nietzsche 1967, 222).

Appealing to Nietzsche's dual legacy again in her later work on Nietzsche, in *Explosion I: De l'"Ecce Homo" de Nietzsche* (Kofman: 1992) Kofman prefers to read a later passage from *Ecce Homo* in which Nietzsche declares that "I consider it a great privilege to have had such a father: it seems to me that this explains whatever else I have of privileges—*not* including life, the great Yes to life" (Nietzsche 1967, 226). Relying on numerous passages in which Nietzsche identifies his mother with rabble, baseness, and decadence, Kofman concludes that the "venom" that Nietzsche "spits" at his mother indicates that he does not think that the privilege of life and the great Yes to life come from her. In Kofman's *Explosion I*, this Yes to life becomes Nietzsche's way to overcome his decadent mother and give birth to himself through his identification with his paternal morbidity. Kofman says that "a privilege is a right accorded to the nobility and to it alone: paradoxically, the source of Nietzsche's noble distinction is identified as paternal morbidity" (Kofman 1994a, 37).

Given the fact that Kofman reads Nietzsche's *Ecce Homo* as a Family Romance true to Freud's, it should not seem paradoxical that Nietzsche's nobility is his paternal morbidity (Kofman 1994a, 39). After all, Oedipus only becomes King by killing his father. Kofman explains that Nietzsche's horror at his mother is the flip side of an incestuous love (Kofman 1994a, 43).[46] He denies his incestuous desires by committing matricide. Kofman suggests that through his Dionysian version of the eternal return, Nietzsche imagines a selective return of active principles and difference which would exclude the return of rabble, baseness, and decadence; it excludes the return of the mother. In fact, she maintains that it is Nietzsche's horror at the idea of the eternal return of his mother that makes him recoil from the idea of the eternal return of the same and invent the idea of the eternal return of difference. Kofman points to an early version of *Zarathustra* in which Nietzsche associates the idea of the eternal return of the same with Medusa's head. The concept of the eternal return of the mother, the mother's sex, incestuous desire, like Medusa's head, turns men to stone. Kofman says that "this capital concept would threaten to decapitate Nietzsche if he did not defend himself immediately through the erection of another head, that of Dionysus, which functions *apotropaically*" (Kofman 1994a, 45, my emphasis). Only Dionysus, whose festivals include a celebration of the phallus, can displace Medusa and the fear of castration that she conjures.

On Kofman's reading, Nietzsche disassociates himself from his decadent maternal genealogy, and from an identification with the castrating mother, by substituting economic metaphors for a biological hypothesis (Kofman 1994a, 48). The eternal return is not the return of biological destiny in some historical cycle; rather, the eternal return acts as a principle of selection through which a great individual is born from "an accumulation of energy necessitating the build up of capital that will burst forth or explode all the more strongly for the time it is kept in check" (Kofman 1994a, 49). Kofman says that "the individual undergoes a process of accumulation and selection that permits him to mature into himself, just as the accumulation and selection of forces over the course of time permit the coming into maturity, the explosion, of great men ... the great man is an outcome and an endpoint, and that a long work of accumulation was necessary for his coming" (Kofman 1994, 49).

Although Kofman does not say as much, her analysis suggests that Nietzsche gives up his maternal genealogy, his biological destiny, in favor of a masculine genealogy through which he can give birth to himself. His self-birth is possible as the result of the sublimation of sexual energy, an accumulation of force, that ends in an explosion where all that has been stored up bursts forth and the great man has come into himself. In this way, Kofman's Nietzsche, unlike Kofman's Freud, finds a way to insist that he is born without a mother; he can give birth to himself and avoid castration and fetishism, if not matricide. Kofman's Freud loves his mother too much to uncover her as the object of his desire, to uncover the key to the riddle of feminine sexuality, to uncover the possibility of maternal sexuality; unlike Oedipus, he refuses to answer the riddle of femininity and prefers to cover up his incestuous/matricidal desires with scientific theories. Kofman's Nietzsche, on the other hand, the Nietzsche of her *Explosion*, covers up his incestuous desires with hateful matricidal desires and a theory that denies his connection to his mother.

The riddle or enigma of Kofman's writing is why the trajectory of her work seems to lead both toward and away from the mother. Why does Kofman work so hard to leave the Oedipal model and Family Romance behind in her earlier work and embrace them so vigorously in her later work? Why does she both criticize and sympathize with Freud's refusal to confront the enigma of woman head-on as the enigma of the mother? In her earlier work, why does she praise Nietzsche's criticisms of the pervert's lack of respect for women's modesty, which he avoids through his dual genealogy, and then insist, in spite of passages to the contrary, that Nietzsche breaks with his maternal genealogy in favor of paternal morbidity in her later work?

Kofman seems fascinated with the figure of enigma or riddle in the texts that she analyzes. Her work on Freud and Nietzsche often touches on their enigmas and riddles. Her strategy is to identify what operates as an *apotropaic* figure or concept in their work. An apotropiac figure is one which displaces another or turns away. She maintains that Freud's notion of penis-envy operates apotropaically to displace the horror of the mother's sex; in Nietzsche, Baubô's stomach operates apotropaically to displace Hades' appropriation of fertility, and Dionysus' head operates apotropaically to displace Medusa or the mother's sex. In what way might Kofman's turn from the mother to the father in her later work on Nietzsche be an apotropaic move? Does the figure of the father function apotropaically in order to displace the mother? Is the figure of the father an enigma which covers up the mother? Or, might the rejection of the mother cover up the rejection of the paternal law?

To begin to think through this enigma of Kofman's work, we might turn back to her reading of the enigma of Ariadne in Nietzsche's

Ecce Homo. In *Explosion I*, Kofman, in passing, asserts that Nietzsche possesses the key to the enigma of Ariadne because he is the only one who has suspected that there was any enigma and that the key is Dionysus' suffering (Kofman 1994, 47). The answer to Ariadne's riddle is Dionysus' suffering. Her riddle is an apotropaic figure for his suffering. Yet, in the passage from *Ecce Homo* cited by Kofman, Dionysus' suffering is never explicitly linked to Ariadne's riddle. Nietzsche begins the section by identifying his writing with the suffering god Dionysus, then he talks about possible redemption from nausea and riddles, and finally he concludes with the exhortation "become hard" because Dionysian creativity is hard. The key to Ariadne's riddle could be Dionysian hardness.[47] Nietzsche suggests that Ariadne is the answer to Dionysian solitude and suffering, and that only he knows what Ariadne is. Kofman *reverses* the riddle and reads Dionysus' suffering as the answer to the riddle of Ariadne. In this section of *Explosion I*, Kofman reads Dionysus as a father figure who operates apotropaically to displace Medusa, the horrifying maternal sex. So, the key to the riddle of Ariadne is the suffering of the father, Dionysus.

Kofman seems to have identified with Nietzsche, perhaps with his suffering, perhaps with his dual genealogy. She wrote at least four volumes on his work. She committed suicide on the 150th anniversary of his birth. Like Nietzsche, she was sick most of her life, suffering from digestive problems from the time of her early childhood, and she lost her father when she was young. Might Kofman identify with what she calls Nietzsche's "fantastic genealogy"? Or, perhaps her identification with Nietzsche, and her philosophical fathers, is her own fantastic genealogy through which she attempts to give birth to herself.

In one of the last works published before her death, *"Rue Ordener, Rue Labat,"* Kofman describes the experience of losing her father during the Nazi occupation of France. She begins her autobiographical essay: "From him, only his pen remains with me. . . . I have used it during all of my scholarly work. It gave out on me before I could decide to abandon it. I have it in my possession always, fixed with scotch-tape, it is before my eyes on my work table and it compels [*contraint*] me to write, write. My numerous books have maybe been inevitable (or obligatory) [*obligées*] routes in order to reach the point to tell 'it' ['*ça*']" (Kofman 1994b, 9; my translation). Her father's pen compels her to write; she writes from her paternal obligation. And all that she has written has been leading up to telling this story, the story of her father's death and her relationship with her mother during the war. Her writing obliges her to tell this story.

On July 16, 1942, Sarah Kofman's father, Rabbi Bereck Kofman, was taken from his Paris apartment by the police and never returned. Later, they heard that he was beaten with an ax by a Jewish butcher in Auschwitz and buried alive. During the war, Sarah Kofman's mother hid Sarah and her five siblings with families in the country. Kofman tells the story of her refusal to eat pork, which she describes as an unconscious obedience to the paternal law as a pretext for returning to her mother: "This refusal which appears as the pretext of obedience to the paternal law comes also, without being completely conscious, to serve as a means to return me to the house, close to my mother" (Kofman 1994b, 30; my translation). Her obedience to the paternal law, which she calls earlier a *supplice paternal* (paternal burden), is practiced for the sake of the mother. For, as she says, "*Le vrai danger: être séparée de ma mère*" (the true danger: to be separated from my mother) (Kofman 1994b, 33; my translation).

Sarah returns to her mother and continues, now consciously, to use the obedience to the paternal law, refusing to eat, throwing up, along with crying, to remain with her mother. After hiding in various places in Paris, Sarah and her mother end up staying with a former neighbor of the Kofman family who had moved two metro stops away to Rue Labat. Sarah calls this woman, who becomes a second mother to her, "mémé." Kofman describes how she turns away from her mother and Judaism and becomes attached to mémé. By the end of the war, Sarah preferred to stay with mémé than be with her mother, who had become intensely jealous of mémé's attentions to Sarah. Mémé introduced Sarah to new books, a new religion, a new diet, new clothes. In the street, Sarah passed as her daughter to avoid the Nazis. Out of her mouth, Sarah first heard of philosophy and various philosophers in the context of mémé's anti-Semitic remarks about Judaism and Jews. After the war, Sarah's mother struggled violently to keep Sarah away from mémé. And, even though she loved mémé or was in love with her, Sarah was relieved when, in spite of a court order that gave custody of Sarah to mémé, her mother took her away.

After she testified against her mother in court, she says that she felt as if she had committed a crime and was wanted; she uses the word *recherchée*, which was the word used to refer to the Jews that were being sought by the Nazis. She describes feeling ashamed of preferring mémé to her mother (Kofman 1994b, 55). She feels guilty for abandoning her mother for another woman. Yet Sarah continues a clandestine relationship with mémé until mémé's death.

Toward the end of *Rue Ordener, Rue Labat*, Kofman compares her relationship to her mother and mémé, her two mothers, to two works of art: a da Vinci painting and a Hitchcock film. Da Vinci's painting *Carton de Londres* depicts the infant Christ with the Virgin Mary and St. Anne. Kofman then quotes Freud's analysis of the painting at length. Freud maintains that the painting reflects the fact that de Vinci's step-mother replaces his real mother in his heart. The Hitchcock film *The Lady Vanishes*, presents a more complicated comparison. Kofman says that this is one of her favorite films because of the visceral anxiety she experiences when the "good 'maternal' face of the old woman" on the train is replaced with the hard and threatening face of another woman, "the bad breast in the place of the good breast . . . the one transforming itself into the other" (Kofman 1994b, 76–77).

In the course of *Rue Ordener*, Kofman's mother undergoes a similar transformation. She begins as the mother without whom Sarah cannot live and will not eat, and she becomes the hard and threatening mother who beats Sarah and with whom she cannot live and will not eat. Mémé becomes the good mother, the desirable mother, close to whom Sarah experiences unfamiliar sensations in her body.

Several times Kofman describes her turn away from her mother and her turn away from Judaism as parts of one movement. She associates the law of her father with her mother; and just as she obeys the law in order to be close to her mother, she abandons the law as she abandons her mother. She rejects her mother and the religion that she always found frightening and burdensome, the religion that keeps her mother prisoner on *Rue Labat* during the war and makes its necessary for her to hide. She says that the true danger is to be separated from her mother because with her mother she is "saved." But she discovers that at the hands of the Nazis her mother cannot keep her safe; her mother becomes associated with danger.

Her mother becomes the true danger. Mémé is the one who keeps her safe. Kofman ends her autobiographical essay with mémé's death; in the last line of the essay, Kofman tells a story recounted to her by the priest at mémé's funeral that on mémé's tomb it is written that she had saved a little Jewish girl during the war.

Like Kofman's Freud, Kofman both kills her mother and saves her by writing her story. Like Kofman's Nietzsche, Kofman associates her mother with everything that drags her down and keeps her from herself. Like Kofman's Nietzsche who identifies with the suffering of his father–god, Dionysus, Kofman identifies with her father's suffering which compels her to write. Like Nietzsche, her creative inheritance is her paternal morbidity. Like her Nietzsche, Kofman creates her own fantastic genealogy.

Kofman's ambivalence to her mother, and the split that she experiences between the good mother and the bad mother in *Rue Ordener*, might help to frame the enigma of the mother in Kofman's work and Kofman's fascination with the ambivalent maternal in both Freud and Nietzsche. Rather than identify with her abject mother who, in both her good and bad forms, becomes associated with the pain of the war, Kofman identifies with her philosophical fathers. Whereas during the war, obedience to the law of her father threatened her safety but also returned her to her mother, obedience to her philosophical fathers provides a world safe from her mother.

Kofman's mother becomes associated with the paternal prohibitions, while her father is associated with suffering and sacrifice. He does not hide; he gives himself up. He is murdered for praying instead of working on the Sabbath. For Kofman, her father's pure relationship to the rites of his religion turns religion into art and law into morality, while her mother's relationship, sullied by the compromises of war and undermined by mémé's anti-Semitism, turns the rites of religion into dangerous convention and arbitrary prohibition.

I present a riddle of my own: What happens when the mother becomes a representative of paternal prohibition? When the separation from the mother is not the result of paternal prohibition, but the rejection of the paternal prohibition results in the separation from the mother? Can Kofman's fidelity to Freud's Family

Romance actually help us to think familial relations outside of the Freudian Oedipal model? I suspect that clues can be found in the stomach.

Recall Freud's dream which he describes as a wish fulfillment for the mother's breast, the place where love and nourishment meet. In his dream nourishment associated with his mother, the dumplings, becomes a visual aid in the lesson of death. Like the dried dumpling dough, we return to the earth. We become what we eat, flakes of dough. The dream that Freud interprets as a wish for the connection between food and love is really a dream about the connection between food and death. The mother is the link between food and love and between food and death. How can she be both what makes food love and what makes food death? How does she go from the good nourishing maternal breast that Kofman associates with the kindly Miss Froy in Hitchcock's film *The Lady Vanishes* to the bad threatening maternal breast?

It might seem that this transition can be explained with Freud's theories on how the infant separates from the mother; the transition from good to bad breast is a necessary step in weaning the child. But Sarah's case is not so simple. In fact, this case challenges Freud's notion of feminine identity. For Freud, the girl separates from her mother when she realizes that her mother is castrated and that she too is castrated and she blames her mother. In the end, she identifies with her mother in the hopes that her love for her father will give her a baby, which is now the symbolic instantiation for the missing penis. Here, however, the girl refuses an identification with her mother in order to separate herself from her father and, in the end, identifies with her father substitutes.

At this point, it might seem that what we have is a girl who moves through the masculine Oedipal situation whereby she refuses an identification with her mother and identifies with her father in the hopes that some day she will have her mother or mother substitute as a love-object. Yet, in this case the prohibited mother becomes identified with the prohibition itself. The move away from the mother is at the same time a move away from the paternal prohibition. So, rather than accept the paternal prohibition in the hopes of receiving a mother substitute, Sarah rejects the paternal prohibition to receive her mother substitute, mémé, with whom she identifies *and* whom she desires. Desire and identification are not the polar opposites that Freud describes.

Identification, Desire, and Abjection

For both boys and girls, Freud describes an original identification with, and desire for, the mother which the Oedipal situation effectively splits. Post-Oedipus, identification and desire lie at opposite poles. The boy discontinues his identification with his mother, identifies with his father, and desires a mother substitute. The girl is forced to identify again with her mother, even after the betrayal of castration, and now desires her father. What Oedipus insures is that desire and identification are split. You desire what you are not and you identify with what you are. But, as I have argued elsewhere, Freud's description of the desire for the feminine is not a description of a desire for something that the masculine is not, but what the masculine negates and rejects in order to be. Freud's feminine is always defined within a masculine economy as castrated or phallic, which insures that man is *not* castrated.[48] It could be said, then, that Freud splits identification and desire, insists that he desire what he negates, the feminine, so that he can insure that he is himself masculine.

But is not desire the excess of identification? Desire is fueled not by an identification that turns the other into the same, you into me. Rather, desire is fueled by an identification that turns the same into an other, that takes me beyond myself towards you. Desire does not say "you are like me so I want you," nor does it say "you are not like me so I can be sure that I am me"; rather, desire says "because you are not me, I can move out of myself towards you." Desire is the excess of the other in one's own identification. I can identify with your desire, but you and your experience are always in excess of that identification. Desire and identification are not polar opposites, neither are they the same. To say that there is no desire without identification is not to say that desire is the annihilation of difference. Rather, desire is the difference in excess of any identification.

Hegel was right that the subject is desire. But desire is not as he describes it. Desire is not the urge to overcome the otherness in the self and to recuperate oneself from the other. Subjectivity does not attempt to close in on itself and fortify itself against the other. Rather, subjectivity opens itself onto the other, multiplies itself but not in the sense of reproducing itself. Desire is the urge to move out into otherness. I do not define myself in relation to a hostile external world against which I am me by virtue of denying everything that I am not. Rather, I am *by virtue* of what I am not. I am by virtue of my engagement with what I am not. Without the difference, desire disappears. Yet, it is not identification with the other that kills desire.

We need to rethink identification such that it is not opposed to differentiation. We need a notion of identification that can navigate between the two extremes that plague contemporary attempts to theorize difference: at the one pole, the position that I can understand anyone by just taking up their position, and at the other, that I can understand no one because of radical alterity which prevents me from taking up their position; at the one pole, communication is unencumbered and we simply say what we mean, and at the other, communication is impossible. The first assumes that we are absolutely identical, which erases our difference, and the second assumes that we are absolutely different, which erases our communion. I maintain that we can communicate or commune only because of our radical difference. This is the reason we do so. Communication across difference is not an attempt to master otherness. Identification, communication, communion, community, are possible only because of our differences. And, while there are wars, oppression, subjugation, hatred, and discrimination, these are not *necessary* to identification, either on the individual or group level.

Psychological identification or identity does not operate like logical identity. Identity within the psyche, conscious or unconscious, does not operate like A=A. Psychological identity is not equivalence. If I identify with someone this does not mean that I make them equivalent to myself. Rather, through the space between us, through our difference, I attempt to find common ground in that which is never the same, our different experiences. These attempts to commune are not part of a hostile Hegelian struggle to recuperate myself from my recognition of myself in you. I do not see myself in you and then try to annihilate the difference that separates us. Rather, I see our differences and try to move out of myself towards you in order to commune with that which ultimately I can never know. And, it is through our relationship and our differences that I can begin to see something of myself. Theories that propose that identity is dependent on the exclusion of difference presuppose that one's sense of oneself needs to be contained, or is containable. But, our experiences of ourselves are not like contained or containable fixed units. We experience our lives as flux and flow, full of surprises even to ourselves.

Contrary to Hegel, who maintains that desire is the attempt to overcome the otherness of the other, desire *disappears* when the self attempts to master the otherness of the other. When the self attempts to master the other in a struggle for recognition which ends in self-knowledge through reason which annihilates its own otherness, this is the death of desire and not its aim. In terms of relationships with others, the illusion that I know myself or that I know another person is an illusion of mastery that kills the possibility of desire. Desire requires a fluidity and openness of subjectivity that charges and electrifies the space between two people. To say that I know you, or that I know that you always behave like that, is to control you and turn you into something that you are not. And, when I am sure that I know you, I am no longer having a relationship with you, but only with myself. Relationships require identification across and through difference, identification that does not reduce the other to the same, identification as compassion and communion.

Theories that identity is constructed through the exclusion or abjection of the other are widespread. Teresa Brennan, Judith Butler, and Julia Kristeva, for example, all propose such theories. In various ways, they all maintain that identity is possible only by abjecting the other. Their theories do not just propose that in order to have an identity we need to exclude some possibilities from our sense of ourselves, but that these exclusions are hostile and that which is excluded becomes abject and threatening to us. If we accept such theories, then relationships with those who are different from ourselves is possible only by turning them into something exactly like us, or experiencing them as a hostile threat, hating them and trying to kill them. While these theories help explain war, oppression, subjugation, hatred, and discrimination, they also *normalize* them. Within what in chapter three I will call a virile economy, identity comes through war; but the virile economy is not necessary or natural. It serves particular ends for certain people. The notion that identity is constructed in hostile opposition also serves particular political purposes.

In *Purity and Danger*, Mary Douglas describes defilement as the danger to identity constituted by filth, which is always defined in relation to the borders of that very identity. Douglas's theory of defilement has been transformed by Julia Kristeva into her neo-hegelian theory of abjection, with which she purports to explain the dynamics of both group and individual identity as constituted through the rejection of otherness. In *Powers of Horror* and later in *Strangers to Ourselves*, Kristeva maintains that our identity and sense of self is built through a process of exclusion. Our individual identity is formed through exclusions which become repressed in the unconscious in order to allow ego boundaries to form. Our national or group identity is formed through exclusions which become associated with rival groups or go unrecognized entirely yet continue to operate as the basis for exclusion; these exclusions set up the border against which we define ourselves as nations or cultures.

Judith Butler expands the theory of abjection when she analyzes the dynamics of exclusion inherent in identification. In *Gender Trouble*, following Kristeva, Butler maintains that "The 'abject' designates that which has been expelled from the body, descharged as excrement, literally rendered 'Other.' This appears as an expulsion of alien elements, but the alien is effectively established through this expulsion. The construction of the 'not-me' as abject establishes the boundaries of the body which are also the firsst contours of the subject" (Butler 1990, 133). In *Bodies that Matter*, she extends her analysis of the exclusion inherent in identification when she describes materiality as delimted through a proceedure which "marks a boundary that includes and exludes, that decides, as it were, what well and will not be the stuff of the object to which we refer. This marking off will have some narmative force and, indeed, some violence, for it can contruct only through erasing; it can bound a thing only through enforcing a certain criterion, a principle of selectivity" (Butler 1993, 11)

The theory of abjection is in the background of Teresa Brennan's notion of a foundational fantasy through which the subject both imitates and envies the original mother. In *History After Lacan*, Brennan describes the way in which the masculine ego recreates the world in its own image, which suppresses and distorts the powers of the

conditions of individuation does not undermine freedom, but makes it possible (20). Law should protect the equivalent chance to become a person for all sexuate beings.

Cornell's theory of equality suggests an alternative notion of identity in which one individual's ability to become a person is not opposed to another's. If every sexuate being can be guaranteed the minimum conditions of individuation to protect their equivalent chance to become a person, then one's self-identity and self-respect can and must be consistent with another's self-identity and self-respect. Although the content of their individuality may vary greatly—how each acts and behaves—their chance at individuation must be equal. This suggests that in principle we can form individual and group identities in harmony, at least on the level of the fundamental structure of identity, if never on the level of the content of identity.

Part of my project here and elsewhere has been to suggest alternatives to the traditional philosophical and psychoanalytic views of individuation and self-identity which are built around the exclusion of otherness and difference. In particular, as an alternative to models of the mother-infant relationship that view the mother as an obstacle that must be overcome in order for the infant to become a social subject, I endorse a model of the mother-infant relationship that views the mother as the first cooperative partner in a social relationship that makes subjectivity possible. The reason why so many traditional theories of the mother–child relationship see the mother as an obstacle to autonomy is that motherhood and maternity are conceived in opposition to everything social and everything fundamental to civil society. Mothers have been imagined as creatures motivated only by instinct and natural tendencies.

With Brennan, Butler, and Kristeva, we could *diagnose* contemporary marginalization and exclusion *using* theories of identity that are built on abjection, but this type of identity is not the only type. There are other ways to construct one's identity, as an individual and a group, besides going to war. Goals that unite people aren't always the destruction of a common enemy. Identity can also be formed in loving relationships, in the spaces between us. Relationships with difference and otherness can give us new perspectives on ourselves; to say that we gain new perspectives on ourselves is not to say that difference is erased. Relationships bring us "out of ourselves" in order to give us a sense of ourselves, to "see" ourselves for the first time. It is only through our relationships that we become who we are.

We don't have a fixed identity that fends off any change by excluding all others and anything different. Rather, as Kristeva says, we are other to ourselves. Our otherness to ourselves comes through our relations with others who are different from us. This does not mean that we contain the other and that the other is really part of us, or the same (which is sometimes suggested in Kristeva's account); rather, through our encounters with others and their differences, we become other to ourselves and in the process become ourselves. Since our lives are social from their beginnings, we always experience this otherness as fundamental to our sense of self. The sociality through which we become individuated is not necessarily or only hostile and antagonistic. It is the otherness or difference inherent in social relations—the space between us—that makes love possible. Meaning is created in the space between social bodies.

Body Language

Bodies Speak

In *The Gift of Death*, Derrida asks, "What does the body mean to say by trembling or crying, presuming one can speak here of the body, or of saying, and of rhetoric?" (Derrida 1995, 55). It seems unusual for Derrida, whose theories incorporate the body only as metaphor, to speak of the metaphorics of the body itself, to speak of body language. Most people would agree that the body speaks through its gestures, through *body language*. And that in face-to-face conversations, we feel the effects of body language; it is what is missing in phone conversations and e-mail conversations. Psychoanalysis has attempted to decode body language. Gestures and affects are focal concerns for analysts trying to read their analysands' unconscious wishes. Repression and psychic disturbance present themselves in and on the body not only through affect and gesture but also through somatic symptoms. *Soma* expresses *psyche*, either through discourse, body language, or somatic symptoms.

Somatic symptoms can also be the result of the lack of adequate discourse and spaces to speak. What cannot be said might be manifest as a somatic symptom. Hysteria might be an example of somatic symptoms that result from the inadequate spaces in which to speak, social restrictions, and social pressures. Irigaray suggests that insofar as patriarchal culture has historically, in a multitude of ways, denied feminine sexuality, proscribed feminine sexuality as solely reproductive, defined feminine sexuality in terms of man's pleasure, all of feminine sexuality has been silenced. There is no language available within patriarchal culture to speak feminine sexualities. To the extent that women's sexuality is repressed within our culture, to the extent to which women's desires are repressed, all women are hysterics attempting to find the language for their desires.

In *This Sex Which Is Not One*, Irigaray says that "the problem of 'speaking (as) woman' is precisely that of finding a possible continuity between [hysterical] gestural expression or [hysterical] speech of desire—which at present can only be identified in the form of symptoms and pathology—and a language, including verbal language" (Irigaray 1985b, 137). This is Irigaray's project: to find continuity between hysterical expressions and language, to find a language with which to speak the desires which have been excluded from phallocratic discourses, including philosophy, psychoanalysis, and medicine.

While hysteria can be paralyzing, it can also be powerful and resistant. Irigaray sees hysterical symptoms as resistance to oppressive social norms. In *This Sex Which Is Not One*, in answer to questions raised by her earlier book *Speculum of the Other Woman*, Irigaray says that "there is always, in hysteria, both a reserve power and a paralyzed power. A power that is always already repressed, by virtue of the *subordination* of feminine desire to phallocratism; a power constrained to silence and mimicry, owing to the submission of the 'perceptible,' of 'matter,' to the intelligible and its discourse. Which occasions 'pathological' effects. And in hysteria there is at the same time the possibility of another mode of 'production,' notably gestural and lingual; but this is maintained in latency. Perhaps as a cultural reserve yet to come?" (Irigaray 1985b, 138).

While Freud identified hysteria as a repressed heterosexual desire which manifests itself in somatic symptoms in the hysteric, Irigaray identifies hysteria with a desire that resists the heterosexual norms defined by patriarchal values. Because the hysteric's desire runs counter to the norms for women proposed in patriarchal culture, there is no language with which to express these desires in that culture. In spite of the fact, as even Freud admits, the girl's first love object is her mother, women are not allowed a proper language with which to express love for other women. Too often the only language available is the language of disease and perversion. Faced with either conforming to the restrictive desires prescribed for her by patriarchal culture, or remaining silent about her desires, the hysteric's desires "speak" through gestures, somatic symptoms, and her physical suffering.

The hysterical gestures are in excess of the language available to patriarchal discourses. Hysterical symptoms are proof that women will not be forced to serve men's desires. Elizabeth Grosz argues that "the hysteric thus attempts to 'cope' with the demands and expectations of a male-dominated culture which relies on women's renunciation of their relations to other women, and of their unmediated relations to their own bodies and pleasures, by summoning up an apparently incapacitating 'illness,' which prevents her from giving satisfaction to men while satisfying herself in a compromise or symptomatic form. . . . In this sense, the hysteric is a proto-feminist, or at least an isolated individual who, if she had access to the experiences of other women, may locate the problem in cultural expectations of femininity rather than in femininity itself" (Grosz 1989, 135).

To argue that hysteria is a mode of resistance to male dominance is not to suggest that it is the most effective mode of resistance. Obviously, in the case of painful physical and emotional symptoms, hysteria is as self-destructive as it is resistant. A contemporary example might be that of anorexia nervosa. The anorexic takes the cultural ideal of feminine beauty past its extreme and thereby undermines the ideal by parodying it. As Elizabeth Grosz points out, "The anorexic seems to be saying: 'Alright, you want me to be slim. I'll be slim. I'll be so slim that you'll no longer find me attractive. This is what you want; but what you'll get is much more than you bargained for'" (Grosz 1989, 136). Yet, even as the anorexic calls into question the ideal of the slender body, she also threatens her own body.

Irigaray reappropriates hysteria and redeploys hysterical symptoms in order to release the power reserve in the hysteric's pent-up desires and to begin to set in motion the cultural reserve yet to come. By reopening the discussion of hysteria in the context of cultural repression rather than individual repression, Irigaray's analysis makes it possible to diagnose the cultural phenomena that cause hysterical reactions. Hysterical symptoms can be reread as the result of oppressive standards for feminine sexuality rather than the result of individual madness or disease.

Just as the hysteric exaggerates what is expected of her and takes on the symptoms of others, so too Irigaray's styles exaggerate the role of woman assigned by the texts of philosophers and psychoanalysts. Like the hysteric, she mimes the texts of others to show how restrictive, even absurd, they are when taken to their limit. Like the hysteric, she does not have the language available to her to speak feminine desire. Still she opens the space for such a language by miming the language that for so long has denied feminine desire. In her texts on Plato, Aristotle, Descartes, Nietzsche, Freud, Lacan, and others, she often merely quotes large bits of their texts and frames these quotes with just a few comments. Within the context of her text, these spokesmen of the Western tradition come off sounding unreasonable, if not hysterical.

At the center of *Speculum of the Other Woman*, Irigaray combines the figure of the hysteric with the figure of the mystic and creates what she calls *La Mysterique*, or the mysteric. In this frenzied essay, Irigaray describes the power reserve or excess of medieval mystics as an hysterical expression of the divine. As Eluned Summers-Bremner points out, like hysterics, medieval mystics often physically mimed the suffering of Christ in ways that resemble "orgasm or childbirth (and frequently both), experiences which are denied symbolic representation in the phallocentric order" (Summers-Bremnar 1995, 40). By identifying their experiences with accepted patriarchal figures, especially Christ, these female mystics could express something of an otherwise forbidden sexuality.

Irigaray suggests that the cultural reserve yet to come may be the divine. If the male traditions have left us without any divinity after the proclaimed death of God, Irigaray maintains that we can recreate divinity through the articulations of the excesses of bodily experience. We do not have to experience the excesses of bodily experience as it relates to the possibilities of our language as a painful lack or somatic symptom. Rather, we can experience bodily excess as the ecstasy and pleasure of divinity. This divinity is not God the father, or a masculine divinity who transcends our feeble and inferior finite embodiment, but rather divinity that expresses embodiment and embodiment that is divine; what Irigaray calls a *sensible* transcendental.

Irigaray's reappropriation of hysteria does not limit us to diseased silent bodies. Rather, she opens the possibility of using language to express sensible, sensuous desires so that they do not have to cause disease or be silent. She imagines the liberation of repressed desires in a language that we speak to each other and through which we conjure the sensible transcendental. By speaking the excess of bodily desire from within the sensible, we speak the transcendental, we experience the divine (Irigaray 1993a, 129).

Language Listens [49]

Psychoanalysis not only proposes that the body's language speaks repressed desires, but also that language proper, discourse, speaks drives, which operate between *soma* and *psyche*, between body and soul. The history of philosophy is full of frustrated attempts to make connections between the body and language, between body and soul. Without a notion of drives, philosophy has been unable to formulate a satisfactory theory of the relationship between body and soul. Many philosophers begin with the assumption that body and soul have nothing in common, they are two different realms, and then attempt to find the point of interaction. Of course, these theories begin with an assumption that ultimately prevents any interaction. Questions about the relationship between body and language continue to trouble philosophers. How does language speak bodily experience? How can we say what we mean?

For example, Derrida continues to struggle with the relationship between language and the living, speaking body. On the most reductionistic and hostile readings, Derrida's critics take the phrase from *Of Grammatology*, "there is nothing outside of the text," out of context to claim that Derrida is a linguistic monist or a nominalist who does not believe in the reality of anything other than language itself (158).

A careful reading of Derrida makes this position difficult to defend. As Derrida says in an interview: "It is totally false to suggest that deconstruction is a suspension of reference. Deconstruction is always deeply concerned with the 'other' of language. I never cease to be surprised by critics who see my work as a declaration that there is nothing beyond language, that we are imprisoned in language; it is, in fact, saying the exact opposite" (Derrida 1984, 123).

Derrida's work is a continual struggle to articulate the "other" of language, which, as he reminds us, is impossible (see Derrida 1989, 60). The other of language is antithetical to language even if it is the call from this other that gives language its meaning. Still, language always only points to that which is absent; it is this absence that makes signification possible. Words can do no more than point to, or conjure, the absence of that about which they speak. That about which they speak—life, love, the material world—is other to language.

On Derrida's account, language does violence to this other (Derrida 1976, 135). At best, language gives us traces of something beyond language, homicidal traces that turn life into death. Although in "Circumfessions" Derrida dreams of a writing that could directly express the living body without violence, for him language is always the dead remains of a living body: "If I compare the pen to a syringe, and I always dream of a pen that would be a syringe, a suction point rather than that very hard weapon with which one must inscribe, incise, choose, calculate, take ink before filtering the inscribable, playing the keyboard on the screen, whereas here, once the right vein has been found, no more toil, no responsibility, no risk of bad taste nor of violence, the blood delivers itself all alone, the inside gives itself up" (1993, 12). Even as Derrida imagines writing that is like a transfusion of the living body into language, he resigns himself to the violence of trying to inscribe the uninscribable. The living body is this uninscribable.

Kristeva's theory more optimistically addresses the problem of the relationship between language and bodily experience by postulating that, through the semiotic element, bodily drives manifest themselves in language. Instead of lamenting what is lost, absent, or impossible in language, Kristeva marvels at this other realm that makes its way into language. The force of language is living drive force transferred into language. Signification is like a transfusion of the living body into language. This is why psychoanalysis can be effective; the analyst can diagnose the active drive force as it is manifest in the analysand's language. Language is not cut off from the body. And, while, for Kristeva, bodily drives involve a type of violence, negation, or force, this process does not merely necessitate sacrifice and loss. The drives are not sacrificed to signification; rather bodily drives are an essential semiotic element of signification.

As I argued in *Reading Kristeva: Unraveling the Doublebind*, Kristeva attempts to bring the speaking body back into discourse by arguing both that the logic of language is already operating at the material level of bodily processes and that bodily drives make their way into language. She postulates that signifying practices are the result of material bodily processes. Drives make their way into language through the semiotic element of signification, which does not represent bodily drives but discharges them. In this way, all signification has material motivation. All signification discharges bodily drives. Drives move between *soma* and *psyche*, and the evidence of this movement is manifest in signification.

Kristeva takes up Freud's theory of drives as instinctual energies that operate between biology and culture. Drives have their source in organic tissue and aim at psychological satisfaction. Drives are heterogeneous; that is, there are several different drives that can conflict with each other. In *Revolution in Poetic Language*, Kristeva describes drives as "material, but they are not solely biological since they both connect and differentiate the biological and symbolic within the dialectic of the signifying body invested in practice" (1984, 167). Nearly two decades later, Kristeva emphasizes the same dialectical relationship between the two spheres—biological and social—across which the drives operate. In *New Maladies of the Soul*, she describes the drives as "a pivot between 'soma' and psyche', between biology and representation" (1995, 30). Drives can be reduced neither to the biological nor to the social; they operate in between these two realms and bring one realm into the other. Drives are energies or forces that move between the body and representation. This notion of drives challenges the traditional dualism between the biological and the social, the body and the mind. Kristeva's attempts to bring the body back to theory also challenge traditional notions of the body; for her, the body is more than material. [50]

By insisting that language expresses bodily drives through its semiotic element, Kristeva's articulation of the relationship between language and the body circumvents the traditional problems of
representation. The tones and rhythms of language, the materiality of
language, are bodily. Traditional theories which postulate that language represents bodily experience fall into an impossible situation by
presupposing that the body and language are distinct, even opposites.
Some traditional theories purport that language is an instrument that
captures, mirrors, or copies bodily experience. The problem, then,
becomes how to explain the connection between these two distinct
realms of language, on the one hand, and material, on the other. [51]

Since traditional theories have not been able to explain adequately
how language is related to the material world, some contemporary
theorists have proposed that language does not refer to some extralinguistic material world; rather, language refers only to itself. Words
have their meaning in relation to other words and not in relation to
things in the world. We can discern the meaning of words by analyzing the structures within which words operate rather than by examining the correspondence between words and things. Whereas
Husserlian phenomenology describes words as windows onto the
meaning constituted by the transcendental subject, structuralism
describes words as elements operating within systems that constitute
their meanings, and post-structuralism describes words as traces of
the processes of difference and deferral that constitute the illusion of
their stable meaning and determinant references, Kristeva describes
the meaning of words as combinations of dynamic *semiotic* bodily
drive force or affect and stable *symbolic* grammar.

Kristeva maintains that all signification is composed of these two
elements, the symbolic and the semiotic. The symbolic element is
what philosophers might think of as meaning proper. That is, the
symbolic is the element of signification that sets up the structures
by which symbols operate. The symbolic is the structure or grammar that governs the ways in which symbols can refer. The semiotic
element, on the other hand, is the organization of drives in language.
It is associated with rhythms and tones that are meaningful parts of
language and yet do not represent or signify something. In *Revolution
in Poetic Language*, Kristeva maintains that rhythms and tones do not
represent bodily drives; rather, bodily drives are *discharged* through

rhythms and tones. In *New Maladies of the Soul*, she discusses different ways of representing that are not linguistic in a traditional sense. There, Kristeva says that the meaning of the semiotic element of language is "translinguistic" or "nonlinguistic" (1995, 32–33; 31); she explains this by describing these semiotic elements as irreducible to language because they "turn toward language even though they are irreducible to its grammatical and logical structures" (35). This is to say that they are irreducible to the symbolic element of language. The symbolic element of language is the domain of position and judgment. It is associated with the grammar or structure of language that enables it to signify something.

The dialectical oscillation between the semiotic and the symbolic is what makes signification possible. Without the symbolic element of signification, we have only sounds or delirious babble. But without the semiotic element of signification, signification would be empty and we would not speak, for the semiotic provides the motivation for engaging in signifying processes. We have a bodily need to communicate. The symbolic provides the structure necessary to communicate. Both elements are essential to signification. And it is the tension between them that makes signification dynamic. The semiotic both motivates signification and threatens the symbolic element. The semiotic provides the movement or negativity and the symbolic provides the stasis or stability that keeps signification both dynamic and structured.

While the symbolic element gives signification its meaning in the strict sense of reference, the semiotic element gives signification meaning in a broader sense. That is, the semiotic element makes symbols matter; by discharging drive force in symbols, it makes them significant. Even though the semiotic challenges meaning in the strict sense—meaning in the terms of the symbolic—it gives symbols their meaning for our lives. Signification makes our lives meaningful, in both senses of meaning—signifying something and having significance—through its symbolic and semiotic elements. The interdependence of the symbolic and semiotic elements of signification guarantees a relationship between language and life, signification and experience; the interdependence between the symbolic and semiotic guarantees a relationship between body (*soma*) and soul (*psyche*). [52]

In addition to proposing that bodily drives make their way into language, Kristeva maintains that the logic of signification is already present in the material of the body. Once again combining psychoanalytic theory and linguistics, Kristeva relies on both Lacan's account of the infant's entrance into language and Saussure's account of the play of signifiers. Lacan points out that the entrance into language requires separation, particularly from the maternal body. Saussure maintains that signifiers signify in relation to one another through their differences. Combining these two theses, it seems that language operates according to principles of separation and difference, as well as identification and incorporation. Kristeva argues that the principles or structures of separation and difference are operating in the body even before the infant begins to use language.

In *Revolution in Poetic Language*, Kristeva proposes that the processes of identification or incorporation, and differentiation or rejection, that make language use possible are operating within the material of the body. She maintains that before the infant passes through what Freud calls the Oedipal situation, or what Lacan calls the Mirror Stage, the patterns and logic of language are already operating in a pre-Oedipal situation. In *Revolution* she focuses on differentiation or rejection and the oscillation between identification and differentiation. She analyzes how material rejection (for example the expulsion of waste from the body) is part of the process that sets up the possibility of signification. [53]

She calls the bodily structures of separation the "logic of rejection." For Kristeva the body, like signification, operates according to an oscillation between instability and stability, or negativity and stasis. For example, the process of metabolization is a process that oscillates between instability and stability: food is taken into the body and metabolized and expelled from the body. Because the structure of separation is bodily, these bodily operations prepare us for our entrance into language. From the time of birth, the infant's body is engaging in processes of separation; anality is the prime example. Birth itself is also an experience of separation, one body separated from another.

Part of Kristeva's motivation for emphasizing these bodily separations and privations is to provide an alternative to the Lacanian model of language acquisition. Lacan's account of signification and self-consciousness begins with the Mirror Stage and the paternal metaphor's substitution of the law of the father for the desire of the mother. On the traditional psychoanalytic model of both Freud and Lacan, the child enters the social or language out of fear of castration. The child experiences its separation from the maternal body as a tragic loss and consoles itself with words instead. Paternal threats make words the only, if inadequate, alternative to psychosis. Kristeva insists, however, that separation begins prior to the Mirror Stage or oedipal situation and that this separation is not only painful but also pleasurable. She insists that the child enters the social and language not just due to paternal threats but also because of paternal love.

At bottom, Kristeva criticizes the traditional account because it cannot adequately explain the child's move to signification. If what motivates the move to signification are threats and the pain of separation, then why would anyone make this move? Why not remain in the safe haven of the maternal body and refuse the social and signification with its threats? Kristeva suggests that if the accounts of Freud and Lacan were correct, then more people would be psychotic (see Kristen 1984, 132; 1987, 30, 31, 125). The logic of signification is already operating in the body, and therefore the transition to language is not as dramatic and mysterious as traditional psychoanalytic theory makes it out to be.

Following Klein and her successors, Kristeva emphasizes the maternal function and maintains that the regulation that sets up the superego and the possibility of language and culture is already operating in the maternal prior to the intervention of the father. Yet, while Klein focuses on the infant's fantasies of the maternal body that become part of the superego, and Winnicott, Bowlby, and Stern focus on the mother's activities around the child that limit and regulate its behavior, Kristeva identifies the structures of signification in the *material* of the body itself. It is not just that the mother–infant relationship is already a social relationship because there is already communication and social exchange between mother and infant, but also that the body itself sets up the structure of social relations.

Against Freud and Lacan, the body and needs are not antithetical to culture; the body, the maternal body in particular, does not have to be sacrificed to culture. Needs, associated with the maternal body, are not left behind once the child acquires language and can make demands. Lacan's notion that language leaves us lacking satisfaction or that it is a necessary but poor substitute for the maternal body, needs, or drives, assumes that drives and needs are antithetical to language (or in Lacanian parlance, that the real is cut off from the symbolic).[54] But what if drives or needs make their way into language? In this case, the maternal realm that Freud and Lacan identify as a hindrance to the properly social realm not only gives birth to the social but is also necessary for the continued operation of the social. We need to be social. And drives are what motivate language. Culture grows organically out of the body.

The drives themselves are also proto-social in that they are not contained within one body or psyche; rather, as Teresa Brennan argues, drives move between bodies; they are exchanged. Affective energy is transferred between people. For example, a person can walk into a room and her mood can affect everyone in the room; it is as if her mood radiates throughout the room. As Brennan explains the physics of psychic energy, originally the fetus *in utero* is literally one with its mother's body. Insofar as there is an intimate connection between psychic and physical processes evidenced by the ways in which emotions, traumas, and repression cause physical "symptoms," we can suppose that the fetus is affected by its mother's psycho-physical states since it is part of her body. It is the distance and delay that result from birth that give rise to a sense of space and time (Brennan 1992, 33). Space and time in turn conceal what Brennan calls the "fleshy memory" of an original psycho-physical connection with the mother's body.

Brennan maintains that this type of *in utero* psycho-physical connection operates *ex utero*, only at a "slower pace" (1992, 34). Human beings exchange energy via these psycho-physical connections. Emotions and affects migrate or radiate between human beings. In fact, for Brennan, it is the exchange of affect in the form of directed energy, or attention, that gives the ego its coherence and identity. She concludes that the ego is neither self-contained nor self-generating but rather the effect of an interplay of intersubjective psychic forces.

Affective energy transfers take place in all interpersonal interactions. The idea that we can transfer affects through contact and conversation resonates with most people who have had the experience of a conversation with a loved one in which s/he is upset during the conversation and after the conversation s/he feels much better—but now the other party to the conversation is upset. This kind of situation suggests a transfer of affect. Even our language in such interpersonal situations suggests an exchange of affect: For example, "I won't take it any more." "Don't give me that." This intersubjective theory of drives points to the sociality of the body.

Brennan's claim that the superego originates with the mother's executive capacities suggests that the mother not only provides the satisfaction of physical needs but also provides a precursor to the Law of the Father. She concludes that it is the *in utero* communication code used between maternal body and fetus, and the infant's fleshy memory of this code, that set up the possibility of language. Following Klein, and like Kristeva, Brennan explains how the superego is set up through the maternal function; there is a maternal law operating before the law of the father.

Like Kristeva and Lacan, however, Brennan believes that a paternal agent is necessary to break up the infant's dyadic dependence on the mother. If, however, the mother possesses this executive function as the law before the law, and if she is a desiring speaking being—that is, if she is social—then the third term is already operating within the dyad; the dyad is already/also a triad. This is significant because now we can take the relationship between the maternal body and the fetus/infant as a model for a social relationship. Unlike Freud, Lacan, or even Kristeva, on this model we can see the mother–fetus/infant relation as exhibiting the logic of a social relation. The move into the social no longer needs to be a violent rejection of the mother or the maternal body. Rather, the mother–infant dyad is modulated by law and regulation and is therefore already a triad which sets up the social relation.

As I argued in the last chapter of *Womanizing Nietzsche: Philosophy's Relation to the "Feminine,"* if the logic and structure of bodily drives is the same as the logic and structure of language, then the primary relation between the bodies of mother and child does not have to be antisocial or threatening. And, if bodily drives are not contained within the boundaries of one body or subject but are interpsychic, then bodily drives are always a matter of social exchanges. These exchanges are *protodialogues* that take place between bodies, bodies that are social even if they are not properly subjects.

Language has its source in the body and not just because it takes a mouth to speak and a hand to write. Language speaks and writes bodily affects and bodily drives, without which there would be no motivation for language. We use language not only to communicate information but also to make psycho-physical connections to others. Lacan might be right that every demand is a demand for love. But he is wrong that these demands are doomed to failure. If we need to speak, we need to make demands, just as we need food; then demands are not cut off from our basic need for satisfaction from our mothers that Lacan associates with love. Also, if drives and bodily needs are discharged in language, then they are not lost and we need not mourn the loss in order to enter culture; the maternal body is not killed and we need not mourn her death. Law and regulation implicit in language are already operating within the body. Law is not antithetical to the maternal body. So, it is not necessary to reject the maternal body in order to enter the realm of law and society.

part two
body politic

no body father

But who is the Father if his will is that flesh
be abolished? . . .

Henceforth, are the sons not obliged to
play weird games of fort-da between mothers
who are by some extraordinary turn virgins
and fathers who are mysteriously absent?

(Luce Irigaray, *Sexes and Genealogies*)

In this chapter, I begin by developing the notions of virile subjectivity and virile Eros. I argue that the history of Western philosophy from Plato to Sartre embraces a virile subject with its virile Eros. The virile subject relates to itself and its world as its property; virility is defined in terms of ownership and ownness. In the second section, "Battle of Wills," I begin by showing that paternal authority is built upon both rejecting nature and appealing to nature; paternal authority is based in the physical strength of the father's body even as it denies the importance of that body. Next, I respond to Ricoeur's analysis of fatherhood in *The Conflict of Interpretations* to suggest that the evacuation of the paternal body in the name of paternal authority is a result of a fear of the contigency of that body's contribution to procreation. I develop a notion of an abject father in order to diagnose our culture's attempts to erase and purify the paternal body. Finally, I analyze recent appeals to fathers' rights and paternal responsibility as another permutation of virile subjectivity.

Virile Subjectivity

Virile Eros

One of the most famous and earliest examples of virile Eros is Socrates' speech on love in Plato's *Phaedrus*. Although Plato associates love with a fourth form of madness, divine madness, he describes love as an exercise in extreme self-control, manly self-control. Reason might guide the soul toward the Good through intellectual and spiritual force—described in metaphors of *physical force*—in order to control the world, starting with its own passions: "Thus when it is perfect and winged it journeys on high and *controls the whole world*" (1987b, 493; my emphasis). The sight of the beautiful boy reminds the philosopher of the Form of beauty and causes his soul to swell and his wings to grow:

> For by reason of the stream of beauty entering in through his eyes there comes a warmth, whereby his soul's plumage is fostered, and with that warmth the roots of the wings are melted, which for long had been so hardened and closed up that nothing could grow; then as the nourishment is poured in, the stump of the wing swells and hastens to grow from the root over the whole substance of the soul, for aforetime the whole soul was furnished with wings. Meanwhile she throbs with ferment in every part, and even as a teething child feels an aching and pain in its gums when a tooth has just some through, so does the soul of him who is beginning to grow his wings feel a ferment and painful irritation. Wherefore as she gazes upon the boy's beauty, she admits a flood of particles streaming therefrom. . . . At last she beholds him, and lets the flood pour in upon her, releasing the imprisoned waters. (Plato 1987b, 497–498)

The sight of the beloved causes a swelling and throbbing of the soul that ends in a flood of particles that releases the soul from its aching and irritation. The soul of the lover does what the body must not; it succumbs to desire. But, unlike the body that desires the pleasures of physical passion, the soul desires the pleasures of intellectual passion, a disembodied passion, the virility of the soul.

Once the beautiful body serves to initiate the process of recollection, it is left behind.

In fact, after the body serves the soul's purpose, it becomes a hindrance in the quest for truth and beauty. The passions are the wanton steeds that try to steer the chariot of the soul in the wrong direction. If the charioteer (reason) cannot control the wanton steed (passion) with the help of the good steed (intellect), then the soul does not see the Form of beauty and may succumb to earthly embodied pleasure instead of divine pleasure. The struggle between reason and passion is described as a gory beating nearly unto death: "the driver, with resentment even stronger than before, like a racer recoiling from the starting rope, jerks back the bit in the mouth of the wanton horse with an even stronger pull, bespatters his railing tongue and his jaws with blood, and forcing him down on legs and haunches delivers him over to anguish. And so it happens time and again, until the evil steed casts off his wantonness; humbled in the end, he obeys the counsel of his driver, and when he sees the fair beloved is like to die of fear" (Plato 1987b, 500).

Plato elaborates this notion of disembodied Eros in Socrates' speech in the *Symposium*. Following older Greek traditions from prephilosophical cosmogonies in which Eros is identified as a force of mediation that draws things together—in Orphic cosmogonies Eros unites all, in Hesiod Eros emerges from Chaos to bring things together, in Pherecydes Zeus creates by changing into Eros who is seen as a kind of cosmological sexual force for unions and births, even for Empedocles Love (philia) unites the elements, and in Parmenides Love or Aphrodite is the daimon or mediator who guides all—Socrates, through his own daimon, Diotima, presents a theory of Eros as mediation between the divine and the mortal, between wisdom and ignorance. Eros as pedagogy of the soul, a mediator that moves the soul from mortal to divine, from sensation to intellection. Next, Socrates reports that with Diotima he concludes that love is love of the good and beautiful and that lovers want to make the good and beautiful *their own*, not just for now, but forever:

> Then may we state categorically that men are lovers of the good?
> Yes, I said, we may.
> And shouldn't we add that they long for the good *to be their own*?

We should.

And not merely to be their own but *to be their own forever?*

Yes, that must follow.

In short, that Love longs for the good *to be his own forever?*

Yes, I said, that's absolutely true. (Plato 1987a, 558; my emphasis)

The desire for ownership, to possess, is the essence of virile Eros. What Socrates and Diotima describe is a love that wants ownership, permanent ownership, to possess forever. Even when they conclude that love is not "a longing for the beautiful itself, but for the conception and generation that the beautiful effects," this longing for the propagation of beauty is founded in the desire for ownership: "And why all this longing for propagation? Because this is the one deathless and eternal element in our mortality. And since we have agreed that the lover longs for the good to be his own forever, it follows that we are bound to long for immortality as well as for the good" (Plato 1987a, 559). Both human propagation of flesh-and-blood offspring and the disembodied propagation of education, works of art, and law are motivated by the desire for eternal life. Diotima asks, "Who would not prefer such [abstract] fatherhood to merely human propagation?" (561). This abstract fatherhood gives birth to itself eternally. What is valued in the fatherhood of education, art works, and laws is the fame that they engender for their creator. His *name* lives forever.

Socrates/Diotima's next proposal is similar to the theory of love and beauty put forth in *Phaedrus*. The sight of a beautiful boy leads the philosopher to ever more abstractions of beauty until he reaches the revelation of the Form of beauty itself: "Starting from individual beauties, the quest for the universal beauty must find him ever mounting the heavenly ladder" (Plato 1987a, 562–563). The philosopher's Eros leads away from the sensual to the idea, away from the body to the soul, away from the earth to the heavens, away from women to men. In Plato's dialogue, however, the body cannot be so easily forgotten; it makes a reappearance at the end of the dialogue in the person of Alcibiades, drunk and full of lust.[55]

With Aristotle love is discussed as *philia*, friendship, instead of Eros. Aristotle identifies self-love as the basis of friendship (1962, 1166a). In making his argument, he lists five characteristics of friendship and maintains that one's relationship to oneself best meets these criteria: 1. a person who does what is good for his friend's sake; 2. a person who wishes for the life of his friend for the friend's sake; 3. a person who spends his time in our company; 4. a person whose desires are the same as ours; 5. a person who shares our joys and sorrows. Who meets these criteria better than oneself? Aristotle also mentions that a mother's relation to her child is characterized by qualities 2 and 5, wishes for life and sharing joys and sorrows. A good man, it turns out, is his own best friend: "All friendly feelings toward others are an extension of the friendly feelings a person has for himself . . . a man is his own best friend and therefore should have the greatest affection for himself" (Aristotle 1962, 1168b).

Even parents' love for their children turns out to be self-love: "Parents love their children as themselves: offspring is, as it were, another self" (Aristotle 1962, 1161b 25). Aristotle also describes the love between parents and children as a type of exchange of property and debt: "For parents love their children as something which belongs to them, while children love their parents because they owe their being to them." Parents (mothers at least) love their children as soon as they are born because they belong to them immediately in the way that "a tooth, a hair, and so forth belongs to its owner."[56] *Philia* in the family is based on ownership; the parents love their children as their possessions, as their own teeth or hair. *Philia*, both friendship and family relations, come back to love of the self. Aristotle presents us with another form of virile Eros, love as ownership and love as love of oneself.

Plotinus returns us to Platonic Eros, only for him it is a solitary force and not Plato's dialogic journey of lovers. While even Socrates' speech about love in the *Symposium* is recounted as a dialogue between Socrates and Diotima, for Plotinus the project of love or philosophy to return to the One is a "flight of the alone to the Alone" (Plotinus 1918, VI, 9, 11). Like Plato, Plotinus describes an ascent to the Good that begins with sensible beauty and passes through practices and sciences to pure beauty. This process is the purification of the soul, a catharsis of everything sensible and passionate that may have contributed to the revelation of the Good, but has nothing in common with it (1, 6, 6). The Beautiful is revealed through an interior vision that makes us one with it (1, 6, 9). The ascent to the Beautiful is no longer through Platonic dialogue but through solitary introspection that requires denying the body. And, the body is a shameful impediment on the way to the Beautiful. Eros is catharsis, manly purification of the soul. Love of oneself at the expense of all others.

In her study of love, *Tales of Love*, Julia Kristeva identifies a narcissism at the heart of Western conceptions of love. In the first century, Ovid invents the myth of Narcissus who falls in love with his own image and dies from the frustration of his unconsumatable love. Kristeva argues that we see Narcissus throughout the history of love. "We are confronted with what we can but call the vertigo of a love with no object other than a mirage. Ovid marvels, fascinated and terrified, at the sight of a twin aspect of the lure that will nevertheless continue to nourish the West's psychological and intellectual life for centuries to come" (Kristeva 1987, 104). While many of the characters in her love story could be described as virile subjects—Narcissus' love as virility—I want to look at one in particular, Don Juan, who moves self-love and/as ownership toward a love of one's own agency. The control implicit in descriptions of love as ownership becomes explicit in Kristeva's reading of the character of Don Juan, for whom the chase is about conquest and not about possession.

In a chapter entitled "Don Juan, or Loving to Be Able to," Kristeva asks, "What makes Don Juan chase and run?" (1987, 191). Her answer is as ambiguous as the figure she describes. Some of her remarks, however, complement the notion of virile subjectivity that I am developing here. She focuses on the likable Don Juan of Molière and the amoral Don Juan of Mozart; "it was not until Mozart came along with the 1787 Prague production of his Opera Buffa, *Don Giovanni*, that the fearsome seduction of [Tirso de Molina's] Spanish nobleman was freed from the moral condemnation that accompanied it" (191). In both Mozart and Molière, Don Juan is a conqueror of women who is likable and comic even as he is reprehensible. Don Juan does not wish to keep women as his possession, but to seduce them, triumph over them, win them over, in *his* game. He does it to prove that *he is able to*.

He does not relate to women as objects "but as stages of his own construction . . . with an array of mistresses and wives he multiplies his universe" (Kristeva 1987, 193). He constructs himself against the paternal prohibition; he laughs at the prohibition. The castration threat turns him on. As Kristeva says, *"seduction is sublimation . . . a necessarily phallic power that integrates the petrified strength of the moral stereotype, takes nourishment from it, goes beyond it"* (199). Kristeva sees Don Juan's attitude towards transgression and prohibition as evidence of his missing ego; that he is "a being without internality" (197). Yet, if what Don Juan wants, as she also says, is paternal punishment, this suggests that it is not that his ego is missing, but that his ego's boundaries can absorb others. In terms of Freud's egology, it is the superego and not the ego that is malfunctioning. Without the *threat* of paternal punishment, the superego loses its effect and the ego loses its proper boundaries. So, Don Juan can relate to women as stages of his own construction; they are his; they feed his ego. And, the paternal prohibition or paternal punishment is not experienced as a threat so much as a challenge; Don Juan's ego is formed through the challenge to swell up and consume others.

Kristeva claims that Don Juan does not relate to others as subjects with their own internalities; his "jouissance is not a jouissance of subjects, it is the jouissance of One master" (1987, 200). Don Juan takes pleasure in the mastery of the art of seduction. "He is not exhaled by sensuality, even autoerotic, but by evidence of his being able to place under his power by diverting them from their own path (*se-ducere*) all the women he meets" (201). He takes pleasure in his power and control over women whom he experiences as part of his own identity. His seduction is not based on his body except insofar as it is the conveyer of the seductive words through which he takes control of his conquests. Only in the contemporary "imitators of Don Juan," as Kristeva calls them (following Braunschweig and Fain), does the penis come to represent phallic power. Imitators of Don Juan seduce with the power of their sexual prowess; they control women through the mastery of their own bodies, which have become instruments of seduction.

Don Juan himself seems captive to his desire; he cannot control his desire to conquer every woman he meets. He controls his conquests, but who controls him? "Fanatic in desire, is not Don Juan, in the final analysis, also possessed by someone?" asks Kristeva (1987, 196). Who or what is the ideal that keeps him searching, never spending too much time in one place? Kristeva conjectures that "the absolute of beauty that excites him continuously is finally none but *she* [his mother]: primal, inaccessible, prohibited. A mere supposition, it is nevertheless confirmed by everyday 'don juans' who truly adhere to the maternal image. The phallic, combinatory power of the seducer would thus be intended to act as a counterbalance to the power of an unnamable mother" (1987, 201). Don Juan's seductions, then, are sublimations of his desire for (or identification with) his all-powerful mother. The mother's power—to create and give gratification—is taken over as phallic power.

In Jeremy Leven's recent film version of the Don Juan story, *Don Juan DeMarco*, Johnny Depp plays (a character who thinks that he is) Don Juan DeMarco, the world's greatest lover. When Don Juan describes his life to the psychiatrist (Marlon Brando) assigned to his case, he begins with recounting his mother's beauty. He describes a scene, which the audience sees, where as a toddler he is sitting in a bathtub watching his mother combing her hair before a mirror; his mother notices the *loving* way that he is looking at her and covers herself. In his fantasy, from his childhood Don Juan has an aura that girls and women find compelling. As a young man he loses his father in a duel over his mother's honor which he must finish. For Don Juan his mother's beauty is always the purest; after she loses her husband, she joins a convent. He also describes his inaccessible love Dona Ana (who happens to bear a very strong resemblance to his mother) as potential mother, a woman in whose eyes he sees his "unborn children." Even when discussing loving women in general he uses maternal images. He asks his psychiatrist, "Have you ever loved a woman until milk leaked from her—as if she had just given birth to love itself, and now must feed it or burst?" Our contemporary Don Juan DeMarco's seduction can easily be read as the sublimation of his desire for, and identification with, his mother and her perfect inaccessible beauty. We find out that the beloved Dona Ana is really a pin-up girl that catches the eye of our masked hero; she is as inaccessible as she is beautiful.

In various ways, some contemporary theorists have analyzed what seems to be the widespread "seduction as sublimation" through which patriarchal culture appropriates the creative power of the maternal. Women are no longer creators; only men are creators. The creator of the cosmos is God the Father. Woman's place in the creation and reproduction of life is erased and covered over by man's fantasies of power over life. In *History After Lacan*, Teresa Brennan describes the way in which the masculine ego recreates the world in its own image, which suppresses and distorts the powers of the mother and the powers of its environment, the earth. Brennan calls this recreation in its own image the "foundational fantasy" through which the ego annihilates heterogeneity in favor of more of itself in order to control its environment: "The subject is founded by a hallucinatory fantasy in which it conceives itself as the locus of active agency and the environment as passive; its subjectivity is secured by a projection onto the environment, apparently beginning with the mother, which makes her into an object which the subject in fantasy controls" (Brennan 1993, 11). The subject's fantasies affect material reality and transform the environment, which he continues to cover over but not in ways that he controls.

On Brennan's account it is only because of the foundational hallucination that we experience ourselves as contained entities, contained in terms of our energies and affects. Earlier, she argued in *Interpretation of the Flesh* that energy and affects migrate between people; they are never contained within one ego. In order to explain the psyche, Brennan suggests that we have to reconceptualize the relation between the flesh and the social sphere: "Psychical factors have to be conceived in energetic, physical terms. The relation between physical and social determination had been conceived as a one-way street, when it should allow for two-way traffic. The social actually gets into the flesh, and unless we take account of this, we cannot account for the extent to which socio-historical realities affect us psychically, and how we in turn act in ways that produce and reinforce them" (Brennan 1993, 10). In this way, patriarchal explanations of energy, creativity, and force become naturalized.

In much of her writing Luce Irigaray has also suggested that woman/mother is the silent support for man's representation of himself as manly. He *is not* castrated because she *is*; he is whole because she is fragmented; he is mind because she is body; he is rational because she is irrational. Irigaray diagnoses this tendency to identify woman with lack so that man might guarantee his identity as her opposite, that is, as complete. Woman has been placed in the no-place of man's other. This other, it turns out, is not truly other because it is merely man's projection of *his* other; so it is the other of the same. Everything comes back to him and his. And, it is through the suppression and erasure of woman–mother that he props up his own identity. His sense of himself is built on the sacrifice of the other, an other that always belongs to him. The maternal body, his first home, is the first to go. "Man's self-affect depends on the woman who has given him being and birth, who has born/e him, enveloped him, warmed him, fed him" (Irigaray 1993b, 60). He creates myths and fantasies in which he gives birth to himself, so that he can pretend to control the forces of life and death (see Irigaray 1991, "When the God are Born"). His love is always a self-love that is possible only because he sees himself reflected in her. He is Narcissus, she is the water upon which he is reflected.

Following Irigaray, in *Womanizing Nietzsche* I examined the ways in which Nietzsche and Freud's writings exhibit this tendency to create masculine identity through the covert sacrifice of the feminine. There, I argued that Nietzsche attempts to control the maternal by presenting images of man giving birth to himself. He values the maternal in the strong virile manly artist, but denigrates maternity in women. He identifies everything base in himself with his own mother and everything noble in himself with his father. Like a twisted version of Platonic Eros, Nietzsche suggests that noble begetting comes from virile Eros, while base begetting come from women's bodies. In his attempts to control the maternal, Freud's theories of female sexuality also manifest a fear of birth and a fear of femininity. Freud fears an identification with the feminine; the enigma of femininity is really "how can a man be a man when he is born from a woman?" The mother is a black hole in Freud's theory. The literature and myths of Western culture are full of images of males giving birth to themselves through the power of their own virility. In these fantasies virility is an attempt to control that which cannot be controlled, the creation of life.

The virile body becomes a representative of control and power. It is an antibody insofar as its virility defies the uncontrollable passions and flows of the body. It is the body that represents the overcoming of body. The virile body is the symbol of manliness; manliness is associated with culture; culture is associated with overcoming the body. As Alphonso Lingis says in *Foreign Bodies*, "the virile body figures as the incarnation of law, reason, power, directions, directives, not because of the use-value of the specifically male nervous circuitry and musculature, but because of its force as the incarnate sign of civilization" (1994, 130). Manliness symbolizes power and the virile body symbolizes manliness.

Perhaps body building is the virile body taken to the extreme. The goal of body building is *definition*; body builders want well-defined bodies, borders within their own control. While body builders value the body, they value it as an object that can be manipulated and controlled. They wear their bodies like the latest fashion. Body builders develop strong bodies that, as Lingis says, have no use-value. For Lingis, theirs is a gratuitous virility, a virility that makes a mockery of virility, virility as display, the *feminization* of virility. Manly virility embodies law, reason, power, courage, virtues associated with overcoming or sublimating the body. Physical strength should be in the service of manliness and manly virtues. The virile body is virtue so long as it is an instrument for the soul or the chariot of the soul. When it becomes an accessory, however, we must confront the return of the repressed: the body comes back to virility. The repressed body comes back in a monstrous form, objectification at its limit, but not to be ignored.

Lingis maintains that body building exhibits virility that is not a challenge to death and therefore does not manifest courage:

> The public does not see in body builders ferocious and destructive brutes which offend its sacralization of civilization—they are known to use their massive power as guardians of bourgeois property, taking jobs, typically, as night watchmen and bouncers in night clubs, where the rich idle, and are suspected of being steroid-pumped eunuchs from whom the debutantes have nothing to fear. The resentment senses in them a virility insulated from death. Years of training that led to no corrida, only to the footlights of a high-school stage. Not a brave contest with death, but a sentimental fantasy of immortality on glossy photographs, fetishized into the metal figures of trophies. . . . There is a feeling at large that the musculature gained in work and in rule-governed contests, the bodies of construction workers, deep-sea divers, and boxers, is virile and virtuous; the musculature built in the rituals of the body builder's cult, grotesque. (Lingis 1994, 36–37)

Yet, we are fascinated with those monstrous bodies. We can't stop looking at them. We are mesmerized by the movements of Arnold

Schwarzenegger. Whether he is a human-machine, a giant in a room full of kindergartners, or the first pregnant man, we wonder at the movement of that body that seems so stationary and solid. His comic roles play on the size and solidity of his body, pairing it with Danny DeVito, small children, and pregnant women. Most of Arnold's characters are self-sufficient; he needs no one. His body is a shield that protects him and makes him inaccessible. It is solid and impenetrable. His strength is the control that he has over his own body.

Virility signifies control and containment of the body. Virile subjectivity is the notion of a subject that is contained and in control of itself and its environment. Virile Eros loves itself because the virile subject relates to the world and others as his own possessions or creations. Even his body becomes his possession. The solidity and hardness of the virile body represents the control and containment of bodily fluids. Virile Eros is the love of what is fixed and unchanging, what does not flow or change. The flows of the male body are repressed within discourses of virile subjectivity and virile Eros. Seminal fluids, which also seem to signal virility, are transformed into solids: sperm counts and babies. The virile subject's *manly* fluids become objects and possessions. As Elizabeth Grosz points out "there are virtually no phenomenological accounts of men's body fluids" (Grosz 1994, 198).

Grosz asks, "Could the reduction of men's body fluids to the by-products of pleasure and the raw materials of reproduction, along with men's refusal to acknowledge the effects of flows that move through various parts of the body and from the inside out, have to do with men's attempts to distance themselves from the very kind of corporeality—uncontrollable, excessive, expansive, disruptive, irrational—they have attributed to women?" (Grosz 1994, 200). She points out that for boys puberty marks the end of childhood with its body out of control and the beginning of manhood with the promise of sex and virility. For girls, on the other hand, puberty marks the beginning of womanhood and reproduction rather than sexuality, and the menstrual flows which cannot be controlled signal another body out of control instead of the end of childhood: "The first issuing forth of sperm, the onset of nocturnal emissions, signals coming manhood for the boy, the sexual pleasures and encounters fantasized and yet to come; but the onset of menstruation is not an indication at all for the girl of her developing sexuality, only her coming womanhood. And moreover, whereas the boy is able to psychically solidify the flow of sperm, connecting it metonymically to a corporeal pleasure and metaphorically with a desire object (or at least place), for the girl, menstruation, associated as it is with blood, with injury and wound, with a mess that does not dry invisibly, that leaks, uncontrollable, not in sleep, in dreams, but whenever it occurs, indicates the beginning of an out-of-control status that she was led to believe ends with childhood" (205).

Grosz argues that it is only by excluding men's bodily fluids from their self-representations and controlling those fluids through various forms of solidification, that men can mark their own bodies as clean and proper (Grosz 1994, 201). The logic of this fantasy is that, unlike women's bodies, men's bodies do not secrete fluids and become subjected to flows that are out of their own control, so their bodies, unlike women's bodies, are clean and have proper boundaries. Ultimately, their bodies are erased from their discourse in an exercise of extreme control. Grosz suggests that "men have functioned as if they represented masculinity only incidentally or only in moments of passion and sexual encounter, while the rest of the time they are representatives of the human, the generic 'person'" (198). Humanity has become synonymous with masculinity; masculinity signifies rationality, control, and containment.

Grosz identifies several ways that men separate themselves and their own identities from their sexual functions and flows. One way is to represent their sex organs as separate from themselves, "on the model of the homunculus, a little man within the man, with a quasi-autonomy of its own" (Grosz 1994, 200). Although there are few discourses on male flow, the homunculus model of the penis is evidenced by the fact that there are probably a hundred different names for the penis, many of them proper names.[57] Other ways of controlling bodily flows and separating themselves from them include abstinence and chastity vows, washing or ritual cleaning immediately after intercourse, and representing the fluid as a solid, as emanating from a solid and producing a solid, as millions of little homunculi engaged in a virile struggle for dominance.

Recent accounts of sperm in medical and biological discourse describe sperm as anthropomorphized little warriors engaging in battle against two enemies, the DNA of females and competing sperm from other males. Evolutionary Biologist Robin Baker's new book, entitled *Sperm Wars: The Science of Sex*, describes sperm engaged in a Trojan war-like situation, encouraged by women, in which different sperm take up different positions in battle.[58] Some sperm perform the work of fertilization while some "kamikaze sperm" take out the sperm of their competitors. Baker and his colleague Mark Bellis "found evidence that *women* promote sperm competition just as do *females* of other species" (my emphasis).[59]

An article in the *New York Times*, "The Biggest Evolutionary Challenge May be the Other Half of the Species," pieces together research from several biologists who maintain that females and males are fighting for evolutionary control of the species.[60] For example, biologist William Rice found that if female fruit flies' "hands were tied" in this evolutionary war, then males would develop increasingly toxic sperm that would shorten the females' lives. Sperm is figured as a "weapon" in deadly "chemical warfare." While the article asks us to believe that these studies on fruit flies and animals apply to human beings, in conclusion the journalist reassures us that we need not take the analogy so far that we become concerned about the toxicity of sperm killing women. These biologists seem to base their conclusions about the evolutionary "war between the sexes" on the fact that males and females' reproductive systems adapt in relation to each other. But rather than see this adaptation as a form of evolutionary communication through which the sexes might be working together for the survival of the species, they choose to interpret it as a war. Their accounts are full of inconsistencies as they try to avoid the fact that the notion that males and females are engaged in an evolutionary war seems to challenge central tenets of the theory of evolution. How could killing off the other sex of your own species serve the survival of the species, or your own survival for that matter? Have these biologists forgotten that "it takes two to tango," so to speak? This *forgetting* is fundamental to the virile subject's fantasy of control.

The virile subject maintains the fantasy that it is the only one, the only subject. All others are merely objects or alter egos controlled or constructed by the virile subject himself. Images of solidity protect the virile body from external forces. So, virility extols solids over fluids, and the penis and individual sperm cells over seminal fluids. Elizabeth Grosz describes what is at stake in this "phallicizing of the male body, of subordinating the rest of the body to the valorized functioning of the penis, with the culmination of sexual activities occurring, ideally at least, in sexual penetration and male orgasm." She says that this solidifying of the male body "involves the constitution of the sealed-up, impermeable body," which she diagnoses as a guard against the horror evoked by loose fluids and flows, the fear that "flow moves or can move in two-way or indeterminable directions . . . the possibility of not being an active agent in the transmission of flow but also a passive receptacle" (Grosz 1994, 201). The virile subject is afraid of relationships, which in the virile fantasy threaten his control.

In "The 'Mechanics' of Fluids" (a response to Lacan), and elsewhere, Luce Irigaray has identified the tendency to solidify fluids with the masculine subject who represents himself as autonomous and contained within the boundaries of his own ego. She postulates that woman is the invisible fluid element that makes it possible for him to have relationships to his *possessions*. She suggests that the tendency to reabsorb fluid into a solid form presupposes a notion of space as discrete points in which the intervals between objects are fixed and calculable (see Irigaray 1985, 110). This notion of space and the subject contained within it makes relationships impossible. There is no exchange, especially exchange of fluids, within this space. All flows and energies are reduced to particles and ever smaller discrete units whose integrity depends on the maintenance of these boundaries. The clean and proper individual is *one* who is not permeated by his environment or those around him. He is the impenetrable virile subject who loves to reproduce himself.

Gestating Body of Phenomenology

In *Totality and Infinity*, Emmanuel Levinas distinguishes virility from fecundity. He describes the virile or heroic *I* that posits itself as a fixed subject in relation to the world as a fixed object. In his brief discussion of virile subjectivity, Levinas alludes to Husserl's transcendental *I* that constitutes its world and Heidegger's *Dasein* who is concerned with illuminating Being and standing out in the light where Being can be seen. The virile subject attempts to know the world by lighting the darkness of being. Everything in his world is defined in terms of his relationship to it. He is defined in terms of knowing and willing and being able to. He is an "I know," "I will," "I can"—the philosopher as would-be Don Juan. He is a powerful subject who dominates everything in the world with his knowledge of it. His relationship to all others is one of knowing and domination. Through his intellect he possesses others. As a result, the virile subject always and only returns to himself. Even his experience of himself is an experience of self-domination and knowledge. He attempts to control himself, especially his body, by knowing himself. As Levinas says, he becomes encumbered with himself and drags himself along as a possession (1969, 270–271). Virile subjectivity experiences the world as its possession. Everything is a matter of ownership.

Just as in Plato's and Aristotle's accounts of love, in Phenomenology we see the subject defined in terms of ownership and ownness. In this section, I return to Husserl's notion of intersubjectivity to point out how even his transcendental subject is both dependent upon its embodiment and upon its relationship to something other than itself. Within Husserl's philosophy, there is already a split within the subject whereby the very act of conscious ownership necessitates the activity of disowning. This split in the subject between owning and disowning becomes more explicit in Heidegger.

What I will do here is show that behind the ownership so dear to Phenomenology is something other, something that cannot be possessed. In the face of this otherness, the virile subject loses his control. The history of Phenomenology from Husserl to Levinas can be read as the attempt to come to terms with this otherness, at first by appropriating it as yet another object constituted by the ego and eventually by making it the origin of possibility for the ego. It is not an accident that within this history the otherness that cannot be owned or controlled is often figured with metaphors of maternity.

Husserl

Although there are three volumes in the *Husserliana* entitled *On the Phenomenology of Intersubjectivity* [*Zur Phänomemologie der Intersubjektivität*], Husserl's theory of intersubjectivity is best known from his discussion in the fifth *Meditation* of the *Cartesian Meditations*. There, Husserl founds his theory of intersubjectivity on the ownness of consciousness. He maintains that ownness is the eidetic structure of consciousness (Husserl 1977, 93). What I do not experience as part of my primordial ownness—what I can imagine as other than myself—is other or alien. The other is constituted through my relation with the ownness of my consciousness and the connection between that ownness and my body. Husserl describes the other as a mirror of my ownness, an analog of me, my alter ego (94). The other's subjectivity or consciousness cannot be directly perceived or presented to me, so it is apperceived or appresented. It is only indirectly perceived or presented as an analog of my own consciousness.

While the other is known through analogy, Husserl insists that the process of constitution is not one of analogical reasoning but analogical transfer (Husserl 1977, 111). Upon perceiving the body of another we immediately transfer the sense of an animated organism with its own subjectivity onto that perception. The perception of the other is constituted as a perception of an animate conscious organism. And although the other is my alter ego or my analog, Husserl maintains that I do not apperceive the other as a duplicate of myself; rather, the process is a type of reproduction: "I do not apperceive the other ego simply as a duplicate of myself and accordingly as having my original sphere or one completely like mine. . . . Its manner of appearance does not become paired in a direct association with the manner of appearance actually belonging at the time to my animate organism (in the mode Here); rather it awakens *reproductively another*, an immediately similar appearance included in the system constitutive of my animate organism as a body in space" (117–118; my emphasis).

Husserl describes a type of association that is indirect and reproductive. What is an indirect reproductive association? The ego and alter ego are always paired through association, which we discovered in the fourth *Mediation* is the result of a passive synthesis (Husserl 1977, 112). Because the association is between my body and the body of another, pairing is always a pairing of my concrete or personal ego with a concrete alter ego (123). Wherever the alter ego appears, I am its companion. It never appears without me. This is because all sense is constituted through my transcendental ego (99, 115, 136). And all intersubjectivity is founded on egology (155). That is to say, the other is always an other *for me*. Husserl as Don Juan.

What troubles Husserl is how I can distinguish my own ego from that of another. Yet, if I can separate the two, then how is empathy or communion with another possible? What guarantees that my ego is mine and not yours is that my ego is presented to me and yours is always only appresented to me (Husserl 1977, 119). In the fourth *Meditation*, Husserl concludes that through the epoché and then the phenomenological reduction, which is performed through imaginative or fictive variation, I can bracket out my personal ego and intuit the eidetic structure of the transcendental ego. The transcendental ego is whatever is left over, what cannot be doubted or imagined away; it is what I cannot imagine to be different than it is. This indubitable remainder is the sphere of my ownness; it is what I cannot doubt is my ego. While I have direct access to my ownness, I have only indirect access to your ownness.

In spite of the radical separation of my own ego from yours, communion is possible through empathy. Husserl maintains that I can put myself in your place and view the world from your perspective. This operation is possible through the same kind of imaginative variation that allowed me to perform the transcendental reduction. Leaving aside the obvious problems with the notion that I can empathize with someone by occupying their space, or imagining occupying their space, leaving aside the fact that as Husserl sets it out the other is no threat to my sense of ownness because it is always *my* other and therefore never truly other, I want to suggest that not only is ownness the result of the other, but also that the alter ego is first *within* my own ego. In other words, it follows from Husserl's analysis that ownness is only possible through disowning.

First, my experience of ownness is only possible through an experience of otherness. As Husserl describes it, it is through the process of imaginative variation that I intuit my ego by excluding all that could belong to some other. What remains after I identify what is not my own or other than me, and exclude it, is undoubtedly mine. It seems that I must first have this imaginative relation with what is other than me before I can intuit my ownness. Derrida makes an analogous argument in *Speech and Phenomena* when he points out that ownness is possible because of internal time consciousness and yet the movement of time undermines the self-presence of ownness:

Does not everything that is announced already in this reduction to "solitary mental life," (the trancendental reduction in all its stages, and notably the reduction to the monadic sphere of "ownness"— *Eigenheit*—etc.) appear to be stricken in its very possibility by what we are calling time? . . . Is not the concept of pure solitude—of monad in the phenomenological sense—*undermined* by its own origin, by the very condition of its self-presence, that is, by "time," to be conceived anew on the basis now of difference within auto-affection, on the basis of identifying identity and nonidentity within the "sameness" of the *im selben Augenblick*? (Derrida 1973, 68)

Husserl's notion of the alter ego is another appearance of "difference within auto-affection" or nonidentity within the ownness of the ego. Husserl maintains that "in a free variation, I can phantasy *first of all myself*, this apodictic de facto ego, as otherwise and can thus acquire the *system of possible variants of myself*, each of which, however, is annulled by each of the others and by the ego who I actually am. It is *a system of apriori incompossibility*. Furthermore the fact, 'I am,' prescribes *whether* other monads are other for me and *what* they are for me. . . . If I phantasy myself as a pure possibility different from what I actually am, that possibility in turn prescribes what monads exist for him as others" (Husserl 1977, 141). I have a sense of the other by freely varying myself and discovering that such variations are not compossible with who I am. The other is who I am not and cannot be. Yet as Husserl describes the process of finding the other as it is founded in, and constituted by, my own ego, the rupture in my own ego becomes more pronounced.

With his distinction between the personal, psychological, concrete, or empirical ego and the transcendental ego, Husserl already splits the ego. He insists that the ownness of my transcendental ego is primary and the ownness of my psychological ego is secondary (1977, 100). Still, it is only on the basis of a pairing of *concrete* egos (as they are embodied) that I can apperceive the other (123). In what sense, then, is my experience of the other constituted by the transcendental ego? It must be constituted in the same way that my experience of my own concrete ego is constituted by the transcendental ego. The other, as Husserl says, "is therefore conceivable only as an analog of something included in my peculiar ownness" (115). But what is there present in my ownness of which the other is an analog? Indeed, how is the ownness of my own embodied concrete ego constituted from within the transcendental reduction except through an analogical transfer of sense from the ownness of my transcendental ego to the ownness of my empirical ego? What I am suggesting is that in the Fifth *Meditation*, the other can appear as alter ego only because I find the alter ego already within my sphere of ownness.

My alter ego is all of those accidental empirical qualities that I bracket off in order to uncover the eidetic structure of my consciousness. In addition, my alter ego is all of those possibilities that I imagine for myself that allow me to delineate my sphere of ownness. I am who I am by virtue of my relation with my own alter ego. It is through a fundamental split in my ego that I am. It is through a process of disowning the alter ego that I intuit my ownness. In order to apperceive an other I merely reproduce this experience of disowning to redefine myself, my ownness, in relation to my other alter ego. The alter ego is not only "demonstrated precisely within the experiencing intentionality of my ego" in the sense that it is constituted through a relationship with my ego, but also in the sense that it is experienced in the intuition of my ego itself (Husserl 1977, 148).

The way in which my ego *reproduces* the otherness of the other from the otherness of myself takes on new connotations when in *On the Phenomenology of Intersubjectivity* Husserl uses the mother–child relation as an illustration of the relation between the other and the I:

> [There] is an excellent [example in the case] where the other is interpreted as [intentionally] related to my "I" and to that which pertains to my "I" [*mein Ichliches*] and [where] I actually experience this. Thus, the unity within the multiplicity of interpretational experience here finds a point of fulfillment in my specific self-experience. . . . In any case, if we think of the most primordial genetic continuity between **mother and child** and of the importance of the social I-Thou-life [*Ich-Du-Leben*] [it becomes clear that] this mode of fulfillment plays a special role.[61]

The mother child relation is used to illustrate the way in which the other is related to the I. The mother gives birth to the child; they are genetically contiguous. So too, the transcendental ego gives birth to, reproduces, the other. In fact, Husserl figures the realm of pure consciousness out of which all objectivity originates as the realm of Mothers. The constitutive activity of consciousness is likened to procreation:

To express it in the myth of Goethe, find the way to the Mothers of knowledge, to discover their realm of pure consciousness, in which all being originates constitutively and out of which all knowledge as knowledge of what is must draw its ultimate intelligible explanation . . . one is dealing with nothing other than the science of the formations of the essence of consciousness as such, as the science of the Motherly origins.[62]

In Goethe's *Faust*, "the Mothers" is the name given to the goddesses who inhabit the realm of the absolute, where there is no finished creature or world, but where the generation of all creatures and everything in the world begins. The path to the realm of the Mothers is lonely and desolate. In his unpublished notes, Husserl asks, "Do we not shudder in the presence of these depths? Who has seriously made them a theme in the millennia of the past? Who, in connection with the first reflections of Augustine, has dared to risk his life on the way to the 'mothers'?"[63] James Hart suggests that the transcendental reduction, or the way to the Mothers, requires a form of violence to oneself, even death of oneself. The life that is forfeited is the life of the natural attitude.[64] The Mothers require the death of the natural life, but they promise a new life both before and beyond that forfeited life. The body and empirical ego must be left behind in this Husserlian reunion with the Mothers of knowledge. Like virile Eros, Husserlian phenomenology, with its love of eidetic knowledge, brackets the body for the sake of control over itself and the world.

Heidegger

Against Husserl, Heidegger insists that the ego is in the world. In *Being and Time*, he reverses the order of Husserlian epistemology. The transcendental attitude does not reveal the essential structures of the natural attitude. Rather, in Heidegger's terminology, the structure of reflective consciousness is already implicit in prereflective understanding. Although he rejects the Husserlian transcendental ego, Heidegger does retain a version of Husserlian intentionality with his notion of care. Like Husserl, Heidegger uses a maternal metaphor for the intentional character of consciousness. In *Being and Time*, the centrality of care to *Dasein* is illustrated using the "ancient fable" of the birth of man, shaped by Care from the body of Earth, given spirit by Jupiter, and named by Saturn, who arbitrates a debate between the other three: "Since you, Jupiter, have given its spirit, you shall receive that spirit at its death; and since you, Earth, have given its body, you shall receive its body. But since 'Care' first shaped this creature, she shall possess it as long as it lives. And because there is now a dispute among you as to its name, let it be called '*homo,*' for it is made out of *humus* (earth)" (Heidegger 1962, 242).

In *Being and Time*, Heidegger describes care as *Dasein*'s fundamental relation to the world. On a prereflective level, *Dasein* is engaged with the world; *Dasein* is always oriented in relation to the world. This is to say that *Dasein* is intentional. Yet, this intentionality is not given to reflective consciousness as an essential structure of a transcendental *I*. Heidegger maintains that if we start with the givenness of the *I*, then we soon discover that I am not that *I*, that what belongs to me, what is my own, is also not mine: "Dasein is in each case mine, and this is its constitution; but what if this should be the very reason why, proximally and for the most part, Dasein *is not itself*?" (Heidegger 1962, 151).

The notion of ownness or own (*Eigen*) permeates Heidegger's writings from the earliest, *Being and Time* (1927), to the latest, *On Time and Being* (1964).[65] In *Being and Time*, the most renowned use of *Eigen* is in the derivative *Eigentlichkeit*, authenticity. Heidegger's notion of authenticity should *not* be reduced to the pop-existentialist notion of being true to yourself. Rather, as Heidegger describes *Eigentlichkeit*, and other forms of *Eigen* in his later works, it becomes clear that authenticity not only involves ownness, or what properly belongs to oneself, but also an owning up to the ways in which one is inauthentic. Modes of revealing proper to human beings are those which reveal the process of concealing. In other words, human beings' own, proper, or authentic, relationship to their own existence is to recognize the various ways in which they conceal that their relationship to their own existence is one of concealment.

Like Husserl's notion of ownness, there is a disowning at the center of Heidegger's notion of ownness. The way in which Heidegger's notion of ownness turns in on itself, against itself, in order to open onto something other than itself, becomes more apparent in his later writings. In *Being and Time*, the structure of ownness is set up, but the essence of ownness, still not made explicit, is the recognition of disowning as the operation that defines *Dasein*. In later works, the essence of ownness is the operation of disowning itself (in the full ambiguity of "itself" in this context).

In *Being and Time*, *Dasein* designates the existential structure, or position, of a being who takes its own being as an issue. *Dasein* is unique among beings because it experiences anxiety in the face of its ownness and anticipation of its own death or impending nothingness (see Heidegger 1962, 232, 308). The special position, both ontically and ontologically, of *Dasein* in relation to Being and other beings is clear from the first chapter of *Being and Time*. What is more ambiguous is the relation between authentic and inauthentic *Dasein* and the relation between *Dasein*'s own and what Heidegger calls "the They."

Heidegger concludes that *"authentic Being-one's-Self* does not rest upon an exceptional condition of the subject, a condition that has been detached from the 'they'; *it is rather an existentiell modification of the 'they'—of the 'they' as an essential existentiale"* (Heidegger 1962, 168). This is to say that authentic *Dasein* is a modification of the actual particular existence (an existentiell) of the They as an essential structure of existence (an existential) or as a mode of understanding *Dasein*. The They is an essential part of the constitutive structure of *Dasein* (167). Yet, in the same section Heidegger distinguishes authentic *Dasein* from the They: "The Self of everyday *Dasein* is the *they-self*, which has been taken hold of in the *authentic Self*—that is, from the Self which has been taken hold of in its own way [*eigens ergriffenen*]. As they-self, the particular *Dasein* has been *dispersed* into the 'they,' and must first find itself. . . . If *Dasein* discovers the world in its own way [*eigens*] and brings it close, if it discloses to itself its own authentic Being, then this discovery of the 'world' and this disclosure of *Dasein* are always accomplished as a clearing away of concealments and obscurities, as a breaking up of the disguises with which *Dasein* bars its own way" (167). Is authentic *Dasein* the breaking up of "the They"? Is it born out of the They? Concealed within the They? What is the relation between authentic *Dasein* and the They?

At the beginning of Part I of *Being and Time*, Heidegger identifies both authentic and inauthentic as modes of Being for *Dasein*. *Dasein* has different modes of Being because it is, in a sense, possibility:

"And because *Dasein* is in each case essentially its own possibility, it *can*, in its very Being, 'choose' itself and win itself; it can also lose itself and never win itself; or only 'seem' to do so. But only in so far as it is essentially something which can be *authentic*—that is, something of its own—can it have lost itself and not yet won itself. As modes of Being, *authenticity* and *inauthenticity* (these expression have been chosen terminologically in a strict sense) are both grounded in the fact that any *Dasein* whatsoever is characterized by mineness [*Jemeinigkeit*]" (68). If both authentic and inauthentic modes of Being belong to the structure or essence of *Dasein*, then how can Heidegger identify authenticity as what is appropriate to, or what belongs to *Dasein*'s own? Unless Heidegger is suggesting that to be authentic is simply to own up to *Dasein*'s possibility for different modes of Being, including inauthenticity. On this reading, authenticity is a mode of Being in which *Dasein* admits its possibilities, including the possibility for inauthenticity, which is the concealing of its possibilities from itself in the they-self.

Own and ownness as the admission of disowning is taken one step further in Heidegger's later writings. In most of his texts, Heidegger is concerned with the question of the proper. On closer examination, however, what is proper turns out to be what opens onto its other. What brings something into its own is not what limits or confines, but rather what opens out onto multiplicity. I will give several examples. In *What is Called Thinking*, Heidegger makes a distinction between the common meaning of the word "call," to name, and a rare meaning of the word "call," to command. To command, in turn, in its original meaning is to commend or entrust (Heidegger 1993a, 387). Although Heidegger insists that "the current meaning of the word cannot simply be pushed aside in favor of the rare one, even though the rare signification may still be the proper one" (Heidegger 1993a, 389), what does it mean for Heidegger to identify one meaning as proper or original? How do we determine the proper meaning?

On Heidegger's analysis, the proper sense of call is command, entrust, or call something forth, because this meaning gives rise to its other meanings, including the common meaning, to name. Things come into their own insofar as they are entrusted to words, names. Things become present (to us) when they are given names.

The name calls forth in the sense of command. Thinking is the response to this same sort of call (cf. Heidegger 1993a, 391; 1971, 183). For Heidegger, in some sense, what is proper to thinking is determined by something other than thinking; what is thinking's own does not belong to it. Or, as Heidegger says, "only the peculiar quality of that which demands of us above all else to be admitted [to thinking] can decide about that [what is proper]" (Heidegger 1972b, 72). If what is proper to thinking is to respond, if responding and recalling are its own, then its own is precisely *not* its own because its own is a response to something other. A response is always a response to something prior.

Heidegger's analysis in "The Question Concerning Technology" shows the point more forcefully. There Heidegger identifies enframing—taking everything as ordered standing reserve for our use—as the supreme danger because, among other things, it leads to "one final delusion: it seems as though man everywhere and always encounters only himself" (Heidegger 1993b, 332). The final delusion of the supreme danger is that we will insulate ourselves completely from any other; we will see only ourselves everywhere.

In this essay, Heidegger once again identifies a proper meaning which he relates to a more common meaning. The common meaning of technology, which he calls the instrumental definition, is that technology is a means to an end and a human activity. Heidegger traces the etymology of "technology" back to the Greek *techne*, which he interprets as a bringing forth or revealing. He suggests that this prior sense of *techne* makes even the current sense of technology as a means or instrument possible. *Techne* as a bringing forth can bring forth a multitude of possibilities. While this proper or original sense of *techne* opens onto multiple possibilities, the mode of technology as enframing limits possibilities. In fact, the danger of enframing is that it will become the only possible relationship to the world; it will become the only mode of revealing. It can do this only by concealing the fact that it is a mode of revealing. Once it reveals that it is a mode of revealing, a bringing forth, then it is one mode among many. It cannot dominate.

This same dynamic holds true for the other examples that I have analyzed where Heidegger identifies the proper or authentic. The proper, authentic, or "own most," is that which opens onto possibilities, even possibilities that disown. As Heidegger says in one of his latest writings, translated as "Time and Being":

> Appropriating makes manifest its peculiar property, that Appropriation [*Aneignung*] withdraws what is most fully its own from boundless unconcealment. Thought in terms if Appropriating, this means: in that sense it expropriates itself of itself. Expropriation belongs to Appropriation as such. By this expropriation, Appropriation does not abandon itself—rather, it preserves what is its own. (Heidegger 1972a, 22–23)

In this lecture Heidegger defines Appropriation as that which gives both Being and time and makes possible the relationship between them. He calls *Ereignis* (event, occurrence) the "event of Appropriation [*Aneignung*]" (19). Like Heidegger's central notion from the first part of *Being and Time*, authenticity [*Eigentlichkeit*], and both Appropriation [*Aneignung*] and Event [*Ereignis*] have their root in own or proper [*Eigen*]. The activity of appropriation [*sich aneignen*], of making something its/one's own, determines both Being and time. What is, is determined as its ownself—it is present (in the sense of Being and time)—through the activity of appropriation. The strange thing about appropriation, however, is that what is proper to it is the activity of expropriation. Furthermore, it is through expropriation, disowning, that appropriation preserves its own. This is to say that things become present to us through a process of revealing and concealing. As some things become present or revealed, others recede or become concealed. In order for something to appear, to become present, other things have to disappear. Appropriating, making something its/one's own, necessarily involves expropriating.

Extending his analysis from "The Question Concerning Technology," in "The Principle of Identity" Heidegger claims that enframing or the instrumental view of technology reduces everything down to man (Heidegger 1969, 34). Yet, as in "The Question Concerning Technology," there exists the hope of what he calls there a "saving power." In "The Question Concerning Technology," Heidegger maintains that the supreme danger of enframing brings with it the saving power. In that essay the relationship between the supreme danger and the saving power remains for the most part imbedded in Heidegger's dense language:

The granting that sends one way or another into revealing is as such the saving power. For the saving power lets man see and enter into the highest dignity of his essence. This dignity lies in keeping watch over the unconcealment—and with it, from the first, the concealment—of all essential unfolding on this earth. It is precisely in enframing, which threatens to sweep man away into ordering as the ostensibly sole way of revealing, and so thrusts man into the danger of the surrender of his free essence—it is precisely in this extreme danger that the innermost indestructible belongingness of man within granting may come to light, provided that we, for our part, begin to pay heed to the essence of technology. (Heidegger 1993b, 337)

"The Principle of Identity" may shed light on the relationship between the supreme danger and the saving power. There, Heidegger again maintains that enframing may make it possible to "overcome the mere dominance of the frame to turn it into a more original appropriating" (Heidegger 1969, 37). How can the frame that dominates turn into a frame that frees us up for our essence? By showing itself as frame. "Assuming we could look forward to the possibility that the frame—the mutual challenge of man and Being to enter the calculation of what is calculable—were to address itself to us as the event of appropriation which first surrenders man and Being to their own being; then a path would be open for man to experience beings in a more originary way" (40). If the process of enframing—how a frame takes over our way of seeing the world and becomes naturalized—displayed itself, then that frame could no longer dominate because it would be seen within a larger frame. The process of framing is the result of the activity of appropriation, of the world becoming present to us in a certain way. If we see that it can become present to us in various ways, through various frames, then no one frame can dominate. The frame that borders this way of seeing, the activity or process of appropriation, opens onto the outside rather than holding the interior firmly in place. The self-same, or one's own, necessarily opens onto its other.

In Heidegger's writings, however, it is questionable how the openness to the other carries over to intersubjective or interpersonal experience. Part of the reason may be that Heidegger is attempting to work outside of a phenomenology of subjectivity, and as his writings evolve he moves further away from any notion of subjectivity.

Even so, earlier in *Being and Time*, he did address relations with other people. There, the positive relation with other people is ambiguous. On the one hand he maintains that *Dasein* is essentially Being-with (*mit-Sein*) others, and on the other hand he discusses the isolation inherent in the being towards death which authenticates *Dasein* (see Heidegger 1962, 155–157; 307–308). In addition, the relationship between *Dasein* and the general other levels down and deprives *Dasein* of its answerability—its ability to respond to the other (165). Later, in *What is Called Thinking*, Heidegger suggests the importance of interpersonal relations when he uses the example of hands: "The hand does not only grasp and catch, or push and pull. The hand reaches and extends, receives and welcomes—and not just things: the hand extends itself, and receives its own welcome in the hands of others" (Heidegger 1993a, 381).

Heidegger rejects Husserl's account of intersubjectivity. In *Being and Time*, he alludes to Husserl when he claims that empathy does not provide the first bridge to the other. In fact, empathy is the result of Being-with and not vice versa (Heidegger 1962, 162). In addition, the other is not merely a duplicate of myself; for this disregards the otherness of the other (162). Against Husserl, Heidegger argues that being with others is not a matter of a collection of subjects intending each other (163). Rather, "so far as *Dasein is* at all, it has Being-with-one-another as its kind of Being" (163). Yet, after this brief discussion of Being-with in *Being and Time*, Heidegger rarely directly discusses interpersonal relations.

Levinas criticizes what we might call the virility of Heidegger's philosophy, in spite of Heidegger's attempts to escape the Cartesian subject. Levinas argues that "the 'egoism' of ontology is maintained even when, denouncing Socratic philosophy as already forgetful of Being and already on the way to the notion of the 'subject' and technological power, Heidegger finds in PreSocratism thought as obedience to the truth of Being. . . . Possession is preeminently the form in which the other becomes the same, by becoming mine. In denouncing the sovereignty of the technological power of man Heidegger exalts the pre-technological powers of possession" (Levinas 1969, 46).

Levinas also suggests that Heidegger's emphasis on the lighting of Being gives privilege to vision; and "vision moves into grasp" (Levinas 1969, 191). Ultimately, Levinas criticizes Heidegger because he makes the concrete Other subordinate to abstract Being: "Heideggerian ontology, which subordinates the relationship with the Other to the relation with Being in general, remains under obedience to the anonymous, and leads inevitably to another power, to imperialist domination, to tyranny" (46–47). Levinas argues that Heidegger's notion of Being becomes associated with nature, in which there is no justice. "Ontology becomes ontology of nature, impersonal fecundity, faceless generous mother, matrix of particular beings, inexhaustible matter for things" (46). In his criticism, Levinas reveals Hei-degger's association between the mother and the tyranny of nature.

Merleau-Ponty

Although like Heidegger, Merleau-Ponty rejects Husserl's notion of the transcendental ego, in his early writings he describes intersubjective relations in terms familiar from Husserl. In *The Primacy of Perception*, Merleau-Ponty introduces the notion of the lived body into Phenomenology. All experience is embodied. Although one might think that this radical change in the emphasis of Phenomenology would have drastic effects for the discussion of intersubjectivity, in *The Primacy of Perception*, Merleau-Ponty claims that the body of another is perceived as an object like any other object except that this object has the ability to communicate (Merleau-Ponty 1964, 18). Reminiscent of Husserl, he claims that the relation to the other is a relation to another myself (17). Morality is possible as a result of the interaction between isolated (now embodied) subjects who appear as my alter egos: "Just as the perception of a thing opens me up to being, by realizing the paradoxical synthesis of an infinity of perceptual aspects, in the same way the perception of the other founds morality by realizing the paradox of an alter ego, of a common situation, by placing my perspectives and my incommunicable solitude in the visual field of another and of all the others" (26). Although, unlike Husserl, Merleau-Ponty recognizes the experience of an alter ego as paradoxical, in this early work he still asserts that the subject is primary and the other is constituted in my lived experience (see 31).

As Merleau-Ponty's writing evolves, however, a radically new notion of intersubjectivity begins to appear. This evolution is apparent even within his last and unfinished work, *The Visible and the Invisible*. There, while admitting in the beginning that my perception of the other is in each case mine, and that the world of the other is private, he begins to open up the boundaries between self and other (Merleau-Ponty 1968, VI II, 82). Rather than reject any philosophy of subjectivity, Merleau-Ponty rethinks subjectivity through the body. Like Heidegger's hand that both welcomes and receives welcome, Merleau-Ponty's flesh makes communication and communion possible. Both the thickness of the flesh and the permeability of the skin make communication with the world and other possible (135).

The body itself "solves" the philosophical problem of the relationship between subject and object, self and other. The body is both subject and object "because a sort of dehiscence opens my body in two, and because between my body looked at and my body looking, my body touched and my body touching, there is overlapping encroachment, so that we must say that the things pass into us as well as we into the things" (Merleau-Ponty 1968, 123). The thickness of flesh and the permeability of skin makes "intercorporiety" possible (141). Merleau-Ponty asks, "If my left hand can touch my right hand while it palpates the tangibles, can touch it touching, can turn its palpation back upon it, why, when touching the hand of another, would I not touch in it the same power to espouse the things that I have touched in my own?" (141). This raises once again Husserl's problem that if I cannot distinguish my own experience from the other's, then either everything becomes part of me or my experience becomes lost to the other.

Merleau-Ponty addresses this problem by distinguishing between Husserl's conception of my own and the other experienced through consciousness, and my own and the other experienced through the body. The problem only arises when consciousness is seen as the source of experience. Consciousness relates to objects; and to make either the self or the other an object makes them identical in this regard. For Merleau-Ponty, the body is not an object, but a synergeric; and "consciousness" is inherent in the body's experience. "My consciousness" is not a Husserlian synthetic unity of "consciousnesses of" (Merleau-Ponty 1968, 141). Rather, it is the unity of the body that makes the unity of consciousness possible (141–142). So, my experience of the other is not a consciousness of another object; rather, my experience of the other is embodied.

As Merleau-Ponty describes it, the unity of my experience of my body is possible through my body's relationship to other bodies. All my experiences are bound together within my body "in such a way as to make up with them the experience of one sole body before one sole world, through a possibility for reversion, reconversion of its language into theirs, transfer, and reversal, according to which the little private world of each is not juxtaposed to the world of all others, but surrounded by it, levied off from it, and all together are a Sentient in general before a Sensible in general" (Merleau-Ponty 1968, 142). Just as all of my singular experiences are linked to each other, so too are my experiences linked to the experiences of others. Merleau-Ponty asks, "Now why would this generality, which constitutes the unity of my body, not open it to other bodies? . . . Why would not the synergy exist among different organisms, if it is possible within each?" (142). He maintains that it is possible to think about this kind of synergy between bodies only if we give up the notion of "belongingness to one same 'consciousness' the primordial definition of sensibility, and as soon as we rather understand it as the return of the visible upon itself, a carnal adherence of the sentient to the sensed and of the sensed to the sentient" (142).

Merleau-Ponty describes the reversibility of the flesh through which flesh folds back onto itself and makes all communication with the world and others possible. We are not consciousnesses cut off from the world trying to find an adequate bridge to our objects. Rather, we are part of the flesh of the world; and we are one body by virtue of our relations with others. The reversibility of the tangible opens up an "intercorporeal being" which extends further than any one individual and founds the "transitivity from one body to another" (Merleau-Ponty 1968, 143). There is no longer a problem of an alter ego because egos are merely by-products of fleshy relations. The thickness of the flesh guarantees relations, while the skin insures that we can distinguish our experience from the other's. Yet, since the flesh and skin are not objects, but synergetic, we are never cut off from the other. The skin is a boundary, but a permeable boundary.

Merleau-Ponty suggests that I can almost experience something of the other's embodiment in the same way that I experience my own embodiment. He gives the example of the difference between hearing my own voice and hearing the voice of another. I have a different relation to my own voice because it emanates from my body and I am affected by the vibrations of my body as I speak. "But if I am close enough to the other who speaks to hear his breath and feel his effervescence and his fatigue, I almost witness, in him as in myself, the awesome birth of vociferation" (Merleau-Ponty 1968, 144). At this point, Merleau-Ponty suggests the radical notion that I can feel the other's pain. There can be an exchange of synergy between bodies and if I am close enough to another person, I can experience the movements of their body in the same way that I experience the movements of my own. More than this, I can feel their effervescence and fatigue. The boundary between self and other has been opened. It is through the reversibility of the flesh that visible meets invisible (see 152).

Sartre

Influenced by German philosophy, particularly the work of Hegel, Husserl, and Heidegger, Sartre devoted a large section of *Being and Nothingness* to a phenomenology of intersubjectivity. Going beyond Heidegger's suggestions of a fundamental Being-with others, Sartre rejects Husserl's notion that the other is known by analogical reasoning from my own experience: "The Other is given to me as a concrete presence which I can in no way derive from myself and which can in no way be placed in doubt nor made the object of a phenomenological reduction or of any other epoché" (Sartre 1956, 362–363). Contra Husserl, Sartre denies that the other is ever given in my experience (309). Sartre describes a dialectical movement between self and other that constitutes my self-awareness through the look of the other. He maintains that I see myself only when I see another person looking at me; once I am captured by the look of another person, I am revealed to myself. Yet, as he describes it, this dialectical movement is not teleological or linear, but circular; neither the experience of self nor the experience of other is primary, but they are co-constituative.

For Sartre, the primary experience that brings me to myself is the experience of shame that results from being caught in the act by another person. Although he insists that both pride and shame are the result of the look of the other, he does not analyze pride.

Instead, he spends much of his discussion describing shame in front of the other. In fact, as it turns out pride is only the antithesis of shame; even pride is derived from the primary feeling of shame: "Pride does not exclude original shame. In fact it is on the ground of fundamental shame or shame of being an object that pride is built" (Sartre 1956, 386). In his analysis of the concrete relationship with others, Sartre devotes most of his discussion to feelings of conflict; even love is ultimately the experience of conflict (477). Even in love, the other is an enemy in a virile struggle for control.

Like Hegel's theory of the onset of self-consciousness through the master–slave relationship, Sartre's theory is premised on the claim that even in concrete relations each person is attempting to enslave the other: "While I seek to enslave the Other, the Other seeks to enslave me. We are by no means dealing with unilateral relations with an object-in-itself, but with reciprocal and moving relations. The following descriptions of concrete behavior must therefore be envisaged within the perspective of conflict. Conflict is the original meaning of being-for-others" (Sartre 1956, 475). As Sartre describes the conflict, it is a conflict over freedom. The other both takes my freedom, possesses it, and is the catalyst for my recognition of my freedom (473). I am imprisoned by the look of the other, yet through the look of the other I am aware of myself as a subject; by being an object for another, I become aware of myself as a subject for myself; I become aware of myself as a subject who escapes objectification, even my own attempts at objectifying myself.

The other can exist in different capacities, but insofar as it is dialectically engaged with my own consciousness of myself, it exists primarily as the bearer of the look. In fact, it exists as the look itself since in the look the other recedes; the eyes of another person give way to the look. When I am caught in the act, I don't see the eyes of the other: "The Other's look hides his eyes. He seems to go *in front of them*" (Sartre 1956, 346). I only see the accusing look. This look is totalizing. Although the other is not given to me as an object of my experience, my experience of the other is a total experience, an experience of the world. Sartre says that "the world announces the Other to me in his totality and as a totality . . . the Other's presence to me as the one who produces my object-state is experienced as a subject-totality" (390). I am overwhelmed by this other, who within this experience is all there is.

For Sartre, in spite of the totalizing presence of the other, the experience of the look, the experience which totalizes the other, is always *for me*. The look of the other always refers back to me: "The look which the *eyes* manifest, no matter what kind of eyes they are, is a pure reference to myself" (Sartre 1956, 347). The other's look is always directed *at me*. In this regard, Sartre follows Husserl's notion of the intentionality of intersubjective relations. Unlike Husserl, Sartre gives up the notion of the transcendental ego. He attempts to retain the notion of intentionality free from the transcendental ego (Sartre 1957, 38–40).

In *Transcendence of the Ego*, he suggests that he replaces the Husserlian egological structure with the notion of consciousness as a nothing (Sartre 1957, 93). Consciousness is not a type of being determined in advance. Consciousness aims at not-being; it aims at what has yet to be, it projects itself into a time yet to come. This is the essence of human freedom:

> Human-reality is free because it is *not enough*. It is free because it is perpetually wrenched away from itself and because it has been separated by a nothingness from what it is and what it will be. It is free, finally because its present being is itself a nothingness in the form of the "reflection-reflecting." Man is free because he is not himself but presence to himself. The being which is what it is can not be free. Freedom is precisely the nothingness which is *made-to-be* at the heart of man and which forces human-reality *to make itself* instead of *to be*. As we have seen, for human reality, to be is to *choose oneself*. (Sartre 1956, 568–569)

Sartre proposes a radical notion of freedom in which each human being is responsible not only for his or her actions but also for his or her emotions, beliefs, and desires. Our freedom and our responsibility are not limited to voluntary acts (Sartre 1956, 572). We are responsible not only for what we do but also who we are, what it is to be human: "In choosing myself, I choose man" (Sartre 1979, 37). Indeed, in choosing myself, I choose the world, since for Sartre all truth, meaning, and value have their source in human subjectivity (see, e.g., Sartre 1979, 32, 34, 61). Don Juan as a Sartrian hero who can.

Although in his discussion of freedom in *Being and Nothingness* Sartre stresses an individual's freedom and responsibility, we know from earlier sections that the other plays a crucial role in my free-dom. It is the look of the other which gives rise to my own recognition of my freedom. The look of the other turns me back on myself so that I can see the way in which I always escape myself; I see my possibilities. The look of the other confronts me with the nothingness at the core of my being when I see myself as an object for the other and realize that who I am is constituted in that look at the same time that I refuse to be reduced to that look. I both am and am not the object seen by the other. So begins my struggle with the other which supports Garcin's conclusion in *No Exit* that "there's no need for red-hot pokers. Hell is other people" (Sartre 1976, 47).

Levinas
In an important sense, the work of Emmanuel Levinas is motivated by the Husserlian problematic which insists on a sharp distinction between my experience and the experience of the other in order to guard against either everything becoming part of me or my experience becoming lost to the other. If Husserl tends toward the pole of the *I* over the other, Levinas tends toward the pole of the other over the *I*. Levinas insists on the radical alterity of the other such that I cannot presume anything about the other from my experience of myself; indeed, I cannot know the other at all. Recall that for Husserl although my experience of the other is based on my experience of myself, I do not know the other through reason; rather, I experience an analogical transference to the place of the other. This analogical transference is unique amongst my cognitive experiences. Merleau-Ponty criticizes the Husserlian transference because it is disembodied. He insists on an embodied experience of the other which, like Husserl's transference, is based on a relationship to the place of the other. For Merleau-Ponty, however, the place of the other is the location of the other in space, and not the location of the ego of the other. Physical proximity, especially intimacy, allows for my experience of the other.

Like Merleau-Ponty, Levinas develops a philosophy of intersubjectivity based on physical proximity; for Levinas I cannot put myself in the place of the other. Unlike Merleau-Ponty or Sartre, Levinas maintains that this relationship is not a matter of intentionality. Husserl's notion of intersubjectivity and consciousness itself is centered on the notion of intentionality. Whereas Heidegger takes over the Husserlian notion of intentionality in *Being and Time* with his notion of care, and Merleau-Ponty and Sartre embrace Husserl's notion of intentionality even while challenging his notion of the transcendental ego, Levinas rejects the notion of intentionality as auto-affection and self-possession (Levinas 1991, 111). Levinas responds that our relationship to an other, to our neighbor for example, is not an Husserlian "consciousness of." To describe relations between people in terms of consciousness is to reduce them to knowledge; another person becomes an object of knowledge for me.

Levinas objects that "the hypothesis that the relationship with an interlocutor would still be a knowing reduces speech to the solitary or impersonal exercise of a thought, whereas already the kerygma which bears its ideality is, in addition, a *proximity* between me and the interlocutor, and not our participation in a transparent universality. Whatever be the message transmitted by speech, the speaking is contact. . . . Speech and its logical work would then unfold not in knowledge of the interlocutor, but in his proximity" (Levinas 1993, 115). Like Merleau-Ponty, Levinas insists on proximity; but unlike Merleau-Ponty, Levinas also insists that proximity is not intentional. Proximity cannot be reduced to "a noetico-noematic structure" (119). Proximity engenders sensibility, tenderness, caresses, none of which are reducible to subjects knowing or intending objects.

Like Sartre, Levinas insists that my experience of the other as other is never an experience of an object. But, whereas Sartre describes the experience of the other as an experience of a subject-totality, Levinas describes the experience of the other as a nontotalizable experience of infinity. For Sartre, the experience of the other is defined in terms of vision, I am captured by the look of the other. For Levinas it is discourse and not vision that defines relations with others: "The face speaks. It speaks, it is in this that it renders possible and begins all discourse. I have just refused the notion of vision to describe the authentic relationship with the Other; it is discourse and more exactly, response or responsibility which is this authentic relationship" (Levinas 1985, 87–88). And this "saying is a way of greeting," not Sartre's hostile or guilty glance (88). Whereas Sartre emphasizes a radical subjectivity at the center of the universe who is limited by others, Levinas emphasizes a radical alterity at the center of the universe of which subjectivity is a by-product. For Sartre, all meaning is the product of human subjectivity, while for Levinas all meaning comes from the other. For Levinas, subjectivity is a relational product of the other, who cannot be experienced as an object of my consciousness.

Although Husserl does not maintain that another person or consciousness is an object of rational knowledge, he does posit that another consciousness becomes an intentional object of my consciousness through analogical transfer. My consciousness is the active agent in the intentional relation to the other. In "Language and Proximity," Levinas points to the passivity upon which the seemingly active Husserlian subject operates. The fact that consciousness can intend objects is the result of what Husserl calls "passive synthesis," which insures that various moments of consciousness are synthesized in time; the result is what Husserl calls internal time consciousness. What Levinas argues is that if consciousness is dependent upon a passive synthesis, then it cannot be intentional: "Consciousness as the passive work of time which no one activates cannot be described by the categories proper to a consciousness that aims at an object" (Levinas 1993, 114). Active, intentional consciousness is dependent on this passive nonthematic consciousness.

In *Otherwise Than Being*, Levinas points to another nonthematic element of Husserl's thematic intentional consciousness. There, he maintains that within Husserl's notion of empty intentions and the possible fulfillment of intentions there is a desire in excess of intentionality itself. If intentionality is merely the thematic by which everything is a consciousness of, then what is it that motivates the fulfillment of intentions? What motivates thematization? Levinas identifies the Husserlian movement from empty to full intentions as desire, tendency, hunger, which is nonthematic and nonintentional (Levinas 1991, 66).

Levinas suggests that the Husserlian notion of intentionality cannot account for sensation and that the relationship with others begins in sensation (see for example Levinas 1991, 67). The relationship with an other begins not with intentional consciousness, but in the proximity of two bodies. As Levinas says, "Only a subject that eats can be for-the-other, or can signify" (74). Embodiment is necessary for any thematization or signification, not just in the obvious factual sense that we need eyes to see and mouths to speak, but in the ontological sense that signification is a response to "an infinite which commands in the face of the other" (97). This infinite which calls for a response cannot be aimed at; it is not an intentional object for consciousness. Thematization by intentional consciousness "undoes" this approach of the other which calls for response (94). This is why Levinas insists that ethics, rather than epistemology or ontology, is the first philosophy. The relation that makes signification possible can only be described as an ethical relation (94).

This relation which makes signification possible, whose necessary consequence is signification, is a relation of responsibility. Subjectivity and signification—these two cannot be separated—are the result of responsibility to the other: "The knot of subjectivity consists in going to the other without concerning oneself with his movement toward me. Or, more exactly, it consists in approaching in such a way that, over and beyond all the reciprocal relations that do not fail to get set up between me and the neighbor, I have always taken one step more toward him—which is possible only if this step is responsibility. In the responsibility which we have for one another, I have always one response more to give, I have to answer for his very responsibility [*Moi j'aie toujours une réponse de plus à tenir, à répondre de sa responsabilité* (1974, 134)]" (1991, 84).

It might be helpful to note that the term responsibility (*responsabilité*) is from the Latin *respondere*, to respond, to answer, to answer's one's name, appear to be present, and *responso*, to keep answering. Subjectivity is fundamentally intersubjective if I *am* by virtue of my response to the other. I am by virtue of my responsibility to answer, even for the other's very answerability. This responsibility to answer is not a moral responsibility and it cannot be described in terms of ethics (Levinas 1991, 120). Rather, this responsibility is an ontological responsibility that makes the ethical relation with an other the foundation of ontology.

My subjectivity is continually constituted through my response to an other. This response is not a Sartrian defense of myself against the other nor a Hegelian struggle for recognition. Neither is it Husserl's or Merleau-Ponty's exchange of places with the other.

But communication would be impossible if it should have to begin in the ego, a free subject, to whom every other would be only a limitation that invited war, domination, precaution and information. To communicate is indeed to open oneself, but the openness is not complete if it is on the watch for recognition. It is complete not in the opening to the spectacle of or the recognition of the other, but in becoming a responsibility for him. The overemphasis of openness is responsibility for the other to the point of substitution, where the for-the-other proper to disclosure, to monstration to the other, turns into the for-the-other proper to responsibility. The openness of communication is not a simple change of place, so as to situate a truth outside instead of keeping it inside oneself. . . . [I]s not the ego a substitution in its solidarity as something identical, a solidarity that begins by bearing witness of itself to the other? (Levinas 1991, 119)

The response commanded by the other is to answer for the appearance of myself as a solitary ego. The response "here I am" is not only to answer for one's presence but also to turn oneself over to the other. The biblical "here I am" not only responds with the location of the *I* in space and time but also turns the *I* over to the other, God (cf. Levinas 1991, 199, fn 11). The responsibility that calls the *I* to the other in this way is not an action taken or chosen by the subject. Rather, subjectivity itself—the possibility of action or choice—is constituted through this responsibility that brings the *I* into being by taking it hostage, calling it forth (see 117). The *I* is by virtue of becoming a hostage to the other: "Subjectivity is being hostage" (127). Yet "the unconditionally of being hostage is not the limit case of solidarity, but the condition for all solidarity" (117). Due to the fact that my subjectivity can substitute for the other, but no one can replace me or my responsibility, I am unique: "Responsibility is what is incumbent on me exclusively, and what, *humanly*, I cannot refuse. This charge is a supreme dignity of the unique. I am I in the sole measure that I am responsible, a non-interchangeable I. I can substitute myself for everyone, but no one can substitute himself for me. Such is my inalienable identity of subject" (Levinas 1985, 101).

Levinas's question ("Is not the ego a substitution in its solidarity as something identical, a solidarity that begins by bearing witness of itself to the other?") suggests that the ego *is* insofar as it bears witness of itself to the other. Bearing witness, in this context, means not only listening to the other but also telling oneself to the other. It is not the content of its testimony that solidifies the ego; rather, it is the bearing witness itself, the relationship of telling oneself to the other, that solidifies the ego. Taking a step away from Levinas, I would say that at the level of phenomenology, my experience of myself comes through the narratives that I construct in order to tell myself and my life to another, especially on a mundane, everyday basis. I construct and reconstruct my experiences for another, even if I don't ever actually tell them the narrative that I have prepared for them. It is the bearing witness to the other itself, spoken or not, that gives birth to the *I*.

In *Otherwise Than Being*, Levinas takes maternity as "bearing par excellence" (Levinas 1991, 75). The subject's relation to the other is a relation of maternity, where maternity is seen as hospitality to the point of sacrifice for the other. For Levinas, maternity is a material relation to an other in which the maternal body is held hostage or persecuted by an other; yet, in spite of—or because of—this persecution, she gives herself to the other and takes responsibility for him. This responsibility is prior to her subjectivity and prior to her own awareness of her body. Maternity shows that our subjectivity starts as incarnation: "Incarnation is not a transcendental operation of a subject that is situated in the midst of the world it represents to itself; the sensible experience of the body is already and from the start incarnate. The sensible—maternity, vulnerability, apprehension—binds the node of incarnation into a plot larger than the apperception of the self. In this plot I am bound to others before being tied to my body" (Levinas 1991, 76). "It is because subjectivity is sensibility—an exposure to others, a vulnerability and a responsibility in the proximity of others, the-one-for-the-other, that is signification—and because matter is the very locus of the for-the-other . . . that a subject is of flesh and blood, a man that is hungry and eats, entrails in a skin, and thus capable of giving the bread out of his mouth, or giving his skin" (77). Maternity is one "body suffering for another" par excellence (79). Maternity is the "groaning of entrails, wounded by those it will bear or has borne" [" 'gémissement des entrailles', blessées en ceux qu'elles porteront ou qu'elles portaient"] (Levinas 1991, 75; translation slightly altered; 1974, 121).

Recall that for Husserl the metaphor of the mother represents the constitutive function of pure consciousness unencumbered by incarnation. For Levinas, maternity represents the function of incarnation prior to representation and self-consciousness. Maternity is a figure for a bodily relation that cannot be constituted by intentional consciousness. Whereas Husserl's mothers of pure consciousness require sacrifice from the knowing subject, Levinas's maternity is the quintessential economy of sacrifice for the sake of the unknowable other. Yet, on my reading of Husserl, Levinas's description of maternity as the "gestation of the other in the same" (Levinas 1991, 75) could be a description of Husserl's notion of the relation between the empirical ego and transcendental ego or the relation between my alter ego and my own ego. The history of phenomenology, from Husserl to Levinas, has been a gestation of the other in the same.

Kristeva

Like Levinas, Sartre, Merleau-Ponty, and Heidegger, Kristeva rejects the Husserlian notion of a transcendental ego which constitutes its objects, including other people. As an alternative to traditional notions of the subject, she proposes a notion of a subject-in-process/on trial (*le sujet en procès*). Kristeva criticizes Husserlian phenomenology for taking one stage of the process of subjectivity and fetishizing it. The stasis and stability of the transcendental ego is but one element of subjectivity. In addition, for Kristeva meaning is not the unified product of a unified subject; rather, meaning is other and as such makes the subject other to itself. Meaning is not constituted by a transcendental ego; meaning is constituted within a biosocial situation. Infants are born into a world where words already have meanings. Meaning is constituted through an embodied relation with another person. In this sense, meaning is other; it is constituted in relation to an other and it is beyond any individual subjectivity. Insofar as meaning is constituted in relationships — relationships with others, relationships with signification, relationships with our own bodies and desires — it is fluid. And, the subject for whom there is meaning is also fluid and relational.

Taking poetic language as emblematic, Kristeva argues that signification is "an undecidable process between sense and nonsense, between *language* and *rhythm*" (Kristeva 1980, 135). The Husserlian transcendental ego cannot account for nonsense or rhythm within signification; it cannot account for the unconscious. But, heterogeneity within signification points to heterogeneity within the speaking subject; if language is a dynamic process, then the subject is a dynamic process. Like signification, the subject is always in a constant process of oscillation between instability and stability, conscious and unconscious. The subject is continually being constituted within this oscillation between conscious and unconscious as an open system, subject to infinite analysis.

The unconscious, although part of the subject-in-process, is also other to consciousness. The unconscious is not just Husserl's, Merleau-Ponty's, or Sartre's alter ego, my ego displaced onto the place of another. Its otherness is not constituted by the fact that it is in another place, a place that I can understand if I just step into it. If I can't understand my unconscious, it is not because it is in another place, a place that I have not yet occupied. The unconscious is an other in the same place; it is the other within. I can't understand the unconscious because it is what is excluded or repressed so that self-conscious understanding is possible.

In *Powers of Horror* and later in *Strangers to Ourselves*, Kristeva maintains that our identity and sense of self is built through a process of exclusion. Our individual identity is formed through exclusions which become repressed in the unconscious in order to allow ego boundaries to form. Our national or group identity is formed through exclusions which become associated with rival groups or go unrecognized entirely yet continue to operate as the basis for exclusion; these exclusions set up the border against which we define ourselves as nations or cultures. These others are the repressed (ultimately the repressed maternal) and psychoanalysis awaits the return of the repressed. For Kristeva, psychoanalysis is a process of coming to terms with, even embracing, the other within.

In *Tales of Love*, Kristeva uses maternity as a model of the other within. She suggests that maternity radically challenges any notion of a unified self-transparent subject. Even as they are subjected to, neither the mother nor the fetus are subjects of, the process of gestation and childbirth. The mother does not relate to her child through an analogical transfer; she does not see herself in the child in the way that Husserl describes an experience of an other as alter ego. If she sees herself in the child it is not as her analog or alter ego, but as her flesh. In the case of maternity, Merleau-Ponty's proximity of flesh is taken to an extreme where the borders between bodies are questionable.

Whereas Husserl, Heidegger, and Levinas all invoke or employ a metaphor of maternity to describe subjectivity and relations, Kristeva suggests that maternity is the quintessential situation of the subject-in-process. Maternity is literally the gestation of the other in the same. The maternal model implicit in the history of phenomenology becomes explicit in Kristeva's writings. The maternal metaphor is in excess of the notions of unified subjectivity proposed in the history of phenomenology. The maternal metaphor cannot be contained within the theories of Husserl or Heidegger; it expands to the point of ripping the fabric of those theories. Even Levinas's self-conscious use of the metaphor of maternity tears at his notion of a sacrificial subjectivity.

Maternity and Subjectivity

Gestation is neither Levinas's maternal sacrifice, where bread is taken from the mouth of the mother and given to the child, nor Sartre's fight against an other who imposes himself on her. The processes of gestation insure that bread taken through the mother's mouth nourishes both the mother and the fetus. The fetus is protected from the maternal body's immune system by the placenta, which signals that the fetus is not a hostile intruder. And the system of exchange set up through the placenta insures that the maternal body is not sacrificed to the fetus. Neither a Sartrian economy of war nor a Levinasian economy of sacrifice, the economy of gestation is a cooperative exchange.

At this level, the traditional phenomenology of the subject breaks down. First, there is no subject–object relationship. Maternal body and fetus cannot be separated into subject and object, self and other. Second, there is no constitutive consciousness. Neither maternal body nor fetus is conscious or constituting the other. This is not a conscious relation and therefore not an intentional relation. While Levinas stretches phenomenology with descriptions of the experience of a face-to-face relation which is beyond knowledge and intentionality, he still attempts to describe human experience *as* experienced. The relation of the maternal body to the placenta takes us out of the realm of our experience *as* experienced and into a prior realm within which the possibility of our experience, both physically and ontologically, is set up.

In the last chapter of *Womanizing Nietzsche: Philosophy's Relation to the "Feminine,"* "Save the Mother," I sketched an ontology of intersubjectivity, or subjectivity as intersubjectivity, using the model of maternity. There, I suggested that the maternal model could provide an alternative to the antagonistic Hegelian master–slave model of intersubjectivity and its contemporary incarnations. The relationship between the maternal body and the fetus is a relationship mediated by communication. It is not a Levinasian face-to-face relationship. Yet, the "third party" in this relationship is not the judging other who transforms Levinas's face-to-face relationship into a political relation. The system within which the maternal body, fetus, and placenta operate—the gestation process—is not a relationship between autonomous beings. Yet these parts of the same process are not identical beings. Stretching Kristeva's terms, with maternity we have subjects-in-process*es*. We can no longer even talk of a subject-in-process as one distinct entity or one fluid subjectivity. Rather, identity and difference flow across subjectivities, which are continually constituted and reconstituted in relationships. With the maternal body, the notion of "one" becomes problematic and so does the notion of "two." Here, subjects are no longer countable entities. And bodies are no longer containers for subjectivity, the chariots or ships of souls. Bodies are no longer the battleships of virile subjects.

Battle of Wills [66]

Paternal Authority

Possibly the quintessential virile subject is the figure of the patriarchal father. He has proven his virility through his paternity and he takes on the control of himself and his family, whom he governs as his possessions. It is commonplace that our traditions associate the father with authority. From Jean-Jacques Rousseau to Jacques Lacan, from John Locke to John Rawls, father knows best.[67] Liberal theorists try to distinguish between legitimate and illegitimate authority by insisting that might does not make right. Yet, there are conflicts in the beginnings of liberal theory between the might of the father and his legitimate authority and the authority of the government. Both Locke and Rousseau present contradictory accounts of the relationship between the family and the state. Locke attempts to distinguish the "master of the family" from the leaders of political society by delineating the limitations of the paternal authority and appealing to a more democratic form of government than that of the patriarchal family. At the same time, he identifies the father as the *natural* ruler of the family "as the abler and the stronger" (Locke 1980, 44). Moreover, he describes the evolution to political society from patriarchal families as the evolution of paternal authority which nourishes political society: "Without such nursing father tender and careful of the public weal, all governments would have sunk under the weakness and infirmities of their infancy, and the prince and the people had soon perished together" (60). Paternal authority, founded in might, takes on the tender maternal role of nourishing and nursing political society.

Rousseau is also concerned that political society be based on legitimate authority and not just the brute strength of natural authority. "The more these natural forces are dead and obliterated, and the greater and more durable are the acquired forces, the more too is the institution solid and perfect" (1987, "On the Social Contract," 163). The father is by nature the authority in the family: "For several reasons derived from the nature of things, in the family it is the father who should command . . . a husband should oversee his wife's conduct, for it is important to him to be assured that the children he is forced to recognize and nurture belong to no one but himself" (1987, "Discourse on Political Economy," 112). Yet, while nature governs the family through the father, the state can only exist against nature. The laws of society are at odds with the laws of nature. "In effect, though nature's voice is the best advice a good father could listen to in the fulfillment of his duty, for the magistrate it is merely a false guide which works constantly to divert him from his duties which sooner or later leads to his downfall or to that of the state unless he is restrained by the most sublime virtue" (113).

Still, in "On the Social Contract," Rousseau maintains that "the most ancient of all societies and the only natural one, is that of the family. . . . The family therefore is, so to speak, the prototype of political societies; the leader is the image of the father, the populace is the image of the children. . . . The entire difference consists in the fact that in the family the love of the father for his children repays him for the care he takes for them, while in the state, where the leader does not have love for his people, the pleasure of command-ing takes the place of this feeling" (Rousseau 1987, 142). In the very next section, he goes on to insist that might does not make right and that physical power has nothing to do with moral or civil duty.

Implicit in the theories of both Locke and Rousseau are the *con-tradictory* claims that the authority of political society is based on right and not might, that only in nature does might constitute authority, that civil society supersedes nature, that the father's authority is based on natural physical strength, and that political society is based on the father's authority. The father's authority is based in nature and physical strength and yet it becomes the basis for a legitimate patriarchal government that is based in right and not might. How does the father come to represent right and not might? How does the father transcend his natural authority based solely in his physical strength in order to take up his civil authority based in his moral and intellectual strength?

This question is answered by Hegel, who, as we saw in chapter one, moves man into the social at the expense of woman. Man can enter culture because woman never leaves nature. In *Philosophy of Right*, Hegel says that man has his "actual substantive life in the state" and woman has her "substantive destiny in the family" (Hegel 1952, 114). Whereas men are capable of higher intellectual life, women inhabit a realm of feelings; "women correspond to plants because their development is more placid and the principle that underlies it is the rather vague unity of feeling" (263). Women are "educated" into this natural realm of feeling "who knows how?—as it were by breathing in ideas, by living rather than by acquiring knowledge. The status of manhood, on the other hand, is attained only by the stress of thought and much technical exertion" (264). Whereas love governs the domain of the family, law governs the state; love, a feeling, is subjective and contingent and therefore the unity of the family can dissolve, whereas law is objective and necessary and therefore the unity of the state is stronger than the unity of the family (265). In

Phenomenology of Spirit (discussed in chapter one above) Hegel describes how man leaves the world of the family and feelings and enters the world of the state and laws through the recognition of the women in his family, who provide the support against which he can pull himself up to a higher level of consciousness. For Hegel, man's nature seems to be paradoxical in itself insofar as man's nature is to go beyond nature. Woman's nature is to love, while man's nature is to lay down the law.

We might think that the association between woman and love and man and law was a nineteenth-century idea that we have outgrown. But these associations have only been fortified in the twentieth century by psychoanalysis. With psychoanalysis, might makes right in that the father's threats set up and fortify the child's superego or moral sense. The authority of the father, based in his physical strength and virility, is internalized to form the moral conscience. While Locke and Rousseau covertly appeal to the father's might in their explanations of the formation of civil society and moral right, Freud openly identifies moral right and civil law with paternal authority, based as it is in the father's bullying castration threats, which lead the son to wish to kill the father and the inevitable guilt associated with that wish. "What began in relation to the father is completed in relation to the group" (Freud 1961, 80).

Freud continues the argument that men are naturally more civilized than women, who belong at home with the children: "Women soon come into opposition to civilization and display their retarding and restraining influence—those very women who, in the beginning, laid the foundations of civilization by the claims of their love. Women represent the interests of the family and sexual life. The work of civilization has become increasingly the business of men, it confronts them with ever more difficult tasks and compels them to carry out instinctual sublimations of which women are little capable" (Freud 1961, 50). Women are not capable of instinctual sublimations because their anatomy does not permit them to *act* on those very instincts that must be sublimated in order to become civilized, namely, urinating on fire and presumably incest with their mothers.

Freud identifies control over fire as one of the primary achievements of primitive man that allowed him to become civilized. In a footnote in *Civilization and Its Discontents*, he hazards a conjecture on the origins of civilization as the origins of control over fire:

> The legends that we possess leave no doubt about the originally phallic view taken of tongues of flame as they shoot upwards. Putting out fire by micturating . . . was therefore a kind of sexual act with a male, an enjoyment of sexual potency in a homosexual competition. The first person to renounce this desire and spare the fire was able to carry it off with him and subdue it to his own use. By damping down the fire of his own sexual excitation, he had tamed the natural force of fire. This great cultural conquest was thus the reward for his renunciation of instinct. Further, it is as though woman had been appointed guardian of the fire which was held captive on the domestic hearth, because her anatomy made it impossible for her to yield to the temptation of this desire. (Freud 1961, 37)

Civilization begins when man curbs his desire to display his virility by urinating on phallic flames. Woman cannot sublimate the desire to pee on the fire because she cannot first act on the desire. We might wonder why Freud doesn't conclude that woman necessarily sublimates this desire since she can't act on it; that her anatomy demands sublimation whereas the male's does not; that in woman, nature has insured sublimation of aggressive instincts and therefore the advancement of the species. Instead, Freud identifies civilization, law, and morality with man's virility and its sublimation, where this sublimation is also described as man's virile act of control over himself.

Like Locke, Rousseau, and Hegel before him, Freud identifies the father as the first authority, upon which the authority of all subsequent government develops: "A Prince is known as the father of his country; the father is the oldest, first, and for children the only authority; and from his autocratic power the other social authorities have developed in the course of the history of human civilization" (Freud 1967, 251). For Freud, the father and his threats of castration intervene in the mother–child relationship to break the son out of this natural bond and propel him into culture. The daughter never fully enters culture since, already castrated, she does not feel the same effects of the castration threat and cannot internalize the paternal authority to the same degree. The internalization of the father's authority marks the child's proper entrance into the social.

Following Freud, Jacques Lacan describes the child's acquisition of language and socialization in terms of the father's authority. The father's "no," or prohibition, along with his name, or symbols, move the child away from the natural relationship with the mother to a social relationship. Lacan reiterates the association between father and culture and mother and nature: "The father is the representative, the incarnation, of a symbolic function which concentrates in itself those things most essential in other cultural structures: namely, the tranquil, or rather, symbolic, enjoyment, culturally determined and established, of the mother's love, that is to say, of the pole to which the subject is linked by a bond that is irrefutably natural" (Lacan 1979, 422–423). Once again the father's threats and prohibitions propel the child into culture and away from its relationship with its mother. The child's identification with the desire of the mother, its image of itself as her fulfillment, must be replaced by the father's name, words, and symbols. The father's name is a symbol that also designates ownership; the children, marked by his name, belong to the father.

Recall that as Lacan describes it, the infant first occupies a realm of needs. It has needs which it experiences as automatically met. Eventually the infant experiences a gap between the feeling of need and its fulfillment; the mother is not always present to meet its needs. This experience of lack or gap, experienced as the threat of castration, motivates the infant to substitute demands for needs. The infant learns that it must ask for what it wants. It learns to make demands using words. But, as a result, there is always something that it cannot get, immediate satisfaction. The infant wants its needs to be met automatically without having to ask; when it must ask for what it needs, then it cannot get it since what it needs is to get it without asking. Recall that this space between need and demand is what Lacan calls *desire*. Desire is produced when the infant substitutes demands for needs and experiences the gap between them, the inadequacy of words to express needs. Once the child moves from need to demand, it has moved from nature to culture and there is no going back; it is forever cut off from the natural world of bodily needs. The body is the real that makes itself felt in traumas that may disrupt the symbolic, but can never be directly accessed through the symbolic. Once we enter the language of culture, we are forever cut off from the language of the body.

For Lacan the father represents law and language, while the mother represents love and need. Once we are forever cut off from the body and needs, we are forever cut off from the mother. Her body, the satisfaction of needs, is lost to culture. But what of the father's body? As far as Lacan is concerned, the father has no body; his body is irrelevant: "For, if the symbolic context requires it, paternity will nonetheless be attributed to the fact that the woman met a spirit at some fountain or some rock in which he is supposed to live. . . . It is certainly this that demonstrates that the attribution of procreation to the father can only be the effect of a pure signifier, of a recognition, not of a real father, but of what religion had taught us to refer to as the Name-of-the-Father" (Lacan 1977, 199). Procreation is attributed to the father through his name; his name is the guarantee that the child belongs to him. And if the real father plays a role in the child's development, that role is dwarfed by the ever-present ideal of fatherhood. The greater the discrepancy between the role of the real father and the ideal father, the more powerful the ideal father becomes in psychic development.[68]

In his discussion of Lacan in *Straight Male Modern*, John Brenkman argues that "fatherhood does not become a metaphor for the norms and rules of interaction because it adequately summarizes them. It is in fact inadequate and is frequently countermanded by them. The paternal metaphor commands its position, rather, because it fulfills the legitimation requirements of male dominance. . . . There is no intrinsic necessity for 'law' and paternity to be linked in this way. The linkage is the product of the historical evolution of male dominance and the modes of legitimating it" (Brenkman 1993, 202).

It is the power associated with traditional paternal authority that makes the father's body and his phallus/penis represent power and authority. In Freud (and Lacan) this power is explicitly associated with the phallus/penis. Paradoxically, the ultimate virility of this masculine power is the sublimation of aggressive sex drives into productive and reproductive social economy. Aggressive instincts turn inward to aggress the self; this becomes self-control. Within this economy the penis takes on tremendous exchange value insofar as it, and control over it, is what makes society possible—recall Freud's account of control over fire. Freud's penis becomes Lacan's phallus, a transcendental signifier that makes economy and exchange possible.

In the words of Alphonso Lingis, "the paternal body presents itself as the supreme value in human commerce, the incarnation of law, reason, and ideals, in the measure that it incarnates the renunciation of the productive libido—infantile, insignificant, and uneconomical—the libido without character—disordered, contaminating, squandering. It governs a domestic economy in which commodities are accumulated as accouterments of the phallic order" (Lingis 1994, 128). The paternal body, then, is the supreme value in human commerce insofar as it represents the *repudiation* of the body.

Yet, the paternal repudiation of the body in favor of law and reason is *based on* the body. For Freud (and arguably for Lacan) it is the anatomy of the male body that makes the repudiation and sublimation of the aggressive sexual instincts possible. The male body is powerful only because it can act on its aggressive instincts in ways that the female body cannot. Paradoxically, for Freud it is not these acts that make men dominant, but the control over and repudiation of these acts. Men can control the body but only because their bodies are so hard to control. The force of the control required to subdue the body is proportionate to the strength of the body.

In philosophy and in psychoanalysis the father's authority as representative of law and culture has been based on his physical strength. Whereas the mother's relationship to the family is natural, the father transcends this natural relationship and engenders society. But it turns out that the father's authority can be justified only by appeals to the very nature that he is said to transcend. From Locke to Lacan, the authority of culture is legitimated in its opposition to the brute force of nature. But, insofar as the authority of culture, ultimately of patriarchy, is justified by appealing to the father's natural authority in the family, culture collapses back into nature. The authority of culture comes from the brute force of nature. Might does make right. And culture is not the antithesis of nature after all. On the other hand, if the law takes us beyond nature's triumph of the strongest, then patriarchy has no justification and there is no necessary connection between law and paternity.

Ricoeur's Symbolic Father

The workings of paternal authority are most obvious, because most tested, in the father–son relationship. Since the myth of Oedipus, the father–son relationship has been associated with murder. Oedipus, the son, is destined to kill his father. The son unwittingly kills his father. Perhaps if he had recognized his father, he would not have killed him. Is it enough for the son to recognize his father as Lacan's spirit in a rock? On the contrary, isn't this recognition necessarily embodied and not merely cognition? Can we think the father–son relationship outside of an economy of murder?

Within the history of Western culture, it is difficult to see the father–son relationship as something other than a fight to the death akin to the Hegelian master–slave dialectic. Freudian psychoanalysis presents us with the prime example of this murderous model. The son must conquer his desires and subject himself to his father's commands so that someday he might take the place of his father, the place of the master. If the son denies his bodily passions he is promised the position of mastery. On some level, the Hegelian master–slave dialectic *only* makes sense as the father–son relation so conceived. The stoicism of the slave only makes sense if someday he will inherit the position of master. In the power play between father and son, the son must defer to the father until he takes the father's place. In this model, manhood requires the death of the father. As the Oedipus story illustrates, there can be only one King. The son becomes complete master only when he is the father who is no longer fathered.

In "Fatherhood: From Phantasm to Symbol," Paul Ricoeur describes fatherhood as a battle of wills struggling for recognition. He brings together what he calls the different perspectives of psychoanalysis, phenomenology, and religion in order to rearticulate the Oedipal situation as a process of recognition which moves from the father as phantasm to the father as symbol and replaces images of real murder with symbolic murder. Through his dialectical analysis, Ricoeur himself attempts to articulate a recognition of fatherhood that moves us away from the phantasm of the father as castrator to the symbol of the father as compassionate. Relying on Hegelian dialectics, Ricoeur outlines a movement from psychoanalysis's fantastic image of an omnipotent father who must be killed so that the son might live to the Christian religious representation of the loving father sacrificing himself through his son for the sake of his children. In this higher stage of the dialectic of paternity, the murder of the father is replaced by his sacrifice. Clearly, however, we are still within a Hegelian master–slave scenario, whereby the only options available to insure the recognition of the father by the son (or the son by the father) are murder or suicide. Recognition requires death, figurative if not literal.

Ricoeur insists that we must move beyond the father as begetter, the embodied father, to reach a recognition of the symbolic father. He argues that at the level of embodiment, the father seems omnipotent and therefore threatening; this threat leads to the son's need to kill him. For Ricoeur, only the abstract disembodied father can be recognized and nonthreatening. I will tell a different story about the perceived need to cover over the father's embodiment with symbols, a need motivated not by the fear of impotence in the face of omnipotence, but by the fear of chance, indeterminacy, and mortality.

In "Fatherhood: From Phantasm to Symbol," Ricouer begins by identifying three stages of the Oedipal process as described by Freud: 1. the formation of the Oedipal complex; 2. the dissolution of the Oedipal complex; 3. the permanence of the Oedipal complex. He sets out his tripartite analysis of fatherhood using this schema. Each perspective both embodies this dynamic which moves from formation, through dissolution, to permanence, and at the same time occupies one of these stages in relation to the other perspectives. So, psychoanalysis both includes a description of these three stages and occupies the first of the three stages in relation to phenomenology and religion. Phenomenology operates according to the same dialectical movement from formation, through dissolution, to permanence, while representing the stage of dissolution in the greater dialectical relation between psychoanalysis, phenomenology, and religion. Religion has its logical analog to the formation of the Oedipal situation, dissolution of the Oedipal situation, and permanence of the Oedipal situation, while occupying the third position of that dialectic in relation to the other two perspectives. Ricoeur insists that in each perspective, in order for the father to be recognized rather than simply murdered, the role of symbolic mediation must be acknowledged. Fatherhood becomes recognized as a designation and not a natural fact only when the mediation of other cultural relationships is acknowledged.

Taking the Freudian model as a point of departure, Ricoeur describes the Freudian Oedipal complex as initiated by the megalomania of infantile omnipotence, which projects a phantasm of an all-powerful father who must be killed so that the infant can maintain its fantasy of omnipotence. In this way, the father becomes a phantasm of the castrator who threatens to take away the infant's power. The dissolution of the Oedipal complex is the dissolution of the economy of omnipotence or all or nothing of the megalomaniac infantile omnipotence. Ricoeur maintains that "the stake involved in the dissolution of the Oedipus complex is the replacement of an identification with the father which is literally mortal—and even doubly mortal, since it kills the father by murder and the son by remorse—by a mutual recognition, where difference is compatible with similarity" (Ricoeur 1974, 471). We could say, then, that the dissolution of the Oedipal complex requires abandonment of the economy of castration, which insists on the impossible identification with omnipotence and the imagined substitution of son for father in relation to the mother's desire.

The paradox of this dialectic as Ricoeur describes it is that the son gives up his patricidal fantasies only when he is able to accept the fantasy of the death of his father; the son gives up the fantasy of the omnipotent immortal father who must be killed so that the son can avoid castration only after he can imagine the death of his mortal father. It is this image of the dead father that allows for the representation of the father. With the mortality of the father comes the designation father. Fatherhood is constituted in the son's call or the son's recognition of his father as father. "It is necessary that the blood tie be loosened, be marked by death, in order that fatherhood be truly instituted; then the father is father because he is designated and called father" (Ricoeur 1974, 471). The image of the death of the body of the father enables a representation of the father as something other than the all-powerful body. Ricoeur identifies this movement as a movement through nonkinship relations which act as the prerequisite for designating or representing the father as "father." In a sense, the infant must be weaned from an identification with the father's body, the "very person of the father," the father as the biological source of life, to see the father as "father" (see 471).

In this dynamic, the Oedipal situation reasserts itself by once again requiring the death of the father, but at this new level his death need not be murder. The perspectives of phenomenology and religion promise not to repeat the Oedipal situation even while they continue to conjure the return of the repressed "by renouncing omnipotence" and assenting "to the representation of a mortal father whom it is no longer necessary to kill but who can be recognized" (Ricoeur 1974, 473). The necessity of the detour through nonkinship relations in order to set up the possibility of kinship relations or fatherhood is more explicit in the perspectives of phenomenology and religion. In fact, in Ricoeur's dialectical analysis, phenomenology stands in the place of the destruction of the Oedipal complex, or the detour through nonkinship relations, which eventually makes a recognition of fatherhood possible.

In his analysis of phenomenology and fatherhood, Ricoeur does not turn to the Ethics section of *Phenomenology of Spirit* in which Hegel describes the dialectic of the family and familial relations. Rather, Ricoeur turns to the Self-Consciousness section of *Phenomenology* and extrapolates its implications for a mutual recognition between father and son. Ricouer emphasizes the importance of the mediation of things in the master–slave relationship; the slave recognizes himself through his labor and his relation to things. Labor is desire restrained and postponed. Ricoeur finds that desire's detour through things promises the recognition of fatherhood: "The *Phenomenology of the Spirit* presents a dialectic between desire and labor for which Freud has designated only the empty mold by speaking of the dissolution of the Oedipus complex. This dialectic permits the introduction of fatherhood itself into a process of recognition; but the recognition of the father and the son takes place by the double mediation of the mastery of men and things and the conquest of nature by labor" (Ricoeur 1974, 476).

Ricoeur sees the master–slave dialectic as a struggle between wills for recognition. So too, he maintains, the father–son relationship is a struggle between wills for recognition. Such struggles are described in Hegel's *The Philosophy of Right*, where two wills struggle for possession of property and rights. Ricoeur sees this struggle over possession as a repetition of the master–slave relation on another level; even contracts are motivated by desire. The confrontation of wills for possession necessitates compromise and contracts. The struggle is mediated by a third will, a third party, and a thing, the contract. Ricoeur concludes that "now, we can very well say that neither fatherhood nor sonship could take on a consistency beyond simple natural generation if they were not mutually bound together, one in relation to the other, not only as two self-consciousnesses, as in the dialectic of master and slave, but as two wills, objectivated by their relation to things and by their contractual ties" (Ricoeur 1974, 477). Father and son are recognized as such only through the mediation of relations of nonkinship with other persons and things, particularly contracts.

The father–son relationship comes back into its own through the mediation of third parties, but it goes beyond such contractual relationships. Contractual relations are concrete relations which instantiate the abstract relation between individual rights. On Ricoeur's reading of Hegel, family relations go beyond these abstract relations of individual rights. Family relations properly recognized move us from the realm of individual wills and rights (*Moralität*) to the realm of collective spirits and ethics (*Sittlichkeit*) (Ricoeur 1974, 479). Although it is based in the marriage contract between spouses, the family itself does not proceed from a contract. But as individuals give themselves over to the collectivity of the family and are born into this community, what Hegel calls morality gives way to ethics, and family relations are more than negotiations between individual wills.

Ricoeur maintains that ethics makes the family possible and the family makes the father possible: "There is a father because there is a family, and not the reverse. And there is a family because there is *Sittlichkeit*, and not the reverse" (Ricoeur 1974, 479). Family relations are recognized as such due to the mediation of contractual relations involving persons outside of the family. The family can be recognized as a collective only by virtue of the mediation of other collectivities *outside* of the family. The family operates as a knot between immediate life and life mediated by both morality and ethics, social life. Insofar as family relations are not voluntary and we are born into our families, the family repeats something of the immediacy of life. On the other hand, insofar as we recognize ourselves as members of a family, we recognize ourselves as mediated by social life and relations with others outside of our family.

For Ricoeur, it is the union of desire and spirit, or sex and ethics, or body and representation, circumscribed by law, that makes the recognition of the father possible. The father can be recognized in his bodily role as progenitor only if this role is mediated by the contractual or social relation. The body of the father can be brought back into the father–son relationship through its union with the body of the mother: "A father who is a spouse is no longer a progenitor (begetter), nor is he any more an enemy to his sons; love, solicitude, and pity carry him beyond domination and severity" (Ricoeur 1974, 489). The mediation of the contract with the mother/wife transforms the father from an omnipotent body that terrorizes the son to a loving equal who recognizes the son through the son's recognition of him. For Ricoeur, the recognition of fatherhood requires that the physical generation retreats in favor of the word, that the destructive identification between father and son is replaced with mutual recognition, and finally, that the access to the symbol of fatherhood is detached from the person of the father (497). The body of the father is replaced with a word of designation, a symbol of fatherhood.

The father is a father in the family community as it is first recognized as a community through the marriage contract, which is recognized by the larger community (Ricoeur 1974, 480). Ricoeur adds that to recognize the father with the mother through their contractual union is also to recognize them through their sexual union. Certainly, fatherhood and motherhood are dependent upon sexual union (or technological intervention). For Ricoeur, sexuality that conceives the family is recognized as the "carnal dimension" of the contract (480). Although he acknowledges the "carnal dimension," he insists that it can only lead to murder. To prevent murder, we must move beyond bodies and fantasies to symbols. "Begetting is a matter of nature, fatherhood of designation. It is necessary that the blood tie be loosened, be marked by death, in order that fatherhood be truly instituted" (471).

Why must the body of the father, and its role in procreation, be replaced so that the father can be recognized? Why can the father's body only be acknowledged in its relation to the body of the mother? Ricoeur suggests that in psychoanalysis the father is associated with his body and it is this association that leads to the son's threatening fantasy of an omnipotent father. In Freudian theory, the son is envious of the father's physical power to possess the mother. The son feels impotent by comparison. The threats of castration from the father cause the son to murder him in order to take his place in relation to the mother. For Ricouer, this murder becomes a compassionate suicide when we move from psychoanalysis to religion. God the father sacrifices himself, "and this death would no longer be a murder but the most extreme abandonment of self" (Ricoeur 1974, 495). In all cases, the death of the father's body is necessary.

In the case of Divine fatherhood, the identification between the father and son transforms the father's death. The son dies for the father, as the father; God dies for his children. Ricoeur concludes that "there is, therefore, a death of the father which is no longer a murder and which belongs to the conversion of the phantasm into symbol . . . the meaning of death is reversed: by becoming 'dead' for another; the death of the Just One achieves the metamorphosis of the paternal image in the direction of a figure of kindness and compassion" (Ricoeur 1974, 492). Death is no longer a murder, but an offering, a sacrifice, made for the other. The son dies for his father so that the father may die for his children, not out of resentment but out of compassion. This death that is self-sacrifice is "at the same time a murder on the level of the phantasm and the return of the repressed, and a supreme abandonment, a supreme dispossession of self, on the level of the most advanced symbol" (493). Only on the level of fantasy, at the level of the imaginary, is the death of the father always either murder or suicide. On the symbolic level, this "death" represents the dispossession of the self for the sake of another, the dispossession of the self as compassion. On the symbolic level the scenario is radically different than on the imaginary level. On the level of phantasm we are stuck at the initial stages of Hegel's master–slave relationship where the only alternatives appear to be murder or suicide, me or you. For Ricoeur, on the symbolic level through the mediation of cultural symbols we can recognize the father and avoid murdering him. More than this, we can revalue the life and death of the body so that the body of the father gives itself over to the life of the son. The father is a promise beyond compromise, the promise of the life to come for the son.

Ricoeur concludes that "the final theme, for each of these three disciplines [psychoanalysis, phenomenology, religion] would be the inclusion of the death of the father in the final constitution of the symbol of fatherhood. And this death would no longer be a murder but the most extreme abandonment of self" (Ricoeur 1974, 495). Recognition of the father requires his death, but this death need not be murder; it can be what Derrida calls "the gift of death." But, it can be something other than murder only when it is mediated by figures outside of the family.

According to Ricoeur, the requites for fatherhood are: 1. the retreat of the physical, 2. mutual recognition must replace identification, 3. the symbolic father must be detached from the person (Ricoeur 1974, 497). Ricoeur suggests that it is through the access to a *symbol* of fatherhood detached from the *person* of the father that we move from murder to sacrifice. He insists that the separation between symbol and person or phantasm of the father introduces contingency and death into the symbolizing process. Overcoming biological necessity, the process of recognition itself, which is the process of symbolizing, becomes a contingent process which requires death. Symbolic contingency is opposed to biological necessity. Culture is opposed to nature. Yet, the contingencies of nature, the contingencies of the paternal body, are put to death through symbols.

Even the death of God, the sacrifice of the body of the son, repeats the Oedipal killing, only this time there is a compassionate suicide rather than a vengeful murder. For Ricoeur, divine fatherhood is analogous to the return of the repressed. Ricoeur ends his essay with the question of the relationship between death and the symbol, a question that he does not attempt to answer. How can we explain the paradox set up by Ricoeur whereby it is necessary to recognize or designate the father in order to avoid murdering him, but that very process of designation or symbolization requires the death of the father? Why does the process of symbolization require death, particularly the death of the father's body?

Abject Father [69]

Why is the father's body seen as such a threat to the son? As philosophers and psychoanalysts maintain, does the son suffer from the illusion that the father is omnipotent? Or, is the substitution of abstractions, law, and symbols for the father's body a screen for the fear that the father is not omnipotent? Without postulating the reign of his will, what is determinant about the father's relationship to the child? Behind the Oedipal story and the Hegelian struggle for mastery is the fear of the father's body, not because its omnipotence threatens to kill the son, but because its lack of determinacy threatens the son's very existence; the contingency and chance of its contribution to procreation is a threat to the son. The son becomes an accident of chance, a contingency as precarious as any individual sperm cell once it leaves the father's body. Even more disturbing, in this fantasy the child may become merely a waste product expelled from the father's body. The fantasy of the father's omnipotence protects the child from a more terrifying fantasy, the fantasy of the father's impotence, which threatens not just the child's death, but the child's coming to be. The threat of what I will call an *abject father* is more terrifying than the threat of an omnipotent father. At least the omnipotent father promises omnipotence for the son who one day can take his place. An identification with an abject father, on the other hand, promises indeterminacy and contingency with regard to even life and death. In the end, both the fear of the omnipotent father and the terror of the impotent father operate within the same economy of virility, which trades on the fear of a male body.

In *Powers of Horror*, Kristeva develops a notion of abjection based on Mary Douglas's notion of defilement. In *Purity and Danger*, Douglas describes defilement as the danger to identity constituted by filth, which is always defined in relation to the borders of that very identity. The identity of the subject is tied to the identity of the borders of the body, which are threatened by bodily secretions: "Matter issuing from them [the orifices of the body] is marginal stuff of the most obvious kind. Spittle, blood, milk, urine, feces or tears by simply issuing forth have traversed the boundary of the body. . . . It follows from this that pollution is a type of danger which is not likely to occur except where the lines of structure, cosmic or social, are clearly defined" (Douglas 1969, 113). Notice that Douglas does not mention semen, which for Kristeva becomes a special case.

Kristeva describes those things, which are not quite objects, that threaten the boundaries of our identities, both individual and social, as abject. Following Douglas, she maintains that the abject corresponds to the attempt to clearly delineate borders. In order to delineate borders, a line must be drawn between the inside and the outside, between the clean and proper self and the abject other. That which threatens identity must be jettisoned from the borders and placed outside. In this sense, identity is constituted through a process of abjection. As Kristeva describes it, both individual and social identity are constituted by abjecting *maternal* elements. The maternal body threatens the borders of the individual and social subject. It threatens the individual subject who was born out of another body and must deny this in order to establish its own proper identity. It threatens social identity insofar as the maternal body is associated with nature, and the social must distinguish itself from the forces of nature. So, those bodily secretions—blood and milk—associated with the maternal body are the most strictly regulated by cultural and religious rituals. Kristeva discusses food prohibitions that revolve around blood and milk, always associated with the maternal.

Although she does not explain why, Kristeva exempts semen from the types of dangerous fluids which call into question the boundaries of identity. Perhaps the exemption of semen stems from Kristeva's premise that it is the fluids associated with the maternal body that are the most dangerous for identity. In any case, she identifies two types of polluting objects, excremental and menstrual, both of which she associates with the maternal body: "Those two defilements stem from the *maternal* and/or feminine, of which the maternal is the real support. That goes without saying where menstrual blood signifies sexual difference. But what about excrement? It will be remembered that the anal penis is also the phallus with which infantile imagination provides the feminine sex and that, on the other hand, maternal authority is experienced first and above all, after the first essentially oral frustrations, as sphincteral training" (Kristeva 1982, 71). In the infant's imaginary the phallic mother has an anal penis and maternal authority governs excrement, so, like blood, excrement is associated with the mother.

Language and culture are born out of this presymbolic maternal authority but only after this authority is repressed. "If language, like culture, sets up as separation, and, starting with discrete elements, concatenates an order, it does so precisely by repressing maternal authority and the corporeal mapping that abuts against them" (Kristeva 1982, 72). Bodily fluids associated with maternal law and maternal power are repressed so that paternal symbolic culture can legitimate its own authority by denying maternal authority. As

Kristeva asks, "What happens to such a repressed item when the legal, phallic, linguistic symbolic establishment does not carry out the separation in radical fashion," or, we might add, cannot carry out the separation in radical fashion? After all, the maternal and feminine, while repressed and denigrated, abjected and defiled, cannot be completely eliminated or even culture and its reproduction would be sacrificed. And it is precisely at this point, where culture is dependent upon that which it denies, that it begins to employ Freud's *kettle logic*. Freud tells the story of a man who borrows a kettle and tries to deny that he broke it by telling its owner first that he didn't break it and next that it wasn't broken and finally that he did not borrow the kettle.[70] These zealous denials produce inconsistencies that betray the culprit.

Semen is a broken kettle. How can semen be exempt from the category of dangerous fluids?[71] Recall from my analysis in "Virile Eros" above that recent research has in fact *determined* that the seminal fluid of fruit flies is toxic to female fruit flies; and while the scientists try to convince us that human beings are analogous to fruit flies, they draw the line at toxic semen. Given their arguments about the similarities between reproduction and evolution in fruit flies, their conclusion should be that semen is also toxic to human females; but like Kristeva, they make an exception for human semen.[72] Semen (and its danger) is invisible within our cultural imaginary in which the virile male body is a purifying force. I am not suggesting that we accept these biologists' conclusions that semen is toxic and the sexes are engaged in a deadly evolutionary war. In fact, earlier I challenged these metaphors of war and battle and the experimental methods (tying the hands of female fruit flies) that produce "toxic semen." Rather, my point is that semen is invisible and purified in our culture. And its invisibility and purification merely cover up its abjection and indeterminant status in our culture.

The earliest theories in Western biology and medicine proposed that male semen is purified by the heat of the male body while female semen (menstrual blood) is cooler and less pure. They took the difference in color as evidence; male semen, once as impure as female semen, is translucent because of the purification process.[73] This physical purification process corresponds to the male's cathartic purification of passions and lusts from his clean and proper self. The separation of the male body from the mess of reproduction, the separation of masculine identity from the male body's role in reproduction, allows masculine identity to be constituted by abjecting everything messy about reproduction and associating it with the female body. In this way, males maintain their own clean and proper selves. But a broken kettle leaks regardless of the anxious stories one tells in order to cover one's mess.

Anxieties about male bodies are projected onto female bodies: Female bodies leak, male bodies do not.[74] The male body absents itself in favor of solid objects that do not flow and a mind that is eternal and without corporeality. Fatherhood is not defined in terms of the paternal body or its contribution to procreation, but in terms of the father's name or law, contracts (or physical surveillance) that guarantee that the child is his. Fatherhood is made determinant by denying the body. The paternal body is absent from discourses about fatherhood because the paternal body necessarily leaks and brings with it indeterminacy and chance.

Within the Western imaginary, the abject father, the father of chance and contingency, is counteracted in the union with the mother's body which provides some regularity and determinacy. For Ricoeur, for example, it is through the union with the mother's cyclical and determinant contribution to procreation, that random chance becomes reality; the child becomes determinant. If the father's body can only be acknowledged in its relation to the mother's body it is because of the fear of the indeterminacy and random chance that comes with the father's dissemination of himself in his bodily fluids. Yet, recall that the maternal body has been associated with nature rather than culture. Because the maternal body is not associated with *social* necessity and *human* agency but *biological* necessity and *natural* determinism, any refuge in the image of the maternal body cannot guarantee that the child is chosen or loved, because choice and love require human agency. As a result, within these dominant fantasis, a child has neither a loving mother nor a loving father.

Virile subjectivity and the image of a disembodied father are attempts to contain the abject paternal body with its flows and contingency. But, these images cannot counterbalance the threat of the abject father. The repressed paternal body returns to haunt virile philosophical discourses on (male) subjectivity. Fantasies of a virile subject leave us feeling alienated and unloved. Ricoeur's notion of the father's body as mediated through the mother's and of father-hood as a battle of wills mediated by contracts is an example of such a virile Eros tied to a virile subjectivity.

Ricoeur's insistence on the mutual recognition of father and son which comes through the Hegelian struggle of wills reinserts deter-minacy and control into the father–son relationship. For him, fathers and sons are products *not* of bodies, but of the determina-tion of the virile will, mediated by contracts: "Fatherhood itself is entirely disassociated from begetting" (Ricoeur 1974, 487). Bodies themselves are possessions regulated by contracts (478). The self-dispossession and abandonment of self that Ricouer identifies with the highest stages of fatherhood are possible as the result of self-recognition that comes through a self-possessed battle of wills. Even divine fatherhood becomes determined by the designation by the son and the result of a contract, God's covenant with Israel. But is it cause for celebration that today so many paternal relationships are *literally* mediated by custody contracts and forced child support?

It may seem strange to think, as Ricoeur does, that the marriage contract determines fatherhood; after all, many children are con-ceived outside of marriage. But until relatively recent technology made it possible to determine paternity, *unwed fathers* merely denied paternity, while married fathers assumed paternity in the face of possible uncertainties. The awkwardness and unfamiliarity of the phrase "unwed fathers" points to the strangeness of attributing fatherhood outside of marriage. *Illegitimate* children were seen as the products of mothers alone, unwed mothers, while *legitimate* children were seen as the products of husbands and wives even if the hus-band was not the biological father.

Michael Caton-Jones's recent film *Rob Roy* (1995) gives the classic example of a woman, Betty, who becomes pregnant out of wedlock and is spurned by her lover, Archibald Cunningham, who denies paternity. Mary McGregor, on the other hand, is raped by Archibald Cunningham and becomes pregnant. Although Betty loves Archibald and wants their child, she commits suicide because of Cunningham's denial, while Mary, who hates Archibald, gives birth to his child because her husband, Rob Roy McGregor, claims paternity. The very notion of *legitimacy* suggests that motherhood and fatherhood are defined in terms of the marriage contract and not in terms of biological conception or sexual intercourse.

Advances in reproductive technology have made conception possible without sexual intercourse. These technologies have complicated the attribution of paternity. Still, the courts consistently define fatherhood within the confines of the marriage contract. If his wife is artificially inseminated, the husband is considered the father of the resulting child even though he is not the biological father. Artificial insemination through medical institution requires the anonymity of the donor, which, among other things, insures that a husband whose wife is artificially inseminated does not have to vie for paternity. Many states have laws that guarantee that husbands have priority as the fathers of their wives' children.[75]

While Ricoeur moves the recognition of fatherhood from the family into the social in order to formulate a notion of recognition between father and son as equals that does not reproduce the power hierarchy of the Oedipal scenario with its murderous revenge, he does not analyze the inequities in these legal and social contracts that might make this type of recognition impossible.[76] We see Ricoeur's analysis in a different light when we consider that most father–son relationships are mediated by contracts, child-custody contracts. State welfare agencies spend much of their time trying to track down fathers in order to collect child support. The contracts that mediate these relations do not necessarily result in equality or recognition. In fact, the legal and economic mediations in the relation between father and children can lead to further alienation and resentment. In addition, the marriage contract, not to mention the social contract in general, which for Ricoeur is the contract that defines fatherhood, has a history of defining its parties unequally. Men and women have not been equal parties to the social contract. When Ricoeur discusses mutual recognition and equality, it is always only between fathers and sons, fathers and sons who become brothers through the social contract which excludes full participation by, or recognition of, their mothers and sisters.

Father's Rights

Many of the conflicts embedded in current discussions of fathers' rights, paternity tests, and custody battles, come to the surface in Thomas Laqueur's "The Facts of Fatherhood" (1990), where he intends to put forth a labor theory of parenthood based on emotional labor. With a critical tone he highlights some of the history of the notion of fatherhood as a disembodied idea, pointing out conflicts in ancient accounts of the male's contribution to procreation. After an overview of medieval views of paternity, he concludes that "much of the debate about the nature of the seed and of the bodies that produce it was in fact not about bodies at all but rather about power, legitimacy, and the politics of fatherhood" and the politics of fatherhood mobilizes accepted facts which are "but shifting sand for the construction of motherhood or fatherhood" (Laqueur 1990, 211). Yet, after discussing several paternity disputes in the courts, including the case of "baby M," Laqueur brings us back to a notion of fatherhood as a disembodied idea.

First, in the few remarks that he makes about the labor theory of parenthood proposed at the beginning of the essay, he is clear that he means emotional labor and not physical labor: "If a labor theory of value gives parents rights to a child, that labor is of the heart, not the hand" (Laqueur 1990, 212). If Laqueur were to emphasize physical labor involved in procreation, childbirth, and child rearing, he would have to acknowledge that in procreation and childbirth (and usually in child rearing as well) the mother's labor is more significant than the father's. But Laqueur discounts maternal labor by claiming that the fact that women give birth and go through labor is a fact of the *flesh* and not a fact of *motherhood.* In his interpretation of the Baby M case, Laqueur says that all fathers are at a material disadvantage because mothers "contribute so much more matter" than fathers, but matter is not what is at stake in parenthood; rather, claims to parenthood "arise from the intense and profound bonding with a child, unborn and born, that biological kinship might spark in the moral and affective imagination but which it does not entail" (219). That being said, he can go on to suggest a notion of parental labor that is based on imaginary connections and affects which allows the father an equal share of parental labor at a distance from the messes and pain of birth and child rearing if he so chooses.

For Laqueur, gestation and birth seem irrelevant to parenthood. And the possibility that a woman might develop a strong emotional bond with the child *through* the material processes of gestation and birth is discounted. In fact, the connection between affect and material is discounted. Laqueur wants to describe a loving, caring, nurturing *ideal* father. He has an *idea* of a father who feels strong connections to his children. But ultimately, like the fathers of Aristotle, Galen, and the medieval notions analyzed by Laqueur, his own notion of father is a disembodied idea. He maintains that "because fatherhood is an 'idea', it is not limited to men" (Laqueur 1990, 217). And that "having the idea or the plan is what counts" (219). But if fatherhood is an idea, it is limited to the imagination or intellect. Where is the paternal body? Where is the physical work that it takes to have a child? Having the idea of a child or the plan for a child is far removed from caring for, or even loving, a child. We are back to the ancient idea of men planting their seeds and planning for the future of their families.

There are instructive conflicts in Laqueur's analysis. He imagines a caring, loving, nurturing father to counteract the stereotype of the affectless father. But his essay edges towards a defensiveness about the importance of fathers and their contributions to emotional labor—there is an undercurrent that fathers (if we ignore bodies) can be just as important as mothers in having children. There is also a certain anxiety in his analysis of the court cases about fathers losing control over their children or their right to control reproduction. These issues point to the various directions of the men's movement.

Some strands of the men's movement are seeking to restore men's paternal authority. They want back the control over the family and women that they have lost. An article in the *New York Times* entitled "What Fathers Want" says it all: "We want our intrinsic authority back. This essential prerogative of fatherhood has been stolen from us by children who want us to be their friends and by those children's mothers who insist on shared paternalism . . . the sources of parental power is not the same. Motherpower is rooted in love, fatherpower in authority. . . . Beyond the pleasures of watching their seed miraculously develop, fathers who make the family effort need recognition as 'head' of a household."[77]

Other strands of the men's movement are asking men to express their *feminine/maternal* side and arguing that men can be nurturing and sensitive. Complex social factors make it possible to imagine different roles for mothers and fathers. The effects of the increase in women in the work force (which is partially motivated by an economic situation that necessitates two-income families), the women's movement, and new reproductive technologies open up new images of mothers and fathers. Mothers work to support the family and fathers take care of the kids.

The sensitive maternal father and the working mother have become popular characters in television and film, and these media representations are telling. The first thing that one notices about most representatives of nontraditional roles for mother or father is that they are single parents. If mothers work or have careers, it is because they do not have a man to support them or to hinder them (*Murphy Brown*, J.C. Wiatt in *Baby Boom*). And if a man nurtures a child, it is because the child is motherless (*Full House, Mr. Mom, Three Men and a Baby*). There are very few representations of fathers nurturing when a mother is present to do the job, or mothers having careers when they have a mate. Many other popular representations of the nontraditional roles of mothers and fathers portray them as conflicts, another manifestation of the war between the sexes (*Kramer vs. Kramer, Mrs. Doubtfire*). Mothers and fathers cannot coexist.

The next thing that one notices about most representations of nontraditional roles is that they are funny. Popular stories about men raising babies are comedies. In a comparison of *Baby Boom* and *Three Men and a Baby*, Ann Kaplan describes the comic effect:

> Unconscious anxiety about men in the domestic may be glimpsed here [in *Three Men and a Baby*]—an anxiety that surely has to do with historical women's new demands that men share child care. But the anxiety is defused through the comedy, and through making sure that nothing is actually at stake for these men in relation to the baby. Fathering is not seen as part of any identity they *need* to assume. . . . The case is very different for Diane Keaton [in *Baby Boom*]: since women are still *assumed* to be linked to child-bearing and rearing, the film shows Keaton quickly altering her personality and life-style; indeed, the focus of her life changes completely to absorption in the baby and neglect of her work, until she is fired. This is what we expect of women, as against men. . . . Men cannot be truly invested in a baby, and their yuppie city jobs are never in jeopardy: this would deny their masculinity, their virility . . . (Kaplan 1992, 197-198)

Part of the humor in representations of fathers nurturing is the contrast between their *true, manly, virile nature* and the maternal role.

Men look funny behaving like women. The humor in Robin Williams's *Mrs. Doubtfire*, for example, revolves around jokes about women's bodies and the discrepancy between William's manliness and the woman's body that he *inhabits*; he is found out when Mrs. Doubtfire is seen urinating standing up. Even *Three Men and a Baby* has its cross-dressing scene when Jack dresses up like a pregnant woman by putting the baby Mary in a sling under his coat in order to fool the drug dealers. The humor in these representations comes as a continual reminder that men are just *pretending* to be maternal fathers; they are really still virile men.[78]

In addition, these representations of men performing nurturing roles dressed as women invite the conclusion that, rather than redefining paternity or manhood, these are representations of the appropriation of maternity and womanhood. As Tania Modleski points out, *Three Men and a Baby* both shows men usurping the roles of women and denigrating women at the same time. She argues that the baby Mary is sexualized and then her genital area is represented as dirty and defiled; many of the movie's central jokes have to do with shit. Modleski insightfully concludes that "envy of woman can coexist with castration anxiety and with the profoundest misogyny—that men can want to be women and still hate and fear them—and, second, that this envy is in fact concomitant with a fear of feminization, even though existing in logical contradiction to it, so that male identification with woman is hedged about with many varieties of 'masculine protest'" (Modleski 1991, 78).

One of the most dramatic representations of womb envy is Ivan Retiman's film *Junior* (1994). *Junior* stars Arnold Schwarzenegger as Dr. Alexander Hesse, who is persuaded by his research partner (Danny DeVito) to try their experimental fertility drug on himself after their funding is canceled. An egg, which was stolen from Emma Thomson's character Dr. Diana Reddin, is fertilized with Dr. Hesse's sperm and implanted in his abdomen (?), resulting in Schwarzenegger's pregnancy. They prove that the drug works, but Arnold decides that he wants to keep his "unborn baby." Here the joke is the contrast between Arnold's musclebound manly body and his maternal emotions and pregnant condition. Arnold's morning sickness, labor, C-section, and emotional swings are funny. In a review of *Junior*, Roger Ebert says that "there is something oddly heartwarming about the sight of this macho guy melting with feelings of protectiveness and maternal concern." He advises that *"Junior is a good family movie, for parents and adolescents to see together, and then to discuss in terms of male and female roles and responsibilities"* (Ebert 1995, 377)!

This science-fiction story suggests a future where women have no more to do with reproduction that donating eggs—of course in this story the egg was stolen. This is a story of men stealing all control over reproduction from women. At a time when more women are refusing traditional roles as housewives and mothers, those roles are being revalued both within conservative rhetoric and feminist rhetoric. As the roles are revalued, they are appropriated by men. At a time when biologists are establishing the active roles of women's bodies in producing the child's DNA, the maternal body becomes masculine, virile. Conan the Barbarian becomes the sensitive man and our model of motherhood.

The Right to Procreate

The desire for control can also been seen in men's fights for the so-called *right to procreate* and control over reproductive choices. Some strands of the men's movement are fighting for more control over reproductive choices. They feel that women have too much control and men not enough control over reproduction. In a statement on oral birth control for men, the Executive Director of Free Men claims that "we always treat reproductive rights as a women's subject and something they control. . . . I think the fact that women carry a womb in their body is an accident of biology. It could just as easily have been men. We have just as much at stake in reproductive subjects as women do." In response to the same issue, the Executive Director of another men's activist group, Men's Rights, says that the "idea that, 'It's my body, I'm bearing the risk, therefore I'm the one who will make the decisions,' [is] the female chauvinism version of men who think women shouldn't have the vote because they weren't the ones who fought in the fields to get democracy."[79] Some men are also fighting for the right to make decisions about when *their* women can have abortions. These debates indicate that men are fighting for control.

In cases of reproductive freedom and reproductive technologies, the discourse of rights hides structural inequalities and injustices behind the rhetoric of equality. Rights-based legal arguments and rights-based ethical arguments overlook social factors central to the issues of reproduction. For example, the most famous case where the *right to procreate* became an issue is the *Matter of Baby M*, as it was called by the New Jersey Supreme Court. The *Matter of Baby M* is the appeal that Mary Beth Whitehead made to the New Jersey Supreme Court to challenge the earlier superior court decision that her surrogacy contract with William Stern was valid and that custody of Baby M should go to Stern, the contracting father. The original contract between Mary Beth Whitehead and William Stern was signed in February 1985. In March 1986, Baby M was born. Whitehead refused to relinquish the baby to Stern. Early in 1987, Stern sued Whitehead for custody of the baby and sought the enforcement of the surrogacy contract. Both were awarded to him. The New Jersey Supreme Court overturned the superior court's decision that the surrogacy contract was valid, but awarded custody of the baby to Stern anyway.

In the New Jersey Supreme Court, the *Matter of Baby M* was argued as a battle between Whitehead's right to the companionship of her child and Stern's right to procreate. The New Jersey Supreme Court respected Stern's right to procreate, but decided that the right to procreate did not automatically include the right to custody of the child. And the court ruled that procreation through the paid surrogacy arrangement violated state laws prohibiting paid adoptions and was therefore illegal. There is tension in this case between ruling the contract illegal based on laws against paid adoptions and the ensuing custody battle that gave Stern custody of Baby M. Stern's case was not analogous to adoption since he was the biological father, and a father need not adopt his own baby. His wife Elizabeth was not party to the original contract, so she was not paying to *adopt* a baby either. When deciding whether the surrogacy contract was valid, Stern was treated as an adoptive parent, but when deciding who should get custody of the baby, Stern was treated as the biological father with rights equal to those of the birth mother. The ability to claim biological paternity when it is convenient is a legacy of court cases before the availability of technology to test paternity.

In the rights debate, proponents of surrogacy argue that an infertile couple has the right to procreate and that a woman has the right to use her body as she pleases. But whose right to procreate is protected in the surrogacy arrangement? The wife of the father of the child produced as a result of the surrogacy arrangement is still infertile. What about her right to procreate? This raises the question, do we really have the right to procreate, even if we have a right to try to procreate? The surrogacy arrangement guarantees that the father can reproduce himself, which is one reason why couples would resort to surrogacy instead of adoption.

Both New Jersey courts questioned Mary Beth Whitehead's right to procreate and to custody because she had agreed to "sell" her baby; the very fact that she agreed to the surrogacy arrangement made her relation to the child suspect. The same was not true of Stern, who also was party to the same contract. His relation to the child took priority over hers. Why? Are mothers expected to behave differently toward their children than fathers? If so, then how can Whitehead and Stern be equal parties to the surrogacy contract? The court assumes that Whitehead and Stern are equal before the law and have equal rights, but at the same time assumes that Stern's rights are more valuable. As Katha Pollit points out, "[Superior Court] Judge Sorkow paid tribute to Mr. Stern's drive to procreate; it was only Mrs. Whitehead's longing to nurture that he scorned" (*The Nation* May 23 1987, 686).

Debates over rights cover up important gender, class, race, and social differences that make the surrogacy contract possible and appealing in the first place. In other words, there are inequalities built into the surrogacy contract that are overlooked by the courts when these contracts are discussed only in terms of equal rights. First, the surrogacy arrangement demands different investments from the biological father and the biological mother. The father provides his sperm, the mother provides not only her egg and womb but also nine months of her life and enduring the pain of childbirth. If the parties to the contract were truly equal, then men wouldn't need women to birth their babies. Second, very few, if any, women would agree to a surrogacy arrangement without payment for their services. Most women who engage in surrogacy do so to make money because they are poor or in debt. Most men who contract surrogates are considerably more financially secure than the women whom they hire. This factor becomes crucial in deciding custody, although it is never discussed in terms of the financial inequality built into the surrogacy contract.

The *Matter of Baby M* is a prime example of a surrogacy case turned into a custody case. Since the contract was found illegal, the case became a fight for custody. In the custody battle over the best interests of the child, the financial and social situations of Whitehead and Stern became major issues. Both New Jersey courts defined best interests in terms of financial security, never acknowledging that the surrogacy contract would not exist if the parties were financially equal. When best interests are defined in terms of financial security, the father owns the child's best interests from the start, since the woman engages in the contract precisely because she is not financially secure.

In the *Matter of Baby M*, the lower court Judge Sorkow noted that the Whiteheads' house was too small and that Whitehead's concern for her daughter's education was suspect in light of her own lack of education. In contrast, the judge points out that the Sterns had a new house and could provide the child with "music lessons," "athletics," and a certain college education (*Stern v. Whitehead* 1987, 74–75). Supreme Court Justice Wilentz also noted the financially superior position of the Sterns, whose "finances are more than adequate, their circle of friends supportive, and their marriage happy," while Whitehead's "finances were in serious trouble" (*Matter of Baby M* 1988, 1258-1259). In addition, the supreme court noted that whereas Whitehead demonstrated contempt for professional psychological counseling, the Sterns endorsed it. Whereas the Sterns were "honest" and learned from error, the court doubted Whitehead's honesty (1258–1259).[80] The court was concerned about Whitehead's "omniscient" attitude toward her child since she claimed to know what her cries meant; as a result, the court concluded that the Sterns would give the child more independence than Whitehead.

All of these factors are the result of differences built into the surrogacy arrangement. College education and music lessons are possible only for those who are financially secure. Class and social difference inherent to the surrogacy arrangement make it more probable that the father will endorse counseling, which can be expensive. Gender stereotypes and biases mean that the surrogacy contract itself makes the mother suspect because she is "willing to sell her child," while it makes the father more capable of "raising an independent child." The contract itself sets up the mother as an evil woman who would give away—worse, sell—her baby, while the father comes to the child's rescue. The discourse of rights creates the illusion that the parties are equal before the law and have equal rights, but in reality the social inequalities insure the outcome before the litigants enter the courtroom.

Taking Responsibility

Some strands of the men's movement are trying to claim responsibility for families. They are trying to counteract the trend towards fatherless female-headed families by taking responsibility. Outside of the men's movement per se, the attention on family values has brought with it the rhetoric of personal responsibility among men, particularly African American men. This was evidenced with the "Million Man March" in Washington, DC, on October 16, 1995, where participants took a pledge to be more responsible fathers and husbands. Hugh Price, president of the National Urban League, called the march "the largest family-values rally in the history of America."[81] The organizers of the march, Nation of Islam leader Farrakhan and former National Association for the Advancement of Colored People secretary, Benjamin Chavis, asked women to stay at home and watch their children and pray while their men attended the march. The primary purpose of the march was for African American men to "atone" for their sins. In an article in *New Statesmen & Society*, Marable Manning described the march: "Farrakhan's call included a demand for 'atonement' that African-Americans should recognize 'wrongs done and make amends,' and apologize for all offenses 'against the Creator.' The march agenda spoke relatively little about contemporary public policy issues, such as affirmative action, immigration and welfare reform. Instead, it emphasized the need for blacks to assume 'personal responsibility' for their own circumstances, and challenged African-American males to provide leadership for their families and communities" (8: 376, p. 14–17, Oct. 27, 1995).

Many people criticized the march because it excluded women and promoted patriarchal visions of men, women, and families. Part of the pledge taken at the march was "I pledge from this day forward I will never abuse my wife by striking her or disrespecting her, for she is the mother of my children and the producer of my future." Women are reduced to mothers and producers of men's futures. He must respect her for the sake of *his* children and *his* future. One marcher said that "we have marched to tell ourselves and the nation that we want to be real men. Real men don't attack their loved ones. Real men don't shirk their duties." [82]

Rhetoric of taking paternal responsibility and wanting to be real men does not address the racism that leaves so many African Americans in poverty. On the contrary, as Kenneth Warren points out, lack of initiative and responsibility is a traditional explanation of poverty: "From the nineteenth century onward we've seen limited efficacy of movements premised on racial uplift. These dismiss claims on the state as symptomatic of a 'slave mentality' and stigmatize blacks at the bottom of the pecking order as lacking initiative. We also know that simplistic readings of race in America will always find the putative lack of self-help, self-improvement and self-reliance among black populations an appealing explanation of inequality" (*The Nation*, 261:15, Nov. 6 1995, p. 524). Racism, social and economic inequality, inequalities in education, discrimination in every sector of society, are all erased by the rhetoric of personal responsibility. The problems of inner-city violence and drugs that are attributed to the fact that black women are the heads of households and fathers are missing are not the result of personal irresponsibility. In this case, reducing social problems to personal responsibility blames those who suffer from racism for the symptoms of a racist society. And this particular invocation of paternal responsibility as paternal authority is yet another call for reinstating patriarchy and virile subjectivity.

In sum, talk of rights and responsibilities presumes contained, autonomous, determinant subjects, virile subjects. The latest links between responsibility and paternity in popular discourse reinforce paternal authority. Paternal authority is established only by denying the body in favor of the soul or ego/agent. At its source, paternal authority is a paradox which requires the brute strength of the male body in order to establish its legitimacy, and yet it claims that paternal authority is not the brute or animal authority of nature but the human authority of culture. Culture is based on the fantasy that man leaves nature/mother/earth behind and creates himself out of himself. This is the virile fantasy par excellence. The virile fantasy is that man controls himself and his environment. He is solid, the solid foundation of the family and the state. His solidity insures that nothing can penetrate his manliness. His lack of permeability, the fact that his body does not leak, also means that he cannot have a relationship. All others are his possessions or his projections. Even in them, he loves only himself.

paternal eros

As for me, behold, my covenant is with thee,
and thou shalt be a father of many nations . . .
thy name shall be Abraham; for a father of
many nations have I made thee. . . . And I will
establish my covenant between me and thee
and thy seed after thee in their generations for
an everlasting covenant, to be a God unto
thee, and to thy seed after thee.

(Genesis 17:4–7)

In this chapter, I critically analyze texts by Ricoeur, Levinas, Derrida, and Kristeva, texts which construct paternity as promise rather than authority, name, or law. Fór Ricoeur, fatherhood promises equality through contracts, while for Levinas, fatherhood promises singularity beyond the law. The tension between equality and singularity, between law and something beyond the law, is what is at stake in Derrida's *The Gift of Death*. There, Derrida describes ethics as a paradox between the universal and the individual, between equality and singularity. I read *The Gift of Death*, with its focus on this story of a father and son, in relation to Ricoeur and Levinas on the question of fatherhood, as the culmination of a dialectical tension between the two. And when I read the Genesis story of Abraham as a legend about father–son realtions rather than just a parable of faith, *The Gift of Death* appears to uncover not just the paradoxical logic of ethics but also the uncompromising logic of patriarchy and paternal authority. I conclude that in the accounts of all of these French thinkers, paternal authority reappears to once again erase the paternal body from our discourses of paternity. Moreover, these discourses of paternity always assume the father–son relationship; why can't the promise of fatherhood be a promise to/of a daughter? In the end, I attempt to suggest ways of refiguring an embodied paternal Eros.

Fatherhood's Promise

Father Time

Both Ricoeur and Levinas reject the Freudian/Lacanian association between father and law and instead associate fatherhood with promise. For Ricoeur, God is not the Father because he gives the law; rather the law, the covenant or contract, enables Him to be recognized as father (Ricoeur 1974, 49). Ricoeur implicitly rejects the Lacanian association of the Father with the Law or the Name. He claims that there is no name of the father. "Father" is not a name, but a designation (485). And the father's proper name is of little significance to his function as father. So too, the father is not the Lacanian "no" or prohibition. The law or covenant is a promise and not a prohibition. Moreover, law does not originate with the father, but makes his recognition possible. The father is not father before the son, but due to the designation "father" by the son. The father becomes father only in answer to the call of his son.

For Ricoeur, God is not properly designated as Father until he is called by the son. It is only after Christ calls Him "Father" that God is frequently referred to as Father in a significant way in the Bible. Once Christ calls to his Father, God becomes Father. We might wonder about the mother of God, Mary. Is she not mother until recognized by the son? Or, is she mother when recognized by the Father, God? Who recognizes her? Her pregnant body suggests motherhood prior to the designation "mother." And if the Father is not father until designated by the son, who is the father of her child before the son's acknowledgment?

For Ricoeur, the father–son relationship becomes one of mutual knowledge and recognition when in Matthew 11:27 Christ says,

"All things are delivered unto me of my Father: and no man knoweth the Son, but the Father; neither knoweth any man the Father, save the son, and *he* to whomever, the Son will reveal *him*." Ricoeur interprets this passage as articulating the mediation necessary for the recognition of the father: "There is fatherhood because there is sonship, and there is sonship because there is community of spirit" (Ricoeur 1974, 491). The father is recognized by the son through the laws of the community. The son's designation, "father," is made possible by those laws that promise the end of murder. In Matthew 11:27 Christ articulates his relationship to his Father in terms of the community and a promise of revelation. The son reveals his father to the community, and it is this designation by the son that institutes fatherhood.

Ricoeur points out that God is referred to as Father in the Old Testament infrequently and not in any significant way; when He is referred to as Father, it is in passages which are not the typical narrative sagas of the Old Testament, but prophetic texts which announce something. Ricoeur suggests that in the Old Testament God can be identified as the Father of Israel through God's covenant with Israel. The covenant, that Israel is chosen by God, is both Law and promise; the covenant is a divine contract of sorts. In the New Testament, allusions to God the Father are allusions to the promise of eternal life and the kingdom of heaven. Christ calls to God his Father as a reminder of a covenant with God. God as the Father is the keeper of the convenant; He is promise. Ricoeur argues that in this sense, the biblical God is not a Father because he begets man or creates man or because he is an origin; rather, He is Father because He is a promise. He is the promise of compassion.

Yet, for Ricoeur, the institution of fatherhood requires the sacrifice of the son for the sake of the Father's other children. Mediated by contracts, the unique relationship between father and son can be annulled such that the force of that relationship applies equally to all other children. Ricoeur's essay suggests that God's promise, his covenant or law, is fulfilled with the sacrifice of His son, which in turn equalizes all God's children in His eyes. Through the fulfillment of the covenant, through Christ, all of God's children are equals. In other words, the contract takes priority away from the bond between father and son; that bond is sacrificed for the sake of equalizing relationships. The father promises that law will replace blood and that the law will equalize.

Ricoeur once again denies the significance of embodiment or physical generation in favor of abstract law/promise. But what he overlooks is that even God's covenant is founded in blood. The promise is a promise made on the basis of blood and constantly reaffirmed through blood, blood as a sign of generation and of fertility. There is no law, no covenant, without blood. The story of Moses, the receiver of the law, is full of blood—the Passover blood, Zipporah's circumcision of Greshom, the ox blood after the tablets are given. The promise that Ricoeur identifies with Christ and God's sacrifice which replaces murder is marked by blood, Christ's blood, which is symbolized by wine in the Eucharist. Law, especially as promise, cannot be separated from the body and the blood.

Like Ricoeur, Levinas proposes a notion of paternity that cannot be reduced to law or threats but must be a promise. Like Ricoeur, he proposes an ontology of paternity that takes us beyond the Freudian psychoanalysis of paternity, which he claims reduces sexuality and paternity to pleasure and egology. Unlike Ricouer, however, for Levinas, the promise of paternity is not recognition but a promise of nonrecognition, of strangeness, of an open future, what he calls infinity. The promise of paternity is not Ricoeur's promise that from a dead father the son will inherit his designation, that the son will also be recognized by his son as father, or the Freudian promise that the son will inherit his father's power. It is not a promise from the past, a promise that returns to itself. Rather, the promise of paternity, as Levinas describes it, is a promise of an open future, the promise that the son is to his father. Although on Levinas's analysis there is an analogy between death and paternity, fatherhood requires neither murder nor sacrifice. Paternity is a special case of alterity that can inform all other relations. For Levinas, it is the only relation in which the self becomes other and survives.

For Levinas, paternity does not reestablish the Hegelian battle of the wills, each seeking recognition from the other. Ricoeur's notion that it does takes us back to a tragic egoity that enables unity only at the expense of multiplicity: There is only one king, father or son. This is why his notion of fatherhood requires murder or sacrifice; for Ricoeur, there is no recognition of fatherhood without death. Here,

Ricouer goes even further than Hegel, whose master–slave struggle stops short of death. For Levinas, paternity does not return us to a battle of wills that reinscribes the subject and turns the self back onto itself even in the operation of self-dispossession and abandonment. Rather, paternity opens up a different structure of subjectivity that opens the self onto the other. The structure of the subject in an erotic relationship moves the self beyond the ego and its exclusivity.

In *Time and the Other*, Levinas moves from an analysis of death, through an analysis of fecundity to his analysis of paternity. He maintains that what all of these relations with alterity have in common is that they cannot be thought of in terms of power, especially in terms of the power of an ego. "Sexuality, paternity, and death introduce a duality into existence, a duality that concerns the very existing of each subject. Existing itself becomes double" (Levinas 1982, 92). This doubling of existing brings the subject to time by making it other to itself. The relation with the other engenders time; and only where there is infinity is there time.

The relation between time and infinity is not only necessary in the simple sense that we cannot think of not-*A* without thinking of *A* or vice versa. Rather, it is the encounter with infinity through the face-to-face relationship which makes time possible. This encounter opens the subject onto itself and separates the subject from the world in a way that makes the counting necessary to time possible. The face-to-face relationship enables subjectivity and there is no linear time without the subject. The tension between the relationship between time and infinity described in *Time and the Other* (1947) and the relationship between time and infinity described in *Totality and Infinity* (1961) might be explained in terms of the different status of the erotic relationship accorded in these two works. As Tina Chanter points out, in the earlier work, *Time and the Other*, Levinas describes the erotic relationship as the primary face-to-face, that is ethical, relationship (Chanter 1994, 196–207). In *Totality and Infinity*, the erotic relationship is beyond the face-to-face, beyond ethics and language. In *Time and the Other*, Levinas emphasizes how time engenders infinity through the erotic relationship, fecundity, and paternity.

In *Totality and Infinity*, the dialectic between time and infinity is more complex than it was in *Time and the Other*. The separation from the world required to experience linear time, the time of subjectivity, is initiated in the face-to-face relationship; this position becomes even more explicit in *Otherwise than Being,* where the subject is described almost as a mere by-product of the relationship with the Other. Yet when the subject experiences his separation from the world as his own enjoyment, he forgets about the relationship with the Other that made it possible. The subject of enjoyment is not the ethical subject, even though the ethical relationship with the Other made the structure of his enjoyment possible. The erotic relationship with the feminine is beyond the ethical relationship; it is paternity that engenders infinity and brings the erotic relationship back within the realm of the ethical. As Chanter points out, within *Time and the Other,* the feminine is an other who can engage the masculine subject in the ethical relationship, whereas in *Totality and Infinity* she is not an other capable of an ethical relationship. In *Totality and Infinity* paternity rescues the masculine subject from the nonethical, nonsocial, nonlinguistic abyss of the feminine.[83]

For Levinas, paternity begins with Eros and fecundity. Yet, Eros and fecundity are ontologically anchored in paternity. Eros is possible because of sexual difference, which is neither a contradiction between two nor a complementarity between two (Levinas 1987, 85). Eros is an event of alterity, a relationship with what is absent in the very moment at which everything is there. Even in an experience that seems to completely fill the universe with itself, the caress seeks something other. The caress is not directed towards another's body; rather the caress is directed towards a space which transcends through the body and a time which Levinas describes as a future never future enough (1969, 254). "The seeking of the caress constitutes its essence by the fact that the caress does not know what it seeks . . . something other, always other, and always still to come [*à venir*]. The caress is the anticipation of this pure future [*avenir*] without content. It is made up of this increase of hunger, of ever richer promises, opening new perspectives onto the ungraspable" (Levinas 1987, 89). In the erotic relationship, the caress anticipates the always about to come of the other, of the future, of a future never future enough. In the erotic relationship the caress is directed towards the future, the forever and always of promises of love, a future that is never future enough to fulfill such promises.

The relationship with the other is such a promise, a promise that cannot be fulfilled, a paradoxical promise whose fulfillment would destroy the promise. And this promise is time. For Levinas, time is not constituted as a series of nows; it is not constituted in the present or by an ego. Rather, time is the absent promise in the relation with the other; it is the not-yet, the always still to come. It is the time of love, the infinite engendered through finite beings coming together. "Love seeks what does not have the structure of an existent, the infinitely future, what is to be engendered" (Levinas 1969, 266). Love seeks what is beyond any possible union between two. For Levinas, love seeks the "trans-substantiation" which engenders the child (1969, 266). Engendering the child is an inherent element in the structure of the erotic relationship; the erotic relationship is defined as fecundity. The caress and voluptuosity are analyzed within this context of fecundity. Through paternity, fecundity opens the masculine subject onto infinite time and returns him to the ethical relationship.

For Levinas, in the masculine erotic relationship, the other beyond the subject's control is the feminine other; fecundity necessitates a relationship with a feminine other. This feminine other is a prerequisite for moving outside of oneself: "But the encounter with the Other as feminine is required in order that the future of the child come to pass from beyond the possible, beyond projects. This relationship resembles that which was described for the idea of infinity: I cannot account for it by myself, as I do account for the luminous world by myself" (1969, 267). The trans-substantiation of the father by the son is only possible by virtue of the feminine other. Man needs woman to beget a son. More than this, it would seem, the infinite time opened up between father and son through paternity is possible by virtue of the movement through the cyclical, nonlinear time of the feminine. Paternity moves the (male) subject outside of time through the mediation of another time, the cyclical time of life. Paternity conquers "father time" by moving through the feminine, what Kristeva might call "women's time."

For Levinas, paternity opens the subject onto infinite time in various ways. The discontinuity of generations brings with it inexhaustible youth, each generation replacing the one before it. In addition to this chronology which stretches indefinitely through time, the ontology of paternity sets up the subject within infinite time. The space between the father and the son opens up infinite time. Not only the discontinuity of generations which promises continued youth, but also the trans-substantiation of the father in the son opens the subject to an other. "The father discovers himself not only in the gestures of his son, but in his substance and his unicity" (1969, 267). In this way the father discovers himself in the son and yet discovers that his son is distinct, a stranger.

Through the trans-substantiation of the I, Levinas says that paternity accomplishes desire. It does not satisfy desire, which is impossible, but accomplishes it by engendering it and by engendering another desiring being, the son. Paternity engenders desire, which is the infinite time of the absolutely other. The time of the other is infinite as compared to the finite time of the self. In relationship with the child, the subject is opened onto infinity: "The relation with the child—that is, the relation with the other that is not a power, but fecundity—establishes a relationship with the absolute future, or infinite time" (Levinas 1969, 268). Paternity, with its generation and generations, literally opens onto infinite time, a time beyond death. That future is the infinite desire which is present as a desire for desire itself infinitely extended into a future that is never future enough. What Levinas calls goodness is associated with the infinity of desire engendered by paternity. "In paternity desire maintained as insatiate desire, that is, as goodness, is accomplished" (272). Paternity is the link between desire and goodness, Eros and ethics. Erotic desire is accomplished (since, unlike need, it can never be satisfied) in engendering a son, a son who embodies desire. In this sense, desire engenders itself (269). For Levinas, the desire of the caress in the erotic relationship is ultimately resolved in paternity: "This unparalleled relation between two substances, where a beyond substances is exhibited, is resolved in paternity" (271). From the beyond, desire, two substances create another desiring substance, the son.

More than the continuation of the substance of the father in the son, as the word "trans-substantiation" might suggest, paternity is a form of trans-substantiation of subjectivity itself. Paternity transforms subjectivity from the subject as "I-can" who sees himself as the center of meaning and values—the constitutor of the world—to a subject beholden to, and responsible for, the other. This form of trans-substantiation takes us beyond substance. The subject or "I" is not a substance, but a response. The paternal subject is not Husserl's, Ricoeur's, or Sartre's virile "I-know," "I-will," or "I-can" but a response to the other who opens up a radically different time, a time beyond the "I-know," "I-will," or "I-can." Levinas says that the relationship with the son through fecundity "articulates the time of the absolutely other, an alternation of the very substance of him who can—his trans-substantiation" (1969, 269).

The relationship of paternity is unique in that the I breaks free of itself without ceasing to be I (Levinas 1969, 278). It is the only relationship in which the self becomes other and survives. The I breaks free of the ego, of what ties it to itself, so that it can reach out to another, even become another, become other to itself. This process of becoming other to itself opens up the possibility of beyond its own possibilities, an openness to an undetermined future: "Fecundity is part of the very drama of the I. The intersubjective reached across the notion of fecundity opens up a place where the I is divested of its tragic egoity, which turns back to itself, and yet is not purely and simply dissolved into the collective. Fecundity evinces a unity that is not opposed to multiplicity, but, in the precise sense of the term, engenders it" (1969, 273).

On Levinas's analysis the father discovers himself in the gestures, the substance, the very uniqueness of his son. This discovery of himself in the son is not Ricoeur's recognition; for Levinas, the father does not recognize himself in his son, but discovers himself, finds himself for the first time. Paternity engenders the father as much as it does the son. Fecundity gives birth not only to the son but also to the father. In relation to his son, who is both himself and not himself, the father discovers his own subjectivity. As he realizes that his son is distinct, a stranger, he discovers that he too is distinct, even a stranger to himself. Paternity challenges what Levinas calls the "virile" subject that always returns to itself, the subject as the "I-know" or "I-can" of traditional phenomenology.[84]

Fecundity engenders the subject as desiring and therefore as an infinite subject who transcends the limits of subjectivity. In fecundity, the I has a different structure from the intentional egotistical virile subject because it has a different relationship to time; and it has a different relation to time because it is not the egotistical subject of need but the loving subject of desire. The virile or heroic subject who takes the world as his possession, for his enjoyments, to meet his needs, is a finite subject (Cf. Levinas 1969, 306–307). For Levinas, fecundity, associated as it is with paternity, is distinct from virility. Fecundity is "a reversion" of the virile subject (270).

Whereas fecundity frees the self from its self-enchainment, virility merely returns the self to itself over again. Virility is the experience of the power of the subject, whereas fecundity is the experience of the limit of the mastery of the subject. The virile subject lives in a world of things that it masters through the initiatives of its own power. Out of the anonymity of what Levinas calls the "there is," or raw being, the virile subject designates existents, beings. In this world, however, the subject continually returns to itself and makes even of itself an existent, a thing, which deteriorates and dies. In the world of the virile subject, "self-possession becomes encumberment with oneself. The subject is imposed upon itself, drags itself along like a possession. . . . *Eros* delivers from this encumberment, arrests the return of the I to itself" (Levinas 1969, 270–271). Eros takes the subject outside of itself, outside of the world of its possessions and power. With Eros, the very structure of subjectivity changes.

While virility indicates a subject closed in on itself, a subject who is self-sufficient, fecundity necessitates a relation with another. The virile subject relates to its future as the future of its possibilities, possibilities determined by its ego or will; the Sartrean subject projecting itself into the future is a virile subject. From the standpoint of the virile subject, the father–son relationship is a conflict of wills. Ricoeur's notion of paternity makes the father–son relationship a virile struggle for recognition in which the father and son mutually recognize their own will and their own possibilities in the other.

In the relation of fecundity, the subject cannot even relate to its own future as the future of its own possibilities. Its future is a future that is not, and cannot be, determined by the ego or will. It is a future that involves relationships with others who cannot be controlled within one's own subjectivity. This future that is not yet calls one out of oneself towards another. Rather than establish the equal and mutual recognition of father and son, or brothers for that matter, Levinas's notion of paternity establishes the uniqueness of the subject in relationship with the other. The father–son relationship is not one of law-bound recognition but of outlaw singularity.

Promissory Love

Levinas's Paternal Election

Levinas holds out paternal love as exemplary: "The love of the father for the son accomplishes the sole relation possible with the very unicity of another; and in this sense every love must approach paternal love" (1969, 279). The father chooses the son after he has had no choice. His love *elects* this particular child in his uniqueness as the loved one, the one meant to be. In this regard, Levinas suggests that all love for another person must approach paternal love insofar as that love elects the loved one from among all others. This love makes the loved one unique, and makes this love necessary rather than contingent. This love is not just for a limited time only, but is for all time, for a future never future enough, for infinite time.

Levinas maintains that just as the lover chooses the beloved when he has no choice, for love is the adventure of what is not chosen, the father chooses or "elects" the son (1969, 254). Yet, the father does not possess his child—"I do not have my child, I am my child." Paternity is the trans-substantiation of the I because the father is not in control; he cannot possess either the feminine other or the child. In these relationships, the father is beyond himself and his will is impotent, even irrelevant.

At this point, we might wonder why the relationship with the lover does not provide the same kind of uniqueness as the father–son relationship. Strangely enough, it seems that for Levinas the feminine lover is neither radically other nor the same and both are required for the uniqueness identified with the father–son relationship. The father says "I am my child" and yet this child is a stranger to him. As I will suggest below, it is the son's *sameness* that engenders the uncanny otherness experience by the father in this relationship. The son's uniqueness comes through paternal election. The son is a unique child because he is elected by his father. "He is unique for himself because he is unique for his father" (Levinas 1969, 279). And, as we will see in a moment, while the feminine lover may be unique and chosen by the father, she is neither other nor the same because she is not fully human.

Paternal election, which chooses from among equals, makes unique precisely by recalling the nonuniqueness of the equals among which this one was chosen:

The unique child, as elected one, is accordingly at the same time unique and non-unique. Paternity is produced as an innumerable future; the I engendered exists at the same time as unique in the world as brother among brothers. I am I and chosen one, but where can I be chosen, if not from among other chosen ones, among equals? . . . If biology furnishes us the prototypes of all these relations, this proves, to be sure, that biology does not represent a purely contingent order of being, unrelated to its essential productions. But these relations free themselves from their biological limitation. (Levinas 1969, 279)

Contingency is precisely what is at stake in Levinas's notion of paternal election. Paternal election seems like an attempt to overcome the contingency and chance of paternity by instituting the father's retroactive choice about that which he had no choice—that is, the choice as to what child is produced. The notion of paternal election seems a counterweight for an abject identification with a father who does not control the products of generation which emanate from his own body. The father's love which elects the son compensates for the lack of choice or control exercised by the paternal body. Levinas's notion of paternal election makes the contingencies of biology irrelevant. All that matters is the father's response to this child; it is his love and not his genetic material that make it determinant and unique. It is as if Levinas is saying that just as biology "selects" one sperm cell from amongst millions, the father (after the fact) selects this child as his son. If biology or paternity does not provide an imaginary selection process, then this child is an accident; he is not unique, not elected, and cannot imagine how he could be loved. Through paternal election the child is unique in that he is "chosen," but this choice is not the result of a virile will.

In this regard Ricoeur's thesis that the father is father by virtue of the son's call or designation might put a new twist on paternal election. The child is unique, not only because it was chosen among "brothers," as Levinas says, but also because it *is* its father and yet *other* to its father. It is the other who calls to its father to recognize it as his unique child. Only after the election has been made does the father respond to the uniqueness of the child. Yet it is the father's response which rescues the child from abject fantasies. He loves this child; he chooses this child even though the choice of this child is not his. He affirms the choice of this child through his love and thereby asserts a paternal election that rescues the child from the contingencies of biology. Whereas Ricoeur assures us that fatherhood mediated through law and contracts makes mutual recognition and equality possible, Levinas assures us that fatherhood is before or beyond the law in that it makes subjectivity unique and at the same time open to its other.

Although Levinas opens up the possibility of an alternative to Hegelian virile Eros, his notion of paternal Eros is grounded in what he sees as a fecund Eros of the lover's relationship. As it was for Ricoeur, paternal Eros is once again channeled through the maternal body. For Levinas, the fecund relationship with a woman has its goal in the child, more particularly, a son. The paternal relationship, however, is higher than the lover's relationship because it is social. The lovers' relationship takes place at the level of laughter and caresses and not language proper. Levinas describes the beloved woman as "silly" and "infantile," her face fading into animality; making love with her is like playing with a "young animal" (Levinas 1969, 263). Although, for Levinas, the erotic is not properly social because it is based in the union of bodies, the caress itself aims at something other than the body.

Once again, bodies are evacuated from love; and the paternal body, as we will see, is even dismissed from sex. In spite of his declarations to the contrary, Levinas's theory is at the threshold of the belief that *embodied Eros* is a contradiction, that feelings and passions are associated with the body which must be overcome for pure Eros. Like Ricoeur's notion of mediated fatherhood, Levinas's notion of paternal election allows for paternal love *in spite of*, and *not through*, the body. For Levinas, even though the father is not the virile subject, his love is not embodied. The body of the father is still absent from paternity and the father's love is still abstract.

Certainly Hegel, and Ricoeur after him, make a distinction between the *natural forces* of sex and procreation identified with the body, on the one hand, and the capacity for love as recognition associated with the social, on the other. For Hegel, sexual and procreative "instincts" are associated with woman, while intellectual and productive activities are associated with man. Just as man's relation to his own body is mediated by woman, the father's bodily relations with the child are mediated by the mother. The father's body must be mediated and controlled. Affective displays are signs of bodies out of control. Our virile notion of fatherhood requires that fathers learn not to express their feelings in order to master control over the body required to enter manhood and culture. As a result, children grow up without feeling loved by their fathers.

The father's control over his affects and feelings compensates for his lack of control over his body by creating the illusion that the body is a thing under his control. Affects and feelings are undeniably fleshy. The body expresses affects and feelings with tears, blushes, sweat. This bodily expression cannot be controlled except by attempts to control or deny affects. Feelings recall our materiality. As such, expressions of feeling and affect are expressions of nature and matter that threaten man's claims to have mastered mind over matter. To admit feelings is to admit the body and to admit the body is to admit that man is not in control of himself or his environment and its effects on him; this is to admit that he is not an active agent but also subject to the whims of the flesh and its contingency.

The repressed fantasy of the abject paternal body—a body out of control—threatens virile subjectivity. Yet it is only because of the notion of virile subjectivity, and the opposition between body and mind or nature and culture, that the father's body can be reduced to the abject provider of chance fertilization. The fantasy of the abject father is both maintained and repressed by a culture that has no antidote or counterweight for such a fantasy. The antidote, I suggest, is an image of paternal Eros—a paternal Eros that is embodied, passionate, and is not just channeled through the maternal body.

Kristeva's Imaginary Father

In *Tales of Love*, Julia Kristeva presents what could be seen as another attempt to counterbalance what I have called the *abject father*. She develops what she calls the *imaginary father*, which she proposes as the counterbalance to the abject mother. On her account, the child has a fantasy of an imaginary father, which is really the fantasy of a "mother–father conglomerate." This fantasy of the mother–father conglomerate allows the child to feel loved even while it is separating from its mother's body. The imaginary father provides a necessary support for the child to be weaned. The idea is that the child must disassociate itself from its mother and her love, but it can still feel loved because of this fantasy of the imaginary father.

While Kristeva's notion of the imaginary father may go some distance to supplement the Lacanian symbolic father of the Law, it still does not provide us with a notion of embodied paternal Eros. Against Lacan, Kristeva maintains that we can give up the stern father of the law without risking psychosis: "Maintaining against the winds and high tides of our modern civilization the requirement of a stern father who, through his Name, brings about separation, judgment, and identity, constitutes a necessity, a more or less pious wish. But we can only note that jarring such sternness, far from leaving us orphaned or inexorable psychotic, reveals multiple and varied destinies for paternity . . . one that can also be playful and sublimational" (1987, 46). In fact, she suggests that if paternity is reduced to law and threats, then we would have no reason to leave the safe haven of the maternal body. The paternal function that introduces the child to language and culture must have some rewards and pleasures or else more of us would refuse to leave the maternal body and become psychotic. The father must promise love.

Although Kristeva's imaginary father is designed to move the child away from the maternal body and into culture, this paternal image is once again channeled through the maternal body and the mother's love. Like Ricoeur's insistence on the mediation of the mother and the marriage contract, and Levinas's description of the fecund erotic relationship with the feminine, Kristeva's imaginary father defines the father only in relation to the mother. It is as if, once again, the contingency of paternity can only be counteracted by the determinacy of the maternal contribution to procreation. The imaginary father is a fantasy of conception which allows the child to feel loved and chosen by its father and mother: if it imagines that it was conceived out of love between its parents, then it too can be loved.[85]

Ultimately, however, Kristeva's imaginary father collapses into the Lacanian symbolic father. Kristeva develops her notion of the imaginary father from Freud's notion of the father of individual prehistory. She finds in Freud the suggestion of a pre-Oedipal father who parallels the pre-Oedipal, or imaginary, mother. Yet, this pre-Oedipal father, as it turns out, is produced by the mother: "Nevertheless, clinical experience has led us to ascertain that the advent of the *Vater der persönlichen Vorzeit* takes place thanks to the assistance of the so-called pre-Oedipal mother, to the extent that she can indicate to her child that her desire is not limited to responding to her offspring's request (or simply turning it down). This assistance is none other than maternal desire for the Father's Phallus" (Kristeva 1987, 40). The identification with the mother–father conglomerate turns out to be an identification with the mother's desire for the Father's Phallus. At the level of the pre-Oedipal, the mother's desire for the Father's Phallus is the mark of the symbolic father of the law on her body. The fantasy that provides the guarantee that the child can be weaned is none other than the father's law in the place of the mother's desire. We haven't moved far from the Lacanian scenario after all.

Where is the father's body in all of this? The mother's desire for the Father's Phallus is not a desire for the father's body except insofar as it represents that power. For Lacan, and Kristeva follows, the Phallus is not the penis. The Phallus is the fraudulent representative of the possibility of all representation, it is the fraudulent representative of the power of culture and discourse. Fraud or not, the Phallus once again covers over the father's body. If, as Lacan says, the Phallus can only be effective when veiled, behind the veil is the paternal body in all of its contingency and uncertainty. Just as within the medical discourse where the paternal body has traditionally provided the seed or form that grows in the maternal soil or matter, within Kristeva's discourse the imaginary father provides the "seed of the Ego Ideal" (1987, 374).

What is abjected in our images of conception is not just the maternal body but also the paternal body. Kristeva argues that the child must reject the maternal body so that it does not become abject by identifying with the maternal body. The maternal body, she says, calls into question the borders of the self; and ultimately the child may imagine itself a waste product expelled from the maternal body. Recall that in Kristeva's analysis excrement and menstrual blood are connected through the maternal body. Yet, insofar as, unlike the female organ, the male organ for reproduction is the same as the organ for urination (a problem that even Hegel identified), it is the paternal issue that can be confused with a waste product expelled from the body. In spite of the association of the maternal body and menstrual blood with chaos and lack of control or containment, the maternal contribution to procreation—the egg—is imagined as determinant and solid. The paternal contribution, on the other hand, is erased or solidified because it is fluid and cannot be contained. It is indeterminate, and the infant produced by the accident of one sperm cell penetrating that egg is a product of chance.

Kristeva's notion of an imaginary father is necessary to counter not the abject mother as Kristeva suggests, but the fantasy that is too much to bear, the fantasy that the child is merely a waste product of the paternal body. Behind the abject projections onto the maternal body is the leaking paternal body not in control of its own production. Yet an imaginary father, especially one who turns out to be another face of the father of the law, cannot replace the real or embodied father. Paternity requires a paternal body. Why has that body been erased from paternity? Why is the paternal body replaced by the fantasy of an imaginary father who turns out to be the mother's desire for a father? An identification with a desire for a father is an identification with the longing for love, which in itself cannot provide the necessary guarantee for feeling loved by a father. Can we return the paternal body to paternal Eros?

Could the Future Be a Daughter?

For Ricoeur and Levinas, paternity is described as a father–son relationship. Even for Derrida in *The Gift of Death*, the paradox and promise of ethics is represented in the story of a father–son relationship, the story of Abraham. But if fatherhood is a promise for the future, could this future be a daughter? Or, does this future have to be a son? Three-quarters of the way through *The Gift of Death*, Derrida makes a short detour through *woman* that suggests these questions. He comments on the absence of women: "It is difficult not to be struck by the absence of woman in these two monstrous yet banal stories. It is a story of father and son, of masculine figures, of hierarchies among men (God the father, Abraham, Isaac . . .). Would the logic of sacrificial responsibility within the implacable universality of the law, of its law, be altered, inflected, attenuated, or displaced, if a woman were to intervene in some consequential manner? Does the system of this sacrificial responsibility and of the double 'gift of death' imply at its very basis an exclusion or sacrifice of woman?"

(Derrida 1995, 76). Derrida doesn't answer these rhetorical questions. In the next section I will discuss the sacrifice of the mother implied in the paternal gift of death. Now, I will take up the question of "can the future be a daughter?" A detour through the distinction between eschatology and apocalypse will set up my critical question.

In *Altared Ground: Levinas, History, and Violence*, Brian Schroeder points out that Levinas separates eschatology and apocalypse. Generally, eschatology is a revelation and apocalypse is a limit or end. For Levinas, eschatology cannot be apocalyptic because it is an opening onto the Other or being otherwise. Rather than the end of history, eschatology is "a *rupture* of linear futurity" (Schroeder 1996, 142). "Instituting a relationship with a radical exteriority, eschatology leaves open the possibility of a radical surprise, a 'breach' of totality, precisely because it is the primordial orientation of subjectivity to the other" (142). Schoeder reads Levinas's notion of eschatology as dependent on "the affirmation of the radical spontaneity of chance, of surprise" (146). For Levinas, paternity, which results from the fecund relation with woman, leads to such an affirmation.

Recall that for Levinas the father discovers himself in the son, who is both himself and a stranger. Through the son, the father becomes other and yet survives as himself. He discovers himself in his son's gestures, substance, and uniqueness. His subjectivity itself is transformed through this relationship with an other who is him and not him. Levinas emphasizes that it is the otherness of the son that pulls the father out of himself towards infinity. Yet, it is the sameness of the son that allows the movement without shattering the father's subjectivity altogether. Ultimately, it is the sameness between father and son that allows for the father to discover himself and his uniqueness through his son. The father identifies with his son. And paternal love is the father's election of this son from among equal "brothers." Paternal election makes biology irrelevant. So, it is not just the biological substance of the son that makes him like and unlike his father; it is something about the son *qua* son. The father chooses this son and that election makes him unique; in turn the son's uniqueness makes the father unique. Through their relationship, they both are singular. Yet, the discovery of their singularity has its basis in their *sameness*.

Levinas suggests that paternity opens onto infinity because it is a relationship with an absolute other in which the I survives. The I survives because paternity is also a relationship with the same. The father is his son and yet the son is a stranger to the father and the paternal relationship makes him a stranger to himself. Yet, how can the son be an absolute other if he is also the same? Is it the son's difference or his sameness that restructures the I through paternity? Wouldn't a daughter be a stranger child? Because of sexual difference and the antidotal effects of feminine time, wouldn't the daughter be other enough to open up an infinite future? For Levinas, desire is possible only in a relationship with an absolute other. Paternity engenders desire and thereby returns the erotic relationship to the ethical. And, yet, doesn't this paternal desire fall back into need if the son returns the father always to himself?

If, however, it is otherness that opens onto infinity and the possibility of radical surprise and the rupture of linear time, then couldn't, shouldn't, the future be a daughter? If paternal election is what makes the son unique and in turn, therefore, what makes the father unique, then could the father choose a daughter? Should we interpret Levinas literally in his discussion of the paternal election of a son? If so, paternal election provides not only an image of the father's choice of this particular child but also the image of the father's choice of a son in particular. Unless the daughter cannot be other because like the feminine in the erotic relationship she is subhuman, more like an animal, then the paternal discovery in her *could* be based on the otherness that opens the future to possibility.[86]

For Levinas, it seems to go without saying that the father chooses a son rather than a daughter. The fact that he is a son is not what makes him unique; he is unique because he is *this* son chosen from amongst *brothers*. All children are brothers, but only this one is my son. Could the trans-substantiation of the father take place in relation to a daughter? Would the father discover himself in his daughter's substance, gestures, and uniqueness? And if the father does not, or cannot, elect a daughter, then doesn't the fantasy that she is unwanted, an accident, unloved, should-have-been-otherwise, become devastating for her? Isn't she forced into an identification with an abject father who refuses to love *her*?

Returning to the distinction between eschatology as openness to alterity made possible by paternity and apocalypse as limitedness implicit in noneschatological teleological philosophy, it seems that

Levinas's preference for a son rather than a daughter moves his philosophy closer to apocalypse. For Levinas, the future that paternity engenders is masculine. Insofar as it is masculine, it is limited. Insofar as it is limited, it is not open to radical alterity. And, insofar as it is not open to alterity, it is not eschatological but apocalyptic. The future that is open only to the masculine is a limited future that marks the end of history. If there are no daughters, then there will be no more sons.

In his discussion of the future as eschatology, Brian Schroeder compares Levinas's notion of fecundity to Nietzsche's notion of the *Übermensch*. Schroeder argues that Nietzsche's *Übermensch* provides another image of an eschatological future that opens onto difference, radical surprise, rupture, and infinity. "It is precisely in the interpretation of future possibility as fecundity that Nietzsche and Levinas converge most in their thinking. . . . What is endemic to both Levinasian and Nietzschean notions of prophetic eschatology (and what is Zarathustra if not a prophet?) is the response to a command issued from alterity, a command to the self to command and obey itself without the promise of reciprocity" (Schroeder 1996, 145). But, isn't Nietzschean fecundity that gives birth to the *Übermensch* just as limited as Levinas's notion of paternity? Could the *Übermensch* be a daughter?[87] Perhaps a feminist reading of Nietzsche could provide the fertile text which engenders a feminine *Übermensch*, the future as daughter. If not, Nietzsche's *Übermensch*, like Levinas's paternity, becomes an apocalyptic end to the promise of otherness and infinity. If not, we always get more of the same and never anything/ anyone different. And, in spite of its illusion that it can, ultimately, without difference, the same cannot maintain itself.

Soul Responsibility

Derrida's Gift of Death

Negotiating sameness and difference or equality and singularity is at the center of Derrida's *The Gift of Death*. Whereas Ricoeur presents the father–son relationship as a relation of mutual recognition through law that insures equality, and Levinas presents the father–son relationship as a discovery of oneself through a relation to the other that insures singularity, Derrida discusses a father–son relationship that puts equality and singularity into conflict. For Ricoeur relations are necessarily mediated by contracts, laws, and ethics. For Levinas, ethics is prior to the law and makes law possible. For Derrida, ethics is a paradox between law and the impossibility of law. Derrida suggests that the father has a duty to his son through the law, which allows for designations as well as names; but the father also has a duty that cannot be named or designated, an absolute duty unmediated by law. These two duties—the duty to respect the equality before the law and the duty to respect the singularity of the individual—conflict. This conflict is the heart of the story of a father caught between his Father and his son, the biblical story of Abraham.

Although it remains in the background of Derrida's analysis, it is significant that Abraham is *promised* a son, Isaac, in his old age. Since his wife Sarah is too old to conceive, Isaac is a miracle. God promises that Abraham will have a son who will be the father of many generations of Israel. For Abraham, Isaac holds out God's promise of generations to come. So why does God asks Abraham to sacrifice Isaac? Does the promise of fatherhood, the promise of generations, require sacrifice? God, the Father, ask his son for a sacrifice. On Kierkegaard's analysis in *Fear and Trembling*, Abraham must give up the ethical or the law for the sake of a higher religious realm. Abraham is in the paradoxical position of believing in the promise of Isaac and believing that he will kill Isaac. Abraham believes the impossible; he believes in what Kierkegaard calls the paradox of faith. So, Abraham is the father of faith. For Kierkegaard this paradoxical belief moves Abraham out of the realm of ethics. For Derrida this paradoxical belief is the core of ethics.

Out of the focus of either Kierkegaard or Derrida's texts is another crucial factor: there are *at least* two father–son relationships in this story, Abraham/Isaac and God/Abraham. Once we see the relationship between God and Abraham as another father–son relationship, then we read a different story. Derrida reads Abraham's relationship to God as the relationship to the wholly other, while he reads Abraham's paternal relationship to Isaac as a relationship of duty to family and law. This is Abraham's conflict: Does he do his duty to his son, family, and society and not commit murder, or does he sacrifice that which he loves to the Absolute, God? Derrida characterizes the dilemma in terms of an absolute duty to God which conflicts with an ethical duty to Isaac, his family, and society. In my exploration of Derrida's analysis of the Abraham story, I will investigate what happens when we reinterpret the relationship between God and Abraham as another Father–son relationship. In addition, I want to expose the secret of Derrida's *The Gift of Death* as the mother's gift of life.

The Gift of Death is about the aporia of ethics, responsibility, secrecy, sacrifice, death, gift giving, and faith. At the beginning of *The Gift of Death*, Derrida uses Jan Patočka's *Heretical Essays on the Philosophy of History* to link secrecy and responsibility. Following Patočka, Derrida concludes that "the history of the responsible self is built upon the heritage and *patrimony* of secrecy, through a chain reaction of ruptures and repressions that assure the very tradition they punctuate with their interruptions" (1995, 7, my emphasis). The secret is a secret inherited from the father, the patrimony of secrecy. The secret is the mystery of orgiastic practices that are repressed and incorporated by/into philosophy. And, as Patočka makes it out, the secret or mystery itself is maternal. Describing the way in which Plato incorporates the mystery, Patočka says "the cavern is a vestige of the subterranean place for gathering of mysteries; it is the lap of the earth-mother. The new thinking inaugurated by Plato involves the desire to forsake the lap of the earth-mother in order to set out upon the pure 'path of light', hence to completely subordinate the orgiastic to responsibility" (Derrida 1995, 11). The earth-mother, it turns out, is kept secret by the patrimony from fathers and sons.

Derrida tells us that for Patočka the demonic mystery is hidden within responsibility and that this mystery is associated with "orgiastic irresponsibility" (1995, 20). The awakening from the mystery is the ability to keep a secret. The idea is that if one is to keep a secret, one needs to have a sense of responsibility and conscience. Now, if we recall that the mystery and orgiastic irresponsibility is associated with earth-mother and that the secret is a patrimony, then the awakening is the ability of fathers to keep the maternal element a secret. The secret of life is that it originates with mothers and the earth. The secret passed down from father to son is the secret gift of life given by the mother and the earth. But this secret is not articulated. Rather, this is the type of secret rendered invisible through practices of repression and incorporation within the patriarchy. In order for fathers and sons to take responsibility, the mother's gift of life must not be spoken. In order for fathers and sons to become responsible subjects, they must forget that earth-mother is responsible for their very lives. Only if "she" is irresponsible can they be responsible.

In Derrida's text, the father (Abraham/God) gives the gift of death, which turns out to be the same as the gift of life. The gift of death is the willingness to sacrifice that which one loves for an other, to give up one's own life or the life of one's son, in this case, for an other. Abraham is willing to sacrifice Isaac, whom he loves (as Genesis reminds us several times), to God. And God sacrifices his son, Christ, for the lives of all of His children. In Christ's case, the gift of death is put forth as a gift of life.[88] Still, to equate giving one's life for another, or dying so that another might live, or sacrificing that which one loves for the other, with the maternal gift of life is to incorporate and repress that fundamental gift. There is no gift of death without the gift of life. In this story, as in many others, the power to give death is the father's. The father can believe that the gift of death, within *his* own power, is the same as the gift of life. He can believe that by giving death it is *he* who gives life. But, as Irigaray says, this belief covers up the truth (1993b, "Belief Itself").

In order for the father to be responsible, the mother can't be. But, as Derrida maintains, the father's responsibility is a paradox. It puts him in an impossible spot. Because of the contradiction at the core of responsibility, he is always guilty and never responsible enough. "Guilt is inherent in responsibility because responsibility is always unequal to itself: one is never responsible enough. One is never responsible enough because one is finite but also because responsibility requires two contradictory movements. It requires one to respond as oneself and as irreplaceable singularity, to answer for what one does, says, gives; but it also requires that, being good and through goodness, one forget or efface the origin of what one gives" (Derrida 1995, 51). Of course, if we reinterpret Derrida's remarks in light of my hypothesis that the secret of responsibility is the life-giving mother, they take on a new meaning.

The guilt inherent in responsibility is the guilt involved in the matricide which makes it possible for the father/son to claim responsibility (for life). He must respond as if he alone is responsible; he is singularly responsible (otherwise the responsibility is not his). Yet, he must forget or efface the origin of that which he gives because that which he gives, the gift of life/death, is also from the mother; he must forget that at its origin he alone is not responsible (for life). Within the frame of Derrida's text, this contradiction is the aporia of responsibility. Responsibility requires both substitution and non-substitution: "For responsibility . . . demands on the one hand an accounting, a general answering-for-oneself with respect to the general and before the generality, hence the idea of substitution, and, on the other hand, uniqueness, absolute singularity, hence nonsubstitution, nonrepetition, silence, and secrecy" (Derrida 1995, 61).

In other words, responsibility has two sides which come into conflict with each other. On the one hand, to hold someone or yourself responsible is to account for and justify his/her/your actions. On the other hand, to be absolutely responsible implies that you alone are responsible, that you have a unique relationship to your obligation which cannot be accounted for, justified, or explained; your responsibility, if it is truly yours, is unique and it cannot be understood in terms of any universal laws, principles, or language. Absolute responsibility requires secrecy because the "secret" obligation defies words; it cannot be spoken even if one were to try. This is why when Abraham speaks, he does so (according to Kierkegaard) ironically. When Isaac asks his father, "Where is the ram for the sacrifice?" Abraham replies, "God will provide." He neither lies, nor justifies the situation to Isaac—he both says something and says nothing at the same time. Irony is what is said and not said at the same time. So it is not by accident, in an apparent digression on woman in the middle of this text, that Derrida quotes Hegel saying "woman is the eternal irony of the community"—she is what is said and not said.

Responsibility is a matter of response. In both German (*Verant-wortung*) and French (*responsabilité*) *responsibility* comes from *respond* (*antworten*, *répondre*) and has a stronger sense of *answer* than in English, where respond and answer are different words. The Latin *respondeo* means to answer and in the legal sense means to answer one's name or be present before the law. When Abraham is called by God, he answers, "Here I am," presenting himself to do God's bidding. His words say everything and nothing about his response to God. Because he is answering to God, the Absolute, out of an absolute responsibility, the appropriate response for Abraham is silence. If, however, he were testifying in a court of law, out of a general responsibility Abraham would be required to speak. In one case the appropriate response is to speak, in the other the appropriate response is to remain silent.

Ethics is "an insoluble and paradoxical contradiction between responsibility *in general* and *absolute* responsibility" (Derrida 1995, 61). General responsibility requires the sacrifice of absolute responsibility and absolute responsibility requires the sacrifice of general responsibility. Various philosophers have told us that both require the sacrifice of women. Recall that for Hegel general responsibility, or ethics, requires the sacrifice of the family, including woman, wife, and sister. And for Freud, women are opposed to civilization and any sort of general responsibility or law of society: "Women soon come into opposition to civilization and display their retarding and restraining influence. . . . The work of civilization has become increasingly the business of men. . . . His constant association with men, and his dependence on his relations with them, *even estrange him from his duties as a husband and father*. Thus the woman finds herself forced into the background by the claims of civilization and she adopts a hostile attitude towards it" (Freud 1961, 50–51, my emphasis). In these scenarios, duties to law, ethics, and society, conflict with duties to women and families.

With Derrida's reading of the Abraham story (following Kierkegaard), we have another conflict of duties between duties to women and family, now seen as part of the law or the ethical, and duties to the Absolute, God. Abraham must leave his family behind. He must be willing to destroy his family for the sake of his absolute responsibility to God. It is almost as if generalizing a law of family relations or sexual relations requires reinstating a higher duty so that women and families will once more be sacrificed. If man's first duty is not to his society, then it is to his God.

Yet, in Derrida's reading of (Levinas's reading of) Kierkegaard's reading of Genesis, God is not outside of the family scene. Rather, in Derrida's text God is also figured as a father. The duty to God as father is not a duty to an absolute and *wholly other*. Abraham is also a father and through fatherhood he shares something with God. In fact, Abraham inherits the patrimony of secrecy, which he must pass on to his own son, from God.

According to the story told by Derrida and Kierkegaard, Abraham's duty to God the father is absolute and cannot be justified. Why? Why can the Father command without justification? Why is the Father's authority without question or accountability? Within patriarchy, isn't it always the father's prerogative to issue commands without justification? When the son happens to talk back and ask why, as in the case of Moses, his Father threatens him with death. The father doesn't have to justify himself. When the child asks "why?" it is enough for the father to say "because I am your father, that's why." Is the command from the Patriarch really the command from the wholly other that resonates from Levinas's texts through Derrida's? Insofar as God is figured as Father, he is not wholly other; rather, he is essentially the same in his relation to his son.

Abraham's conflict is not only a conflict between general responsibility to all others and absolute responsibility to the wholly other God. It is a conflict between duties to Father and son. He has a duty to protect and love his son. He has a duty to obey and love his Father. His Father commands him to sacrifice his son. And, ultimately it is for the sake of his son, for the sake of his patrimony, that Abraham obeys God the Father. If the son obeys the father's absolute, yet outlaw, authority it is because one day he will be the father and inherit that authority. This is the promise of paternity within patriarchy. Once we read God as a Father, isn't the Abraham story another version of Freud's Oedipal drama where the son must defer to the father's authority, must castrate himself, in order to avoid castration? As Kierkegaard says, Abraham is "great by reason of his power whose strength is impotence" (Kierkegaard 1954, 31). The son's impotence is demanded in the face of the Father's potency.

Derrida indicates at one point that Abraham's sacrifice of law and family, of everything that is his own, moves him outside of economy. But,.if his sacrifice is made at the command of the ultimate Patriarch, God the Father, then the son is only protecting what is his own by giving in. His sacrifice is made in the name of fatherhood, for the sake of preserving the authority of fatherhood. He sacrifices the present for the future, his own future and the future of his son. The paradox is that God asks Abraham to sacrifice his son, his heir, for the sake of paternal authority and his/His heirs. The paradox is that Abraham is both father (to Isaac) and son (to God) at the same time. He has the authority to take Isaac up Mount Moriah, bind him, and raise the knife over his head. Isaac goes along with it because Abraham is his father, whom he obeys and loves, just as Abraham goes along with his Father, God, whom he obeys and loves. So, Abraham is the father of faith. But Isaac, the son, also has faith in his fathers. He is the one who lays his life on the line with his obedience and faith. The Abraham story is a lesson in the son's obedience to paternal authority. The father's responsibility for the gift of life, his authorship, is acknowledged through the son's obedience.

The sacrifice of the son is a ritual sacrifice for the sake of patriarchy. It is a sacrifice for the sake of the son himself and his inheritance. Its threats are ritualized. But these ritual sacrifices between father and son work to erase the prior sacrifice of mothers and daughters. The sacrificial economy of patriarchy, with its father–son rituals, protects the patrimony of the *secret* sacrifice of mother earth. These rituals protect the heroes, Knights, and Martyrs of patriarchy who become charlatans if the secret of life leaks out.

Perhaps Abraham is nothing more than a big-time gambler in a game with the highest stakes. Perhaps Abraham doesn't move outside of economy, but moves the possibility of any outside back into an economy of calculation. Sacrifice isn't outside of calculation; it is just the unthinkable, most outrageous, wager. In a cynical moment, Derrida imagines "demystifiers of this superior or sovereign calculation that consists in no more calculating [who] might say that he played his cards well. Through the law of the father economy reappropriates the *an* economy of the gift as a gift of life, or, what amounts to the same thing, a gift of death" (Derrida 1995, 97). The gift of death turns out to be a high-stakes wager in a gamble with life and God.

This scenario is made more plausible, if not irresistible, at the end of *The Gift of Death* when Derrida reads (Kierkegaard's) Christian Abraham in conjunction with a passage repeated several times in Matthew, chapter 6, "thy Father which seeth in secret shall reward thee openly." The paradox of this secret is that God the Father asks his children to give in secret and yet promises them that He will see. How can they hide their gifts knowing that He will see? How can they forget that He is watching when they are giving? How can they help calculating their rewards for these secret gifts? And, if they calculate their rewards, then they are not giving but merely making a financial transaction or investment or betting on a bigger reward. Gift giving requires secrecy, but God is always watching, so a secret, and therefore a gift, is impossible. The paradox: God's secret requires and yet prohibits giving.

In an enigmatic passage, Derrida associates the Father's seeing in secret with the secret of the mother-tongue. He describes the secret of the mother-tongue as that which cannot be translated into another language or law. The untranslatability between duties or responsibilities would be such a secret. The secret of the mother-tongue "is there before us in its possibility, the *Geheimnis* [secret] of language that ties it to the home, to the motherland, to the birth-place, to economy, to the law of the *oikos* [family], in short to the family and to the family of words derived from *heim*—home, *heim-lich* [secret], *unheimlich* [uncanny, eerie], *Geheimnis*, etc" (Derrida 1995, 88). Within one paragraph, Derrida makes use of at least two such secrets. The association between *home* and *secret* in German, *heim* and *heimlich* or *Geheimnis*, is lost in translation. This is a very clever secret of the mother-tongue. And, the multiple meanings of *tout* and *autre* in the French "*tout autre est tout autre*" are lost in translation. Here *tout* can mean some, someone, some other one, totally, absolutely, radi-cally, infinitely other, and *autre* can be a noun or an adjective (see Derrida 1995, 82–83). So, some possible translations might be the opposed formulations "every other is wholly other" or "all others are the same." But the play between these two meanings is hidden or lost in translation. The secret of the mother-tongue is hidden or lost when it is subjected to universal principles of translation. The law of the family, of the maternal, itself shares something with absolute responsibility in that it cannot be translated or justified.

"There is a secret of the mother tongue, the secret that the father's lucidity sees in, and the secret of the sacrifice of Isaac. It is indeed an economy, literally a matter of law (*nomos*) of the home (*oikos*), of the family and of the hearth (*foyer*, hearth, focus); and of the space sepa-rating or associating the fire of the family hearth and the fire of the sacrificial holocaust. A double foyer, focus, or hearth, a double fire and double light; two ways of loving, burning, and seeing" (Derrida 1995, 88). Is the secret, then—the secret of the mother tongue through which the father sees—the secret space, abyss or possible passage, between the fire of the hearth and the fire of the sacrificial altar? Is it the secret of the untranslatablity between these two spaces? Or their secret connection, a secret passageway perhaps? Does God the Father see a secret passage between responsibility to the family and the ethical and absolute responsibility? Is the mother-tongue hiding such a passage? Or, is the mother-tongue itself the hidden passage? Does the mother-tongue circumscribe the alliance with God, the covenant that takes precedence over all other covenants? Does the father finally see a way to translate absolute responsibility into/through the mother-tongue?

God Himself legislates from the shadows. He does not allow His face to be seen. He remains a secret. And His authority is maintained through this secrecy. He commands through His absence. His authority requires absence. *God is our culture's prime example of an absent Father.* "God is himself absent, hidden and silent, separate, secret, at the moment he has to be obeyed. God doesn't give his reasons, he acts as he intends, he doesn't have to give his reasons or share anything with us: neither his motivations, if he has any, nor his deliberations, nor his decisions. Otherwise he wouldn't be God, we wouldn't be dealing with the Other as God or with God as *wholly other*" (Derrida 1995, 57). Otherwise His authority wouldn't be absolute; if He justifies His actions, then they are open for dispute. If He is absent and only His commandments, threats, and laws are presented without any justification other than His own authority, then His authority is self-justifying and it cannot be challenged. Even in His absence, especially in His absence, the Patriarch must be obeyed because He sees into your heart.

At the end of *The Gift of Death*, Derrida uses Nietzsche to suggest that the God of Christianity is not wholly other; or, at least, the Christian relation to God is not a relation to the wholly other. The *economy* of sacrifice which seemed to take Abraham outside of economy turns out to be another version of an economy of exchange with higher stakes. In *On the Genealogy of Morals*, Nietzsche describes the birth of God as the result of a debtor–creditor relationship gone wild. The debt becomes so great that the creditor himself must pay it off. But with Christianity, God's payment of man's debt, the sacrifice of His son, does not eliminate the debt; it merely makes the debt unpayable. An unpayable debt is the extreme of the economy of exchange and not beyond it. The gambler is betting on a return—the higher the stakes, the higher the possible return.

The invocation of Nietzsche puts a new twist on any discussion of responsibility and promise. Nietzsche begins the second essay of *On the Genealogy of Morals* "to breed an animal *with the right to make promises*—is not this the paradoxical task that nature has set itself in the case of man? Is it not the real problem regarding man?" (1967b, 57). Promises require memory, the ability to coordinate cause and effect, and calculations of the future. "This," says Nietzsche, "precisely is the long story of how *responsibility* originated" (1967b, 58). Responsibility begins in calculations and identifying causes in men with their effects. Nietzsche goes on to suggest that moral responsibility requires a uniform calculus with which to measure men's accountability. But, paradoxically, what this calculative responsibility leads to is the "sovereign individual" whose sovereignty conflicts with any moral laws or calculations. Nietzsche challenges Kant's notion of an autonomous moral will by claiming that " 'autonomous' and 'moral are mutually exclusive" (1967b, 59). This is the same paradox identified by Kierkegaard between the individual and the universal, where the individual is higher than the universal (contra Hegel). And, Derrida echoes the paradox in the form of the conflict between absolute responsibility, which comes from one's singularity or individuality, and general responsibility, which comes from the equality of all men.

In another paradoxical turn, however, Nietzsche identifies the sovereign individual's responsibility with his conscience. When responsibility becomes instinct, when it turns inward and one holds oneself responsible, then it becomes conscience. On Nietzsche's analysis, conscience is born out of cruelty and brings with it guilt. This cruelty begins with legal contracts: "It was in this sphere, then, the sphere of legal obligations, that the moral conceptual world of 'guilt,' 'conscience,' 'duty,' 'sacredness of duty,' has its origin: its beginnings were, like the beginnings of everything great on earth, soaked in blood thoroughly and for a long time. And might one not add that, fundamentally, this world has never since lost a certain odor of blood and torture?" (1967b, 65). Guilt (*Schuld*) was originally debt (*Schuld*). And, when debts were not paid, the creditor exacted punishment in lieu of payment; these punishments can be explained only by the enjoyment of torture and cruelty, for they do not in any other way repay the debt.

Contracts turn human relationships into calculative exchanges in which equal value is assigned to unequals (e.g., torture for debt). On this analysis, the mutual recognition that Ricoeur seeks through contracts reduces human relations to an exchange of security at best or a justification of torture as punishment at worst. In the case of the contracts that currently dominate paternal relations, the father's role in the family is reduced to a set amount of money per child that he is expected to pay in child support. If he accepts his paternal responsibility, he provides financial support for his children; if he avoids financial support, he is an irresponsible father sought out by court order.

Since World War II, fatherhood itself has been associated with responsibility. The father is responsible for his family. His responsibility includes financial support, protection, both moral and physical, which involves disciplining children and women. He is responsible for decisions made on behalf of the family. And, he faces the consequences. As these ideals of paternal responsibility continue to break down and more children are left without fathers or their support, manly responsibility has become a rallying cry for both men and women. Witness the "Million Man March" in Washington, DC, where thousands of black men called on themselves and each other to take responsibility for their families.

Coincidentally, responsibility has been a central issue in post–World War II philosophy. Philosophy itself has been a rallying cry to responsibility. While post-war *Analytic* philosophers have been trying to delineate exactly when and why we should hold someone responsible, *Continental* philosophers have been concentrating on the origin of responsibility. While Analytic philosophers ground responsibility in questions of autonomy, Continental philosophers talk about responsibility in relation to questions of subjectivity. Concepts of agency and agents are central to both approaches to philosophy. In 1943 Sartre's *Being and Nothingness* presented a radical notion of responsibility wherein human beings are responsible for creating themselves, both as individuals and as groups; and human beings are responsible not only for their actions but also for their emotions and characters. Levinas ups the ante when in *Totality and*

Infinity he suggests that human beings are responsible not only for themselves but also, and primarily, for the other. And, in *Otherwise Than Being*, he claims that we are responsible not only for our own response to the other but also for the other's response to us. For Sartre and Levinas subjectivity is defined in terms of responsibility.

A return to Nietzsche at this point might be telling. In *On the Genealogy of Morals*, Nietzsche diagnoses responsibility as the result of instincts turned inward that produce consciousness and conscience. There is no responsibility without some notion of a subject to be held responsible. Responsibility comes only with what he calls the interiorization of man. Responsibility is primarily legal responsibility, which has its origins in a type of cruelty that demands punishment. Certainly, insofar as men have been associated with culture and mind, they are responsible subjects; and insofar as women have been associated with nature and body, they are not responsible subjects, but objects. Hegel's women do not become social or responsible subjects. Freud's women are incapable of sublimation and as a result have inferior ego development and an underdeveloped sense of justice; they are not fully responsible subjects. Fathers, then, are held responsible because they are seen as subjects, agents who control their action through their own will power, which entails the sublimation and repression of nature, the body, and women. This responsibility brings with it the promise of rewards and punishment. But, while it can be empowering, responsibility can also be a cruel burden.

Can He Have a Body?

> There has been too much stress on the crisis in paternity as cause of psychotic discontent. Beyond the often fierce but artificial and incredible tyranny of the Law and the Superego, the crisis in the paternal function that led to a deficiency of psychic space is in fact an erosion of the loving father. It is for want of paternal love that Narcissi, burdened with emptiness, are suffering; eager to be others, or women, they want to be loved.
>
> (Kristeva 1987a, 378)

In *New Maladies of the Soul*, Kristeva asks "do you have a soul? . . . In the wake of psychiatric medicines, aerobics, and media zapping, does the soul still exist?" Her question is motivated by what she identifies as the lack of psychic life, which she defines as the representation and interpretation of experiences. She describes a "modern man" who is "losing his soul" and becoming merely "a body that acts" (Kristeva 1995, 7). "We have neither the time nor the space needed to create a soul for ourselves, and the mere hint of such activity seems frivolous and ill-advised. Held back by his aloofness, modern man is a narcissist—a narcissist who may suffer, but who feels no remorse. He manifests his suffering in his body and he is afflicted with somatic symptoms" (7). Kristeva describes a modern man for whom the collapse of time and space has collapsed the psyche, a modern man who has a body but no soul. "The body conquers the invisible territory of the soul" (8).

The life of the psyche, and thus the soul, is inhibited by drugs and media images. These have become the weapons used in the body's takeover of the soul. Kristeva diagnoses the body's takeover of psychic space which leaves modern man without a place of his own. In *Tales of Love*, she calls modern man "an exile, deprived of his psychic space, an extraterrestrial with a prehistory bearing, wanting for love" (Kristeva 1987, 382). Kristeva's discussion suggests that drugs and media images have flattened the psyche. The psyche and soul have become two-dimensional, worn on the skin of a body that suffers from their thinness. The body suffers and the modern Narcissus turns to more drugs and more images to ease the pain. But drugs only regulate the oscillation between pain and relief, and media images reflect false selves which ultimately only exacerbate our feelings of out-of-placeness. Neither can compensate for the "erosion of the loving father."

Kristeva suggests that each individual has a personal malady of the soul which requires an individual discourse in order to articulate it. What analysts should do is help their analysand find his/her own discourses in which his/her own emptiness and his/her own out-of-placeness "become essential elements . . . of a *work in progress*" (1987, 380). Discourse has become normalized and standardized and thus meaningless; it cannot speak *my own* experience (see 1995, 8). So the analyst is in the business of providing a space of ownness that allows the psyche to reinflate, to be filled with individual meaning. The problem with *modern man* is his inability to represent himself which "hinders sensory, sexual, and intellectual life" and "the psychoanalyst is then asked to restore psychic life and to enable the speaking entity to live life to its fullest" (1995, 9).

The problem, it seems, comes down to emptiness or fullness. To be full is to be content; to be empty is to be hungry for something else. Our psyches are hungry and need nourishment, but they receive only artificial nutrients and junk food. For Kristeva, only the loving father can feed and fill the psyche; the mother's body has already nourished the body and been disposed. The same mouth that fed on the mother's milk now feeds on the father's words. But it turns out that those words are abstract; they are used by everyone; they are normalized and standardized. They are all used up and they don't speak to the son's individuality. They do not elect *him* as the chosen one, the only one. They are given equally to everyone and so they don't fit him. As a result, he wants to become other, to become woman, in the hopes of being loved, of being chosen, of having his own discourse, his own space, a womb of his own. But his womb is always experienced as *empty* or *artificial* and therefore never satisfying.

Yet, isn't the desire for one's own discourse and providing individual spaces for each psyche itself a narcissistic desire? Does the attempt to create an individual discourse address modern narcissism? Or, like drugs and media images, does it merely perpetuate its frustration? If Narcissus suffers when he realizes that he sees only *his own* image reflected back to him, that he is alone, then doesn't he need companionship and communion, communication and a shared discourse, instead of *his own* individual discourse? Are modern men and contemporary analysands looking for their own space or a shared space? Are they looking for their own individual language or someone else who understands their language? Are they looking for ownership or the gift of love?

Perhaps if words are cut off from their affective meaning and we cannot represent our experiences, it is not because the body has conquered the soul or because we don't have our own individual languages. Rather, perhaps words are cut off from their affective meanings because our psyches have been colonized by the soul and we are alienated from our own individual bodies. As Nietzsche might say, we are no longer bodies that act but souls that react in ways that are increasingly cut off from the force, drives, and affects of the body. Rather than ask Kristeva's question "do you have a soul," we might ask "do you have a body? . . . In the wake of psychiatric medicines, aerobics, and media zapping, does the body still exist?" In the end, maybe these come down to the same question.

What is it that psychiatry, aerobics, and media images have in common? They all objectify the body. Media images present two-dimensional idealized bodies, often as commodities to be purchased. Aerobics and body building are attempts to control the body and realize the ideals of those media images. And psychiatry turns the body into an object for scientific study. The body with its pains and secretions becomes a laboratory experiment that can be controlled with chemicals. These attempts to objectify and control the body do not signal the conquest of the soul by the body, but the emptying of the body. The body becomes a two-dimensional surface, a container for discrete and removable organs, upon which the symptoms of its own forced silence appear as illness. Our experiences do not find language because we cannot speak (of) the body except in terms of these discourses, which turn it into a dead object. Since we cannot speak the life of our bodies, we become hysterics whose bodies speak for themselves in the painful codes of somatic symptoms. The only discourse that does not shy away from the body is the medical discourse, which renders the body safe by dissecting it.

Aside from the gym, this is where we find men's bodies; and it is the only place that we find the paternal body. The contingency of the paternal body is contained by medical discourse, not only because the paternal body and its fluids are measured and calculated but also because high-tech tests make it possible to determine paternity. As a result, the medicalized paternal body shows up in the courtroom as evidence for rights and responsibilities. The medical discourse translates the flows and secretions of the paternal body into objects. It controls those uncontrollable elements by framing them in terms of productions. It rarely addresses the flows in themselves or as secretions of a body whose pleasures are out of control. The pleasures of the paternal body are measured in terms of the motility of sperm to determine the chances of producing offspring. Or, they are identified in order to assign rights to, or responsibility as a sort of punishment for, those offspring. Elizabeth Grosz points out that when it comes to the male body:

> Phenomenology is generally displaced in favor of externalization, medicalization, solidification. Seminal fluid is understood primarily as what it makes, what it achieves, a causal agent and thus a thing, a solid; its fluidity, its potential seepage, the element in it that is uncontrollable, its spread, its formlessness, is perpetually displaced in

discourse onto its properties, its capacity to fertilize, to father, to produce an object. Man sees that his "function" is to create, and own, at a (temporal and spatial) distance, and thus to extend bodily interests beyond the male body's skin through its proprietorial role, its "extended corporeality" in the mother whom he has impregnated and the child thereby produced, making them *his* products, possessions, responsibilities. (Grosz 1994, 199)

It seems that just as the female body is reduced to the maternal body, so too the male body (although not masculinity) is reduced to the paternal body, but a ghostly absent body. Whereas the female/maternal is reduced to body, the male/paternal is dissociated from his body. He is not his body; rather, his body and its products are his possessions. In this virile imaginary, his body is a thing to be controlled and an instrument for control and for reproducing himself.

If, however, in its beginnings parental love is not some abstract pleasure in reproducing oneself, but it is the pleasure in touching and smelling the infant—already a social pleasure, which becomes the pleasure of intersubjective interaction—then we can imagine a paternal Eros that is not the pleasure in reproducing the self or mastering or possessing the child.[89] We can imagine a paternal Eros that is formed through touch and smells between father and infant which set up the loving relationship between father and son, between father and daughter. This paternal Eros is developed through the exchange of affective drives which sets up the possibility of the infant's *growth* into language and culture through affective attunement and the repetition of bodily dynamics rather than through threats and law. The father's love becomes a support for the developing infant subject.

This notion of paternal Eros would require more than the bodily presence of a father in the child's life; it would also require a new conception of the paternal body and the paternal function. It would have to grow out of a different conception of the subject and a different notion of manhood. Virile notions of subjectivity and manhood that evacuate the body in favor of the will or reason expel the father from the family scene. Virile notions of subjectivity and manhood require an absent father. The paternal body has been evacuated from the family scene and replaced by the father's law, name, or threats. But in order for the child to be loved, the symbolic or imaginary father can never replace a real embodied father.[90]

family values and
social subjectivity

Throughout this book I have been talking about the family, images of maternity and paternity, and familial relations. In conclusion, I would like to speculate on values, values that emerge from reconceiving of the family, maternity, and paternity—family values. Conceiving subjectivity as social subjectivity changes the way that we think about ethics. Ethics cannot be based on the rights or reason of an autonomous subject if all subjects are inherently social in the constitution of their very subjectivity. Discussions of individual rights presume a self-contained virile subject who controls his body and actions. But if we give up our commitment to the virile subject in favor of a social subject, then in order to make ethical or judicious decisions we must examine the relationships between people and the conditions that make these relations possible; we cannot merely assume equality, a surface equality that often masks deeper inequalities.

What happens to our values and our sense of ourselves when maternity is no longer associated with an antisocial nature but with regulation and social exchange, and paternity is no longer associated with authority and disembodied culture but with embodied love? Only when the mother is social and the father has a body can our sense of ourselves develop with the support of love. Only when the mother is social and the father has a body can our identities develop through love and attachment rather than through abjection and exclusion. Only when the opposition between culture and nature is deconstructed can the *war between the sexes* give way to peace.

The subject born out of paternal and maternal love is not Oedipus unwittingly murdering his father and leading his mother to suicide. Subjectivity born out of the bodily relationship of love and tenderness is not the Hegelian master–slave dialectic in which we can choose only murder or suicide. Self-identity is not necessarily bought through the sacrifice, or abjection, of others. Somewhere between the animal body mother and the no-body father is love. Love cannot be reduced to either the realm of nature or culture. Love is between nature and culture and it is the place inhabited by human beings. Neither merely bodily nor merely linguistic, love is flesh and word. The rhythms of dynamic bodies and bodies interacting, the rhythms of affects circulating between bodies at the heart of sociality, becomes language and culture. Love is the support that makes identification and separation possible and gives birth to the subject.

Culture and society need not be seen as the result of the repression of our hostile instincts, instincts directed originally against mothers and fathers. Rather, if we are social, if our instincts themselves are social, our bodies are social, then community is not at odds with subjectivity. Only if we rethink the relationship between nature and culture, between body and language, between mother and father, is community or ethics possible. Ethics requires the possibility of a relationship between different people. Imaging human beings as monadic subjects struggling against each other makes relationships impossible. On the other hand, imagining a total identification between subjects also makes a relationship between different people impossible. Ethics requires a notion of subjectivity that is neither opposed to, nor identified with, the other, a notion of social subjectivity. Ethics requires reconceiving of our primary relationships as loving social relationships, rather than hostile struggles.

If justice requires overcoming war, oppression, and discrimination, we might begin by overcoming the stereotypes that insure that we imagine ourselves born out of war. Theories that propose that human beings are naturally at war, that children are primarily driven by matricidal and patricidal impulses, that subjectivity and identification require hostility, that there is a natural battle between the sexes, that nature and culture are at odds, work not only to explain but also to justify and legitimate war, oppression, and discrimination. I am not suggesting that we go to the other extreme and deny the existence or possibility of war and oppression. Rather, I am suggesting that we need alternative images with which to renegotiate and disarm the cultural landmines that continue to wage war against women as well as other oppressed people. We need a peace treaty in the *war between the sexes*, a war fabricated in order to justify dominance and oppression. That peace can come only by embracing alternative images of who we are and where we come from.

endnotes

1 I give extended analysis to this effect in *Womanizing Nietzsche: Philosophy's Relation to the "Feminine,"* Routledge, 1995.

2 "The Science of the Brain: Why Men and Women Think Differently" (*Newsweek*, March 27, 1995, 48–54).

3 The call from middle-class white feminists to enter the work force prompted reactions from feminists of color and lower-class women who traditionally had to work outside of the home to support their families. Many of these women did not have safe and comfortable houses in the suburbs and husbands to support them. For example, see hooks (1981).

4 Ruth Hubbard suggests that Darwinism and post-Darwinistic theories can be read as reactions to the nineteenth-century women's movements: "The recent resurrection of the theory of sexual selection and the ascription of asymmetry to the 'parental investments' of males and females are probably not unrelated to the rebirth of the women's movement. We should remember that Darwin's theory of sexual selection

was put forward in the midst of the first wave of feminism. It seems that when women threaten to enter as equals into the world of affairs, androcentric scientists rally to point out that our *natural* place is in the home" (Hubbard 1983, 61).

5 For a useful account of various feminist views toward the family and the history of the contemporary women's movement see Nicholson 1986 and Jagger 1983.

6 The attempt to find meaning through new-age religions is particularly interesting. Before the scientific revolution, religion with its sacred mysteries provided meaning for people's lives. After the scientific revolution, science replaced and demystified religion. Recently, science has lost the ability to explain our world. The experts present such conflicting data on everything from oat bran to ozone that people have lost faith in science. New-age religion is a synthesis of sorts of science and religion. It uses the rhetoric of science, with talk of harnessing energies and forces, in order to promote self-esteem and a better future.

While Nancy Reagan consulted an astrologer, Hillary Clinton consults a new age pyschologist, a "global midwife" (*New York Times*, June 24, 1996 1).

7 Veroff, Kulka, Douran, *Mental Health in America,* indicate that the number of people going to therapy has dramatically increased since World War II; see p. 166–167, 176–177. Basic Books, 1981. Robert Bellah, et. al, *Habits of the Heart,* suggests that people go to therapy looking for love. University of California Press, 1985.

8 A version of this section is forthcoming in the *Journal of Medicine and Philosophy.*

9 In *The Use of Pleasure,* Foucault specifically addresses ancient theories of reproduction and embryonic development in the context of sexual pleasure (see 131–133). There he also discusses procreative practices in relation to diet (120–124). In *The Care of the Self,* Foucault includes a chapter on Galenic biology in which he discusses Galen's theories of reproduction, once again in the context of sexual pleasure (105–111). I will follow Foucault in his suggestion in *The History of Sexuality,* vol. I, where he states that "the hysterization of women, which involved a thorough medicalization of their bodies and their sex, was carried out in the name of the responsibility they owed to the health of their children, the solidity of the family institution, and the safeguarding of society" (146–147).

10 Twentieth-century biology classifies the placenta by shape, among other factors, and there are four different placental shapes: 1. diffuse, for example in the pig, where blood vessels are distributed fairly uniformly

over the whole fetal sac; 2. multiplex, for example the cow, where blood vessels are scattered in clusters; 3. zonary, for example the dog, where blood vessels form a complete or partial girdle and; 4. discoid, for example the human, where blood vessels are grouped in a discrete disc. (Ramsey, 1975)

11 In *Reproducing the Womb*, Alice Adams criticizes Hunter's questionable methods and his depiction of the maternal body (see 128–136).

12 Alice Adams specifically questions Hunter's dissection practices in *Reproducing the Womb* (128–136).

13 Alice Adams makes a comparison between Hunter's emphasis on the truth of the seen object and Nilsson's emphasis on the truth of the seen object (Adams 1994, 142–143).

14 Much pyschoanalytic theory at least implicitly holds the mother responsible for the child's pyschological problems. Although I cannot develop the thesis here, I suggest that this responsibility is not only implicit in some of Freud's writings, but also in some of Kristeva's writings and some of Chodorow's writings.

15 Representing the placenta as autonomous renders it easier to address the ethical questions regarding placental research. The placenta is represented as an experimental animal or tissue that can be used in order to learn something about human biology.

16 Natalie Angier, "Fighting and Studying Battle of the Sexes with Men and Mice" (*New York Times*, June 11, 1996, B10).

17 Carol Kaesuk Yoon, "The Biggest Evolutionary Challenge May Be the Other Half of the Species" (*New York Times*, June 18, 1996, B5).

18 Pregnant women are expected not to drink, smoke, or eat certain things. They are held responsible for anything that they might do to harm the fetus. In fact, there have been recent suggestions that children could sue their mothers for harm suffered as a result of improper prenatal care.

19 A version of this section was published as "Antigone's Ghost: Undoing Hegel's *Phenomenology of Spirit*," in *Hypatia, a journal of feminist philosophy*, Spring 1996.

20 The German title of Hegel's *Phenomenology of Spirit* is *Phänomenologie des Geistes*. *Geist* can mean spirit, mind, or ghost.

21 I use "man" and the masculine pronoun "he" throughout this section when discussing Hegel not only because Hegel does so but also because my argument is that the movements into the social described by Hegel are possible, within his system, for men only.

22 Hegel's analysis here makes sense only in terms of Sophocles' *Antigone*, as I explain later.

23 Cf. *Philosophy of Nature*: "In many animals the organs of excretion and the genitals, the highest and lowest parts in the animal organization, are intimately connected; just as speech and kissing, on the one hand, and eating, drinking and spitting, on the other, are all done with the mouth" (Hegel 1970, 404).

24 In the original German text, Hegel mentions Antigone only once in the text; and he mentions Sophocles' *Antigone* once in a footnote attached to this reference in the text (Hegel 1970, 348). In Miller's translation there are two footnotes to Sophocles' *Antigone*: Hegel's original footnote (1977, 284, § 470) and an additional footnote, presumably added by the translator or editor (1977, 275, § 457). This second footnote, which does not appear in the original, is affixed to this sentence: "The loss of the brother is therefore irreparable to the sister and her duty toward him is the highest" (1977, 275, § 457).

25 In Sophocles' play, Antigone defies the order of her uncle Creon, King of Thebes, to leave the traitor Polynices' body to rot. Antigone is the daughter of Oedipus and Jocasta. After Oedipus had discovered that he had married his mother and killed his father, he turned his throne over to his brother-in-law, Creon. Several years later, Creon expelled Oedipus from Thebes. After this, Oedipus's son, Antigone's brother, Polynices, attacked Thebes to take his rightful place as heir to the throne. Oedipus's other son, Antigone's other brother, Eteocles, fought for Creon. Eteocles and Polynices killed each other in battle. Eteocles was buried as a war hero and Polynices was left without a burial. Antigone buries her brother and pays with her life for violating Creon's decree.

26 Tina Chanter presents a thorough analysis of why, in Hegel's scenario, Antigone's relation to Ismene is fundamentally and structurally different from her relationship to Polynices. Chanter concludes: "For Hegel, however, Ismene could never be as valuable to Antigone as Polynices because (1) she is alive, and as such not an appropriate vehicle for Antigone's ethical action—any action Antigone could perform for her would remain contingent and would not address the individual as a whole; (2) she is a woman, and as such she does not act in the political sphere; (3) she has denied her obligation to the family, in the figure of Polynices—but the family is the only sphere of action that, in Hegelian terms, is properly her own" (1994, 102).

27 In *Glas*, Derrida brings a suggestive analysis of Hegel's relationship with his sister, Christiane, to bear on Hegel's claim that the brother is irreplaceable for the sister (see Derrida 1986, 151–65).

28 See chapter one of my *Womanizing Nietzsche, Philosophy's Relation to the "Feminine,"* Routledge Press, 1995.

29 In spite of Freud's theory of drives and Lacan's recognition of the real, both theorists continue to separate nature from culture and the body from language.

30 John Bowlby, *Maternal Care and Mental Health* (1951), New York: Schocken Books, 1966; *Attachment,* Penguin Books, 1971.

31 Daniel Stern, *The Interpersonal World of the Infant: A View from Psychoanalysis and Developmental Psychology*: Basic Books, 1985.

32 Lacan would argue that it is the mother's desire for the Phallus, the representative of law and language, that the child incorporates. In other words, the mother may introduce the child to culture, but that culture is paternal; in a sense, she only introduces the child to the father. For Lacan, the paternal function, which has little to do with the real mother or real father, necessarily intervenes to set up the possibility of a properly social relationship. In chapter two, I will argue that the law and regulation associated with the paternal function is already operating in the maternal function. If Lacan is right that culture or the Symbolic is associated with the power of the Phallus that is only because of the fantasy perpetuated by patriarchy, a fantasy that I will discuss in chapter three.

33 In *Womanizing Nietzsche: Philosophy's Relation to the "Feminine,"* I also identify the mother–infant relationship as an intersubjective relationship. After reading Cynthia Willett's *Maternal Ethics and Other Slave Moralities,* I am convinced that the relationship is a nonsubjective social relationship. This notion of nonsubjective social relations opens the possibility of social relations with other animals.

34 An earlier version of this section is published in *Derrida and Feminism,* ed. Mary Rawlinson, et al., Routledge, 1997.

35 See the Oxford English Dictionary.

36 Quoted from *The Holy Scriptures,* The Jewish Publication Society of America, 1955.

37 *The Book of J,* Trans., David Rosenberg, Grove Weidenfeld Publishers, 1990, p. 144.

38 See, for example, *The Soncino Chumash: The Five Books of Moses with Haphtaroth,* A Cohen, Hindhead, Surrey, eds., The Sancino Press, 1947

39 Dorothy Zeligs, *Moses, A Psychodynamic Study,* Human Sciences Press, 1986, p. 87.

40 Charlotte Berkowitz, *The Dream Is One: Reflections in a Biblical Mirror,* doctoral dissertation, University of Houston, 1995, 217.

41 Charlotte Berkowitz points out that Moses has two mothers in *The Dream is One: Reflections in a Biblical Mirror.*

42 Cf. Harold Bloom's commentary on *The Book of J,* Grove Weidenfeld Publishers, 1990, 247.

43 For a more detailed analysis of Derrida's use of "hymen" and his attempts to undermine the economy of the proper or castration, see my *Womanizing Nietzsche: Philosophy's Relation to "the Feminine,"* Routledge, 1995, especially chapter three.

44 Freud indicates that he is not sure that she actually *said* this in the dream, but in the dream she *shows* him that he will have to wait.

45 In my *Womanizing Nietzsche*, I argue that "having it both ways" is the logic of fetishism. I analyze Derrida's notion of undecidability as a form of fetishism. There I am critical of Kofman's suggestion that, by having it both ways, Nietzsche escapes fetishism.

46 For an alternative reading of Nietzsche's ambivalent relationship to the mother, see my "Nietzsche's Abjection," in Peter Burgard, ed., *Nietzsche and the Feminine*, University of Virginia Press, 1994, 53–67.

47 I am reminded of a passage in *Beyond Good and Evil* where Nietzsche says that good and bad women alike want a stick. See Nietzsche 1966, 89.

48 See my *Womanizing Nietzsche: Philosophy's Relation to the "Feminine,"* Routledge, 1995. See also Luce Irigaray, *Speculum of the Other Woman*, Cornell University Press, 1985a.

49 Some parts of this section are published in my introduction to *The Portable Kristeva*, Columbia University Press, 1997.

50 Kristeva's theory also challenges the narrow conception of the material as it is opposed to the social or linguistic.

51 Traditional theories have tried to address these problems in various ways. Referential theories of meaning have held that the meaning of a word is its reference to something extralinguistic, something in the world. The meaning of a word is either what it refers to (some thing) or the relationship between the word and its referent. But as Frege pointed out, meaning and reference are not the same, since there are many different ways of referring to the same thing; and not all of these linguistic expressions necessarily have the same meaning even if they have the same referent. The most famous example is the reference to Venus as both the morning star and the evening star. Some theorists (e.g., Locke, Husserl, Saussure) have tried to avoid some of the problems of referential theories by supposing that the meaning of a word is determined by the thought that corresponds to that word. The referent in this case becomes an idea or concept and not a material thing in the world. These theories, however, merely displace the problems of reference from the material world to the world of ideas. All of the problems of correspondence still obtain. Some contemporary theorists (Austin, Wittgenstein, Searle) propose that meaning is determined by the use of words and that the use of words must be analyzed as a type of activity

with certain rules and regulations. The way in which words are used, however, varies as much as the thoughts or ideas associated with them and their possible material referents.

52 In the history of philosophy, the distinction between body and soul has also been discussed as a distinction between body and mind, or the mind–body problem.

53 Kristeva's writings themselves can be read as an oscillation between an emphasis on separation and rejection and an emphasis on identification and incorporation. In *Revolution* (1974) and *Powers of Horror* (1980), she focuses on separation and rejection,; in *Tales of Love* (1983) and *Black Sun* (1987) she focuses on identification and incorporation. In *Strangers to Ourselves* (1989) she again analyzes separation and rejection. And in *New Maladies of the Soul* (1993) she again analyzes identification and incorporation. In an interview with Rosalind Coward in 1984 at the Institute of Contemporary Arts, Kristeva claims that, for this reason, *Powers of Horror* and *Tales of Love* should be read together; alone each provides only half of the story.

54 For Freud, drives make their way into language only by tricking the ego and superego.

55 For an excellent interpretation of the role of Alcibiades and the appropriation of the feminine in Plato's Symposium, see Carolyn Bottler's "Sexual Difference in Plato's *Symposium*," master's thesis, the University of Texas at Austin, 1996.

56 Aristotle says that mothers feel greater affection for their children than fathers because they love them immediately when they are born (*Nicomachean Ethics*, 1161b, 25).

57 For a list, see the recent Quentin Tarantino, film, *Four Rooms*.

58 Robin Baker, *Sperm Wars: The Science of Sex*, Basic Books, 1996.

59 Reported in Carol Kaesuk Yoon, "The Biggest Evolutionary Challenge May be the Other Half of the Species" (*New York Times*, June 18, 1996, p. B10). Notice that either the reporter or the scientist use the word *women* rather than *females* when referring to human beings, suggesting intentional behavoir.

60 I discuss this article earlier in chapter one above.

61 Quoted in Bernet et. al. 1993, 163; 504, my emphasis.

62 Hua XII, 233; quoted in James Hart, *The Person and the Common Life*, Kluwer Academic Publishers, 1992, 3.

63 This quotation is from unpublished manuscripts in the Husserl Archives in Louvain, B I 14 XIII, 27; quoted in James Hart, *The Person and the Common Life*, Kluwer Academic Publisher, 1992, 3–4.

64 James Hart, *The Person and the Common Life*, Kluwer Academic Publishers, 1992, 33.

65 It is interesting to note that Husserl's *Cartesian Meditations* were delivered after he had read Heidegger's *Being and Time*. In fact, passages in *Cartesian Meditations* read like a response to Heidegger's criticisms of phenomenology in *Being and Time*. For example, on a page that Husserl inserted after he had delivered the lectures, as a response to Heidegger's criticism of the transcendental attitude, he says: "The all-embracing constitution of the world within the ego is outlined as a problem only/as far as the theory of clues—as far as the consideration of the world (that is to say: the ontological consideration thereof, as transformed into a constitutional-ontological consideration). Somewhere in that context, naturally, the problem man must present itself? But what is the proper order?

"The first procedure in *Meditations* I–IV is to awaken the guiding thought: The world is a meaning, an accepted sense. When we go back to the ego, we can explicate the founding and founded strata with which that sense is built up, we can reach the absolute being and process in which the being of the world shows its ultimate truth and in which the ultimate problems of being reveal themselves—bringing into the thematic field all the disguises that unphilosophical naiveté cannot penetrate" (Husserl 1977, 52 footnote 1).

66 Financial support for time spent writing parts of this section and parts of chapter 4 were generously provided by a summer fellowship from the University of Texas at Austin.

67 John Rawls's notion of justice determined through a veil of ignorance can be read as a conservative strategy that promotes the patriarchal status quo, since it ignores differences in power and positions that cannot be so easily erased by a philosophical thought experiment.

68 John Brenkman makes this argument in *Straight Male Modern*, Routledge, 1993, 192. Lacan's insistence on the association between the father and the name makes Derrida's insistence on the association between the mother and the name all the more interesting; see chapter two.

69 I continue to develop this notion of an abject father, especially in chapter four, § Promissory Love.

70 *Jokes and Their Relation to the Unconscious*, Standard Edition, VIII, 205.

71 Although she does not develop her criticism, Elizabeth Grosz challenges Kristeva's exemption for semen in *Volatile Bodies*, 206–207.

72 "The Biggest Evolutionary Challenge May Be the Other Half of the Species" (*New York Times*, June 18, 1996, B5, B10).

73 See my discussion of the theories of Aristotle and Galen in chapter one above, § Biological Imaging.

74 See Elizabeth Grosz's analysis in *Volatile Bodies*, especially p. 205.

75 For example, in his article "The Facts of Fatherhood," Thomas Laqueur points out that the California Civil Code sections 7005 (a) and (b) "provide that if, under the supervision of a doctor, a married woman is inseminated by semen from a man who is not her husband, that man under certain circumstances is treated as if he were *not* the natural father while the husband is treated as if he were." See Thomas Laqueur, "Facts of Fatherhood," in *Conflicts in Feminism*, ed. Marianne Hirsch and Evelyn Fox Keller, Routledge, 1990, p. 215.

76 John Brenkman points out that Ricoeur assumes that contracts take place between equals. See *Straight Male Modern*, Routledge, 1993, 45.

77 William Safire, "What Fathers Want" (*New York Times*, June 16, 1994, A27).

78 Recent cross-dressing films exhibit the same phenomenon. *To Wong Foo . . .* and *The Birdcage* get laughs by continually reminding the viewer that these women are *really men* pretending to be women.

79 Jean Marbella, "Men Offer Mixed Opinions on Male Birth Control Pill Contraception: Men's Rights Activists Applaud Option, but Others Raise Concerns Over Side Effects" (*Baltimore Sun*, May 14, 1990, 3E).

80 In this case there are in fact reasons to doubt the Sterns' honesty. First, they had arranged for a new birth certificate that would indicate that Elizabeth Stern was the mother of the baby. Second, Elizabeth Stern diagnosed herself with multiple sclerosis and concluded that she could not have children. During the trial it was determined that she could have children, although there could be some health risks.

81 Quoted in Richard Lacayo, "I, too Sing America" (*Time*, October 30, 1995, 146:18, 32)

82 Michael Eric Dyson, "Words Unsaid," *The Christian Century*, 112:34, Nov. 22 1995, 1100.

83 Some of his contemporaries have criticized Levinas for sacrificing the feminine for the masculine subject's ascent into the ethical relationship through paternity. See Catherine Chalier, *Figures du féminin: Lecture d'Emmanuel Levinas*, Paris: La nuit surveillée, 1982; Luce Irigaray, "The Fecundity of the Caress" (1984), in *An Ethics of Sexual Difference*, trans. Carolyn Burke and Gillian Gill, Cornell University Press, 1993, and "Questions to Emmanuel Levinas," in Margaret Whitford, ed., *The Irigaray Reader*, Basil Blackwell, 1991.

84 Levinas reads the history of phenomenology from Husserl through Sartre as the history of a notion of the subject as the center or meaning and value. The subject gives meaning to experience; the subject constitutes meaning. Levinas calls the subject as meaning, giver the subject as "I-can."

85 For substantiation of this reading of Kristeva's Imaginary Father, see my *Reading Kristeva: Unraveling the Double-Bind*, Indiana University Press, 1993, chapter three.

86 In the next section, I will discuss Levinas's description of the feminine in the erotic relationship in *Totality and Infinity*.

87 For a sustained analysis of how Nietzsche's philosophy opens onto difference and yet closes off the possibility of feminine difference, see my *Womanizing Nietzsche: Philosophy's Relation to the "Feminine,"* Routledge, 1995.

88 In the last section of *Marine Lover of Friedrich Nietzsche*, "When the Gods are Born," Luce Irigaray argues that Christ's suffering on the cross and his bleeding side are masculine appropriations of the mother's suffering and the blood of childbirth through which she gives life.

89 Recall my discussion in chapter two above of Cynthia Willett's theory of touch as the foundation of subjectivity.

90 Whether there is a father physically present, our *images* of fatherhood should include an embodied loving father rather than just the stern symbolic father of the law or an imaginary father who collapses into either the symbolic father or the maternal body.

references

Adams, Alice. *Reproducing the Womb*. Ithaca: Cornell University Press, 1994.

Aristotle. *The Generation of Animals*. Trans. A Platt. In *The Complete Works of Aristotle*, ed. J. Barnes. Princeton: Princeton University Press, 1984.

———.*Nicomachean Ethics*. Trans.

Bar On, Bat-Ami., ed. *Modern Engendering: Critical Feminist Readings in Modern Western Philosophy*. Albany: SUNY Press, 1994a.

———.*Engendering Origins:Critical Feminist Readings in Plato and Aristotle*. Albany: SUNY Press, 1994b.

Beaconsfield, Peter, and Claude Villee. *Placenta—A Neglected Experimental Animal*. New York: Pergamon Press, 1979.

Beaconsfield, Rebecca, and George Birdwood, eds., *Placenta—The Largest Human Biopsy*. New York: Pergamon Press, 1982.

Beauvoir, Simone de. *The Second Sex*. Trans. H.M. Parshley. New York: Random House, 1989.

Bellah, Robert. *Habits of the Heart*. Los Angeles: University of California Press, 1985.

Benhabib, Seyla, and Drucilla Cornell, eds. *Feminism as Critique.* Minneapolis: Minnesota University Press, 1987.

Benjamin, Jessica. *The Bonds of Love.* New York: Pantheon, 1988.

Berkowitz, Charlotte. *The Dream Is One: Reflections in a Biblical Mirror.* Doctoral dissertation, University of Houston, 1995.

Bernet, Rudolf, et. al. *An Introduction to Husserlian Phenomenology.* Evanston Illinois: Northwestern University Press, 1993.

Birdwood, George. *Placenta—The Largest Human Biopsy.* New York: Pergamon, 1982.

Bowlby, John. *Maternal Care and Mental Health.* New York: Shocken Books, 1966.

———. *Attachment.* London: Penguin Books, 1971.

Brenkman, John. *Straight Male Modern: A Cultural Critique of Psychoanalysis.* New York: Routledge, 1993.

Brennan, Teresa. *The Interpretation of the Flesh.* New York: Routledge Press, 1992.

———. *History After Lacan.* New York: Routledge, 1993.

Cole, F.J. *Early Theories of Sexual Generation.* London: Oxford University Press, 1930.

Corea, Gena. *The Mother Machine: Reproductive Technologies from Artificial Insemination to Artificial Wombs.* New York: Harper & Row, 1985.

Cornell, Drucilla. *The Imaginary Domain.* New York. Routledge, 1995.

Chalier, Catherine. *Figures du féminin: Lecture d'Emmanuel Levinas.* Paris: La nuit surveillée, 1982.

Chanter, Tina. "Looking at Hegel's Antigone through Irigaray's Speculum." In *Ethics of Eros, Irigaray's Rewriting of the Philosophers.* New York: Routledge, 1994.

Derrida. Jacques. "The Law of Genre." Trans. Avital Ronell. *Critical Inquiry* 17, no. 1: 55–81, 1980.

———. *Speech and Phenomena.* Trans. David Allison. Evanston, Illinois: Northwestern University Press, 1973.

———. *Given Time: I. Counterfeit Money.* Trans. Peggy Kamuf. Chicago: University of Chicago Press, 1992.

———. "Otobiographies." in *The Ear of the Other.* Ed. trans. Peggy Kamuf and Avital Ronell. Christie McDonald and Claude Lévesque, Lincoln: University of Nebraska Press, 1985.

———. *Spurs: Nietzsche's Styles.* Trans. Barbara Harlow. Chicago: University of Chicago Press, 1979.

———. *Glas.* Trans. John P. Leavey Jr. and Richard Rand. Lincoln: University of Nebraska Press, 1986.

———. "Circumfession." In *Jacques Derrida.* Trans. Geoffrey Bennington. Chicago: University of Chicago Press, 1993.

———. *Of Grammatology*. Trans. G.C. Spivak. Baltimore: Johns Hopkins University Press, 1976.

———. "At This Very Moment Here I Am." R. Berezdivin. trans. In *Re-Reading Levinas*, ed. Bernasconi and Critchley, Indiana University Press, 1991.

———. *The Gift of Death*. Trans. David Wills. Chicago: University of Chicago Press, 1995.

———. Interview with Richard Kearney. *Dailogues with Contemporary Continental Thinkers.*, ed. Richard Kearney. Manchester: Manchester University Press, 1984.

———. "Psyche: Inventions of the Other." In *Reading DeMan Reading*. Ed. and trans. Catherine Porter. L. Waters and W. Godzich. Minneapolis: University of Minnesota Press, 1989.

Doane, Janice, and Devon Hodges. *From Klein to Kristeva*. Ann Arbor: University of Michigan Press, 1992.

Douglas, Mary. *Purity and Danger*. New York: Routledge, 1969.

Ebert, Roger. *Roger Ebert's Video Companion, 1996 Edition*. Kansas City: Andrews and McMeel Publishers, 1995.

Fineman, Martha Albertson. *The Neutered Mother, The Sexual Family*. New York: Routledge, 1995.

Foucault, Michel. *The History of Sexuality*, vol. I. Trans. R. Hurley. New York: Random House, 1980.

———. *The Use of Pleasure.* Trans. R. Hurley. New York: Random House, 1985.

———. *The Care of the Self.* Trans. R. Hurley. New York: Random House, 1986.

———. *The Birth of the Clinic*. Trans. A.M.S. Smith. New York: Random House, 1975.

———. *Discipline and Punish*. Trans. A. Sheridan. New York: Random House, 1979.

Freud, Sigmund. *Civilization and Its Discontents*. Trans. James Strachey. New York: Norton, 1961.

———. *The Interpretation of Dreams*. Trans. James Strachey. New York: Avon, 1967.

———. *Jokes and Their Relation to the Unconscious*, vol. 8. In *The Standard Edition of the Complete Psychological Works of Sigmund Freud*. Trans. James Strachey, in collaboration with Anna Freud, 1933.

Galen. *On the Usefulness of the Parts of the Body*. Trans. M.T. May. Ithaca: Cornell University Press, 1968.

———. *On Anatomical Procedures*. Trans. Charles Singer. London: Oxford University Press, 1956.

————. *On Semen.* Trans. Phillip De Lacy. Berlin: Akademie Verlag, 1992.

Grosz, Elizabeth. *Sexual Subversions.* Sydney: Allen & Unwin, 1989.

————. *Volatile Bodies.* Bloomington: Indiana University Press, 1994.

Hart, James. *The Person and the Common Life.* Boston: Kluwer Academic Publishers, 1992.

Hegel, G.W.F. *Phänomenologie des Geistes* in *Werke 3.* Frankfurt: Suhrkamp Tashenbuch Verlag, 1970.

————. *Phenomenology of Spirit.* Trans. A.V. Miller. Oxford: Clarendon Press, 1977.

————. *Philosophy of Right.* Trans. T.M. Knox. London: Oxford University Press, 1952.

————. *Philosophy of Nature.* Trans. A.V. Miller. Oxford: Clarendon Press, 1970.

Heidegger, Martin. *Being and Time.* Trans. John Macquarrie and Edward Robinson. New York: Harper & Row, 1962.

————. *What Thinking is Called.* Trans. J. Glenn Gray. New York: Harper and Row, 1968.

————. "The Question Concerning Technology." In *Basic Writings,* Ed. and trans. David Farrell Krell. New York: Harper Collins, 1993b.

————. "The Principle of Identity." In *Identity and Difference.* Trans. Joan Stambaugh. New York: Harper & Row, 1969.

————. "Time and Being." In *On Time and Being.* Trans. Joan Stambaugh. New York: Harper & Row Publishers, 1972.

————. "The End of Philosophy and the Task of Thinking." In *On Time and Being.* Trans. Joan Stambaugh. New York: Harper & Row, 1972.

————. "The Thing." Trans. Albert Hofstader. In *Poetry, Language, and Thought.* New York: Harper & Row Publishers, 1976.

Holmes, Helen Bequaert, and Laura Purdy, eds., *Feminist Perspectives in Medical Ethics.* Bloomington: Indiana University Press, 1992.

hooks, bell. *Ain't I a Woman: Black Women and Feminism.* Boston: South End Press, 1981.

Hubbard, Ruth. "Have Only Men Evolved?" In *Discovering Reality.* Ed. Sandra Harding and Merrill Hintikka. Boston: Reidel Publishing, 1983.

————. *The Politics of Women's Biology.* New Brunswick, New Jersey: Rutgers University Press, 1990.

Hunter, William. *Anatomy of the Human Gravid Uterus.* 1772.

Husserl, Edmund. *Cartesian Meditations.* Trans. Dorion Cairns. The Hague, Netherlands: Martinus Nijoff, 1977.

Irigaray, Luce. "Love of Same, Love of Other." In *An Ethics of Sexual Difference,* Trans. Carolyn Burke and Gillian Gill. Ithaca: Cornell University Press, 1993a.

————. *Sexes and Genealogies.* Trans. Gillian Gill. New York: Columbia University Press, 1993b.

————. "The eternal irony of the community." In *Speculum of the Other Woman.* Trans. Gillian Gill. Ithaca: Cornell University Press, 1985a.

————. *This Sex Which Is Not One.* Trans. Catherine Porter. Ithaca: Cornell University Press, 1985b.

————. *Marine Lover of Friedrich Nietzsche.* Trans. Gillian Gill. New York: Columbia University Press, 1991.

————. "Questions to Emmanuel Levinas." In *The Irigaray Reader.* Ed. and trans. Margaret Whitford. Cambridge, MA: Basil Blackwell, 1991.

Jagger, Alison. *Feminism, Politics and Human Nature.* Totowa, New Jersey: Roman & Allanheld, 1983.

Kaplan, E. Ann. *Motherhood and Representation.* New York: Routledge, 1992.

Keller, Evelyn Fox. *Reflections on Gender and Science.* New Haven: Yale University Press, 1985.

————. *Secrets of Life, Secrets of Death.* New York: Routledge, 1992.

Kierkegaard, Soren. *Fear and Trembling.* Trans. Walter Lowrie. Princeton: Princeton University Press, 1954.

Klein, Melanie. "The Importance of Symbol-Formation in the Development of the Ego." *The Writings of Melanie Klein,* vol. 1: 219–232, ed. R.E. Money-Kyrle et al. London: Hogarth Press, 1975a.

————. "Notes on Some Schizoid Mechanisms." In *The Selected Melanie Klein,* Harmondsworth, UK: Penguin, 1986.

————. "The Oedipus Complex in the Light of Early Anxieties." In *The Writings of Melanie Klein.* vol. 1: 370–419, ed. R.E. Money-Kyrle et al. London: Hogarth Press, 1975b.

Klopper et al., eds. *The Human Placenta Protiens and Hormones.* New York: Academic Press, 1980.

Kofman, Sarah. "A Fantastical Genealogy: Nietzsche's Family Romance." In *Nietzsche and the Feminine,* ed. Peter Burgard. Charlottesville: University of Virginia Press, 1994a.

————. *Rue Ordener, Rue Labat.* Translations appearing in *Family Values* are my own. Paris: Galilée, 1994b.

————. *Explosion I: De l'"Ecce Homo" de Nietzsche.* Paris: Galilée, 1992.

————. "Baubô: Theological Perversion and Fetishism." Trans. Tracy Strong. In *Nietzsche's New Seas,* ed. M.A. Gillespie and Tracy Strong. Chicago: University of Chicago Press, 1988.

————. *The Enigma of Woman: Woman in Freud's Writings.* Trans. Catherine Porter. Ithaca: Cornell University Press, 1985.

————. *Nietzsche et la scène philosophique.* Paris: Union Générale d'Editions, 1979.

Kristeva, Julia. *Revolution in Poetic Language*. Trans. Margaret Waller. New York: Columbia University Press, 1984.

———.*Desire in Language*. Ed. Leon Roudiez. Trans. T. Gora, A. Jardine, and L. Roudiez. New York: Columbia University Press, 1980.

———. *Powers of Horror*. Trans. Leon Roudiez. New York: Columbia University Press, 1982.

———.*Strangers to Ourselves*. Trans. Leon Roudiez. New York: Columbia University Press, 1991.

———. *New Maladies of the Soul*. Trans. Ross Guberman. New York: Columbia University Press, 1995.

———.*Tales of Love*. Trans. Leon Roudiez. New York: Columbia University Press, 1987.

Lacan, Jacques. *Écrits: A Selection*. Trans. Alan Sheridan. New York: Norton, 1977.

———. "The Neurotic's Individual Myth." In *The Psychoanalytic Quarterly* 48:3, 422–423, 1979.

Laqueur, Thomas. "Facts of Fatherhood." In *Conflicts in Feminism*. Ed. Marianne Hirsch and Evelyn Fox Keller. New York: Routledge, 1990.

Levinas, Emmanuel. *Autrement Qu' Être Ou Au-Dela de L'Essence*. Martinus Nijhoff, 1974.

———. *Otherwise Than Being, Or Beyond Essence*. Trans. Alphonso Lingis. Boston: Kluwer Academic Publishers, 1991.

———. "Language and Proximity." In *Collected Philosophical Papers*. Trans. Alphonso Lingis. Boston: Kluwer Academic Publishers, 1993.

———.*Ethics and Infinity*. Trans. Richard Cohen. Pittsburgh: Duquesne University Press, 1985.

———.*Totality and Infinity*. Trans. Alphonso Lingis. Pittsburgh: Duquesne University Press, 1969.

———. *Time and the Other*. Trans. Richard Cohen. Pittsburgh: Duquesne University Press, 1982.

Lingis, Alphonso. *Foreign Bodies*. New York: Routledge, 1994.

Locke, John. *Second Treatise on Government*. Ed. C.B. MacPherson. Cambridge: Hackett Publishing, 1980.

Merleau, Ponty, Maurice. *The Visible and the Invisible*. Trans. Alphonso Lingis. Evanston, Illinois: Northwestern University Press, 1968.

———. *The Primacy of Perception*. Ed. and trans. James Edie. Evanston Illinois: Northwestern University Press, 1964.

Modleski, Tania. *Feminism Without Women*. New York: Routledge, 1991.

Nicholson, Linda. 1986. *Gender and History: The Limits of Social Theory in the Age of the Family*. New York: Columbia University Press.

Nietzsche, Friedrich. *The Gay Science*. Trans. Walter Kaufmann. New York: Random House, 1974.

———.*Ecce Homo*. Trans. Walter Kaufmann. New York: Random House, 1967a.

——— . *On the Genealogy of Morals*. Trans. Walter Kaufmann and R.J. Hollingdale. New York: Random House, 1967b.

———.*Beyond Good and Evil*. Trans. Walter Kaufmann. New York: Random House, 1966.

Nilsson, Lennart, and Lars Hamberger. *A Child is Born*. Trans. Clare James. New York: Bantam Doubleday Dell Publishing, 1990.

Oliver, Kelly. "Kristeva's Revolutions." In *The Portable Kristeva*. Ed. K. Oliver, New York: Columbia University Press, 1997.

——— . *Womanizing Nietzsche, Philosophy's Relation to The "Feminine."* New York: Routledge, 1995.

——— . *Reading Kristeva: Unraveling the Doublebind*. Bloomington: Indiana University Press, 1993.

Plato. *Symposium*. In *Plato, The Collected Dialogues*. Ed. E. Hamilton and H. Cairns. Trans. Michael Joyce. Princeton: Princeton University Press, 1987a.

———.*Phaedrus*. In *Plato, The Collected Dialogues*. Ed. E. Hamilton and H. Cairns. Trans. R. Hackford. Princeton: Princeton University Press, 1987b.

Plotinus. *Enneads*. In *Complete Works*. Trans. Kenneth Sylvan Guthrie. London: Bell, 1918.

Ramsey, Elizabeth. *The Placenta of Laboratory Animals and Man*. New York: Holt, Rinehart and Winston, 1975.

Rich, Adrienne. *Of Woman Born: Motherhood as Experience and Institution*. New York: W.W. Norton, 1976.

Ricoeur, Paul, "Fatherhood: From Phantasm to Symbol." Trans. Robert Sweeney. In *The Conflict in Interpretations*, ed. Don Ihde. Evanston, Illinois: Northwestern University Press, 1974.

Rouch, Hélène. Interview in Luce Irigaray, *je, tu, nous*. Trans. Alison Martin. New York: Routledge, 1993.

Rousseau, Jean-Jacques. *Essay On the Origin of Languages*. Trans. J. Moran and A. Gode. In *On the Origin of Language*. New York: Frederick Ungar Publishing, 1966.

———. "On Social Contract," and "Discourse on Political Economy." In *The Basic Political Writings*. Ed. and trans. Donald Cress. Cambridge: Hackett Publishing, 1987.

Sartre, Jean Paul. *Being and Nothingness*. Trans. Hazel Barnes. New York: Washington Square Books, 1956.

———. "The Humanism of Existentialism." Trans. from *L'Existentialisme Est un Humanisme* by Bernard Frechtman. In *Sartre: Essays in Existentialism*, ed. Wade Baskin. Secaucus, New Jersey: Citadel Press, 1979.

————.*No Exit.* Trans. Stuart Gilbert. New York: Alfred Knoff, 1976.

———— . *The Transcendence of the Ego.* Trans. Forrest Williams and Robert Kirkpatrick. New York: Farrar, Straus and Giroux, 1957.

Sawicki, Jana. *Disciplining Foucault.* New York: Routledge, 1991.

Schroeder, Brian. *Altared Ground: Levinas, History, and Violence.* New York: Routledge, 1996.

Sophocles. *Antigone.* In *The Three Theban Plays.* Trans. Robert Fagles. New York: Penguin, 1982.

Stern, Daniel. *The Interpersonal World of the Infant: A View from Psychoanalysis and Developmental Psychology.* New York: Basic Books, 1985.

Steven, D.H., ed. *Compartive Placentation.* New York: Academic Press, 1975.

Summers-Bremnar, Eluned. *Speaking as Woman, Female Body Transformations and the Divine.* Doctoral dissertation, University of Canterbury, Christchurch, New Zealand, 1995.

Tuana, Nancy, ed. *Rereading the Canon.* Series. State College: Pennyslvania State University Press, forthcoming.

————.*The Less Nobel Sex.* Bloomington: Indiana University Press, 1993.

Veroff, et. al. *Mental Health in America.* New York: Basic Books, 1981.

Willett, Cynthia. "Hegel, Antigone, and the Possibility of a Woman's Dialectic." In *Modern Engendering: Critical Feminist Readings in Modern Western Philosophy.* Ed. Bat Ami Bar On. Albany: SUNY Press, 1994.

————. "Hegel, Antigone, and the possibility of Ecstatic Dialogue." In *Philosophy and Literature* 14 (2) : 268–83, 1990.

————.*Maternal Ethics and Other Slave Moralities.* New York: Routledge, 1995.

Winnicott, D.W. "The Mirror Role of Mother and Family in Child Development." In *Playing and Reality.* London: Tavistock, 1971.

————. "The Theory of the Parent–Infant Relationship." In *Maturational Processes and the Facilitating Environment.* New York: International Universities Press, 1965.

Wynn and Jollie, eds. *Biology of the Uterus.* 2nd ed. New York: Plenum Publishing, 1989.

index